SOUTHEAST ASIA: A HISTORY

Lea E. Williams

New York
Oxford University Press
1976

Southeast Asia: A History

To John K. Fairbank and the memory of Harry Benda

Preface

An author must begin his labors by asking himself if any useful purpose can be served by the publication of yet another book on a subject previously explored by others. If the answer to the question is affirmative, the writer has concluded either that his book will be an improvement over earlier ones or that it will be constructively different. As suggested in the bibliographies to follow, the considerable number of good histories of Southeast Asia already available makes the odds against producing a better book quite unfavorable. Thus, I have tried to take a fresh approach to the subject by paying more attention to historical themes and currents than to individuals and events. The object of this exercise is to offer readers an analytical framework rather than a body of facts, to generate an awareness of the unity in diversity that is Southeast Asian history.

The chief difficulty in the approach followed here lay in having to decide what to omit from the narrative. Of course, writing history is inevitably a selective process; no historian ever presents a raw, undistilled record. Leaving out material that does not contribute to instructive and, ideally, honest analysis is the track of the trade. In the present book, names, dates, and illustrative data are therefore kept to a minimum. Thus, specialists are likely to be outraged by what may seem to be the cavalier treatment afforded their chosen periods, places, and people.

A further word of warning is also appropriate. No attempt has been made to conceal my feelings while telling a human story. Consequently, the presentation is frankly opinionated. Objectivity and integrity naturally require that all sides of an issue be considered, but an author is not bound to maintain Olympian aloofness, to be emotionally sterile.

The spelling of geographical and personal names is a problem when dealing with Southeast Asia. No system of Romanization is foolproof; and, to make matters worse, numerous systems have been devised. Moreover, political changes have produced new names that are favored by some purists and pedants. The rule followed here is simple, if not fully satisfactory: the spellings and names most commonly in use among English speakers are employed. Penang will not be referred to as Pulau Pinang; Borneo will not be replaced by Kalimantan; here, the capital of Thailand is Bangkok, not Krung Thep.

A few explanatory words on bibliographical practice may be in order. At the end of each chapter, there appears a list of books in English considered particularly relevant to the preceding discussion. The titles of a few general works are given at the end of the book. It must be acknowledged that assigning works to individual chapter listings was quite awkward, for many books cover a broad range of subjects. In essence, then, the chapter listings record the titles of those books that are considered especially, thought not exclusively, useful within a specific context. No attempt was made to include journal articles or similar items in the bibliographies.

There are many to whom I am indebted, including authors listed in the bibliographies. Because of political sensitivities in Southeast Asia, however, the names of many kind people in the region who generously helped me must be left out here. That is the price I must pay for expressing value judgments that may be officially unfashionable.

Two scholarly institutions have earned my special thanks. The Institute of Southeast Asia Studies in Singapore, where a fine library and a highly professional staff gave me months of happy productivity, and my home university, Brown, by granting me sabbatic leave and by providing a congenial working environment, supported the present undertaking. At Brown, the staff of the John Carter Brown Library,

Contents

Contents

Maps

Drawn by Miklos Pinther

particularly Mr. Richard H. Boulind, Curator of Maps, gave most generously of their time and expertise.

Further, I wish to thank Mrs. Gregory Coppa for typing (and retyping) the manuscript. My colleagues, Jerome B. Grieder and Eric G. Widmer are remembered for their editorial guidance and their encouragement. Finally, my daughter, Adrienne, who read proof, my son, William, who processed most of the illustrations in his darkroom, and my wife, Daisy, who kept our household in smooth operation while I was abroad on my latest field trip, are affectionately thanked.

L. E. W.

Providence, Rhode Island
September 1975

Southeast Asia: A History

1
The Setting

Books on Southeast Asia invariably begin with a defense of the idea that the lands bounded by the Indian subcontinent on the west, China on the north, Australia on the south, and the Pacific to the east are capable of analysis as a unique region of the world. Writers on Sub-Saharan Africa or Western Europe or other areas do not display the uneasiness that afflicts those who seek to write on Southeast Asia.

There are two reasons for this state of affairs. First, the term "Southeast Asia" gained currency only during the Second World War as a collective designation for the Japanese-occupied countries south of China. Earlier, the region had been viewed historically as divided between Sinicized Vietnam, the Hispanicized Philippines, and "Farther India"—that is, the other lands of the region, which share a common cultural indebtedness to India. The three-way cultural division seemed to preclude a regional approach to Southeast Asian history. Some scholars focused on one of the three subregions; others limited their efforts to Europocentric studies of the various colonial records. A breakthrough was achieved in the immediate postwar decade with the publication of the first edition of a monumental work, D. G. E. Hall's *A History of South-East Asia*, though tradition and convenience dictated treatment only of the Sinic and Indic lands and the exclusion from consideration of the analytically awkward Philippines. (The omission of the archipelago was most productively corrected in later editions.)

The second reason for the difficulty of a regional approach to Southeast Asian history is to be found in the recent colonial past. There has been relatively little exchange among Southeast Asian countries in modern times. The great decisions of state in the colonial era were made in Western capitals. Economically, the region was fragmented into units, each individually tied to outside, industrialized trading partners. In human terms, the peoples of the region were sharply separated from one another by colonial frontiers. Indonesians sought advanced education in the Netherlands; the Gallicized splinter of Vietnamese society came close to equating France with civilization; Filipino immigrants abroad concentrated in Hawaii and California. Even today, Paris is more familiar than Jakarta to Cambodians; probably more Sarawakians have been to Britain than to the nearer island of Java. It is not odd, therefore, that Southeast Asia has been described as a collection of countries facing outward and turning their backs on each other.

Despite the fragmentation, Southeast Asia is much more than an arbitrary geographical expression. There are influences and processes of geography and history common to all parts. It is on the basis of these shared features that a general approach to the area can be attempted. A regional analysis obviously can no more paper over the diversity and complexity of Southeast Asia than a history of Europe can ignore the variety of the human experience on that continent. Still, the tropical lands of East Asia can legitimately be handled as a collectivity through a thematic treatment of their history. It is useful to begin with the physical environment.

GEOGRAPHICAL CONSIDERATIONS

Southeast Asia, maritime and continental, is washed by warm and generally placid seas. For millennia, men and their goods have moved through the region on great, water highways. Indeed, many technological advances in navigation and shipbuilding can probably be attributed to Southeast Asian ingenuity and experimentation. It is certain that the sailors were both competent and bold, for the seafaring prowess of ancient Malayo-Polynesian speakers carried them and their languages around two-thirds of the world, from Madagascar off Africa to Easter Island near South America. Many centuries before Europeans dared challenge the fierce Atlantic, the South Pacific and the Indian Ocean served man; and Southeast Asia was the central intersection of the sea routes.

The Chinese have long recognized the maritime cohesion of the islands and coasts to their south, for in Chinese the whole region that Westerners have so recently named Southeast Asia has traditionally been called *Nan-yang*, [the lands of the] Southern Ocean. From the Chinese perspective the region was correctly seen as bound together by the sea. The reasonableness of that position is immediately apparent from the map, for Southeast Asia is, in fact, a maritime extension of the Asian heartland.

There is considerable uniformity of climate, so far as heat is concerned, in a region lying within thirty degrees of latitude to the north and ten degrees to the south of the equator. The only significant variations in temperature are attributable to differences in altitude. There is a drop of roughly three degrees Fahrenheit for every thousand feet of ascent in hilly and mountainous country. By and large, however, Southeast Asians are concentrated in the soupy heat of the agriculturally productive lowlands. The delightful coolness of the higher elevations is familiar only to minority hill peoples and visitors to mountain resorts developed by homesick Westerners at places like Baguio on Luzon, Puntjak in western Java, or the Cameron Highlands of West Malaysia.

Though temperatures are generally monotonous, rainfall varies greatly from place to place and throughout the year in some areas. A belt within five degrees of the equator, including most of the Malay Peninsula and Sumatra plus Borneo, Celebes and the Moluccas, experiences a fairly equal distribution of rainfall over any twelve months. Those lands have neither dry nor wet seasons. Rain, typically accompanied by dramatic thunder and lightning, most frequently comes for short periods in the late afternoon and early evening.

Beyond the immediate vicinity of the equator, however, the monsoons are masters. Rainfall arrives when the seasonal winds bring sodden clouds from over the sea. In the cold season of the Northern Hemisphere, a vast flow of air sweeps into Southeast Asia from over the Western Pacific. It is then that much of Vietnam, the Kra Isthmus, Sarawak, and Java, not sheltered by intervening mountain ranges, are

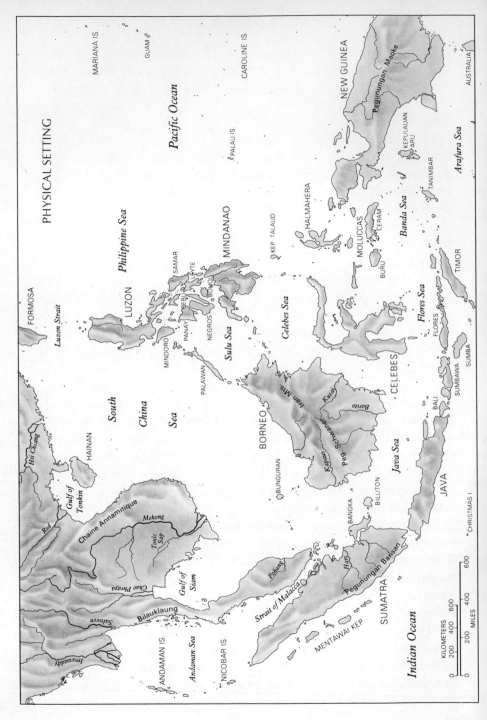

PHYSICAL SETTING

MARIANA IS

GUAM

CAROLINE IS

NEW GUINEA

Pegunungan Maoke

PALAU IS

KEPULAUAN ARU

Pacific Ocean

TANIMBAR

Arafura Sea

AUSTRALIA

FORMOSA

Philippine Sea

LUZON

SAMAR

LEYTE

CEBU

PANAY

NEGROS

MINDORO

MINDANAO

BOHOL

HALMAHERA

KEP TALAUD

MOLUCCAS

CERAM

BURU

Banda Sea

Luzon Strait

TIMOR

South

China

Sea

Sulu Sea

Celebes Sea

Flores Sea

FLORES

SUMBA

HSI Chiang

HAINAN

PALAWAN

BORNEO

Iran Mts.

Kinai

Barito

CELEBES

BALI

SUMBAWA

Java Sea

JAVA

Gulf of Tonkin

Kapuas

Peg. Schwaner

BUNGURAN

Red

Chaine Annamitique

Mekong

BILLITON

BANGKA

Tonle Sap

CHRISTMAS I.

Chao Phraya

Gulf of Siam

Hari

SUMATRA

Batang

Pegunungan Barisan

Indian Ocean

Salween

Bilauklaung

Strait of Malacca

Pahang

ANDAMAN IS

Andaman Sea

MENTAWAI KEP

Irrawaddy

NICOBAR IS

KILOMETERS

0   200   400   600

0   200   400   600

MILES

Map 1.

The watery main thoroughfare of a town on the Thai-Malayan frontier is typical of maritime and riverine areas. (Lea E. Williams)

drenched, while Burma, Thailand, Laos, and Cambodia are parched. When the northern cold gives way to the high temperatures of summer in the Asian heartland, the pattern is reversed. It becomes the turn of most of the previously dry areas to be soaked. There are, of course, also some locations in the shadows of heights which never get heavy rain.

Over countless centuries farmers have waited for the monsoonal shifts to bring life to their fields. Fortunately, Southeast Asia has been virtually immune to the droughts that periodically devastate India and China. Indeed, the lands between those Asian giants have been singularly blessed by nature. The typhoons of the South China Sea in the months from July to November are the only substantial climatic menace, and those great gales, bringing needed rainfall, do not extend southward beyond the Philippines and northern Vietnam.

A further word is in order concerning the cycle of the monsoons. Sailing vessels, still significant in Eastern waters, since earliest times have been propelled by the steady force of monsoonal winds. Voyages under sail from China to the south are swift and secure in the months of the northeast monsoon; return passages are similarly smooth when

7

the winds blow from the southwest. So reliable are the monsoons that Chinese junk skippers for centuries were equipped with rutters that permitted quite accurate predictions on the duration of voyages. It was merely necessary to wait, sometimes for a few months, for the favorable monsoon. Once it came, the voyage was, to borrow from yachting jargon, "downhill." That held for voyages within Southeast Asia and to ports in India and beyond as well as for those to and from China. The monsoons, as much as geographical location, put the tropical Far East at the center of Oriental seaborne trade and have thus been a prime factor in the maritime cohesion of insular and littoral Southeast Asia.

Comparatively benign though the climate may be, other forces of nature have brought great suffering. Volcanic activity in much of insular Southeast Asia is intense. Western Sumatra, the Lesser Sunda Islands, and Java in Indonesia, as well as Luzon, Mindanao, and other Philippine islands, are periodically seared by lava flows and shaken by earthquakes. Indonesia, with some fifty active volcanoes, over half of them on Java, where a smoking cone seems always in sight, is a delight to the tourist or the volcanologist. For Indonesian peasants whose fields and villages have been smothered in ash or molten rock, and town dwellers whose houses have been toppled by tremors, fear is part of the landscape.

Nature, however, seems incapable of manifesting unmixed evil. Just as the typhoons that lash the Philippines bring torrents of rain to sustain crops, volcanic eruptions, particularly on populous Java and Bali, spew out lava that is ultimately broken down to form new soils rich in minerals. For every peasant to fall victim to the volcanoes, there have been untold thousands of others whose survival on land that would otherwise be barren has been derived from the fiery mountains. Hence, Java is able to sustain the world's densest farming population, over seventy million souls packed on the more level parts of an island the size of the Malay Peninsula, England, or New York State.

On the Asian continent—in Burma, Thailand, Cambodia, Cochin China, and Tonkin—and, on a smaller scale, on Luzon and other islands, the monsoonal downpours have not merely watered the fields; they have created them. The alluvial plains formed by silt brought from the interior are bountiful rice bowls. The loss of fertility in upland soils through leaching is the gain of the deltas. Uncounted generations of peasants cultivating the flatlands of the lower reaches of the Irrawaddy, Chao Phraya, Mekong, and Red rivers on the mainland, and along the lesser streams of the Luzon plains have been indebted to the eroded hills of the interior as the source of the minerals that give fertility to their paddy fields. The Southeast Asian wet rice farmer, like the *fellah* of Lower Egypt, has always been dependent upon the renewal of life in his fields by seasonal flooding, though the phenomenon lacks the theatrical majesty of the rise of the Nile.

The deluges that send rich silt to the lowlands of course exhaust the slopes above. The vast stretches of jungle in Southeast Asia carpet lands that offer little to man, except timber and the potential of mining. With the mineral riches of the topsoil largely washed away, the clearing of forested land is a costly, all but fruitless task of enormous difficulty. Even where the impenetrable mass of plants, trees, ferns, vines, and creepers is somehow removed, the fields opened up are, at best, of dubious promise. Moreover, the processes of leaching and erosion are greatly accelerated by the removal of the jungle cover.

Westerners seem to have had foisted upon them, presumably by novelists and film-makers, the myth that the Southeast Asian jungle is a tropical Eden, where exotic fruit is never beyond reach and meat is waiting for the campfire. Nothing could be more remote from bleak reality. The forests of Southeast Asia are dark and oddly barren of life. Insects and small reptiles are usually the sole inhabitants to be seen; birds and mammals are normally heard only in the distance of the matted forest ceiling or in the tangled undergrowth. For man, the jungle is a green desert. The ecological adjustments of the recently discovered Tasaday of Mindanao, in the Philippines, exemplify the poverty of the tropical forest, for that tiny band of humans must subsist on a diet featuring edible roots and tadpoles wrested from a mean environment.

Niggardly though the jungle may be, an ancient form of farming known as swidden or slash-and-burn agriculture is carried on across wide areas of Southeast Asia; and, everywhere, the governments of today are hostile to the practice as allegedly wasteful of resources and, one assumes, an embarrassment in the age of modernization. It must also be noted that current official efforts to drive upland peoples into settled farming can be regarded as but the latest manifestation of a contest waged since distant and unrecorded times, when the first confrontation

Jungle trees in combat with ruins at Angkor Wat. (Lea E. Williams)

occurred between the more technologically advanced, and far more numerous, peasants of the plains and the roving hill tribes. Land hunger is not a twentieth-century development.

As the term slash-and-burn makes clear, swidden agriculture depends upon the clearing of jungle plots by mortally wounding the trees and later setting fire to their dead trunks. The charred area, temporarily enriched by wood ash but not cleared of stumps and rocks, is planted in dry upland rice, occasionally in other grains, legumes, or tubers, and—with distressing frequency nowadays in northern Burma, Thailand, and Laos—in opium poppies. The plow would be of no service in the rough fields. Only the planting stick is used to puncture the soil. This is neolithic farming, but it seems to represent a most efficient use of resources under present circumstances of technology and capital availability.

The land area required to support a population of swidden farmers is necessarily vast, for the fertility of their cultivated plots is soon dissipated and new patches of forest must be burned off. The old plots lapse quickly back into jungle to wait for a later generation of semi-migratory hill people to come and extract subsistence with machete, torch, and planting stick.

FOLK MIGRATIONS

While the geographical centrality of Southeast Asia in Eastern trade and navigation has been of incalculable significance, the place of the region as a crossroads of peoples has been and remains even more decisive. It is likely that no other region of the world has been traversed and settled by such human variety. The sea routes have carried some of the flow, but it was probably the courses of the great rivers and the Indo-chinese coastal plain that served the bulk of the migrants.

The topography of East and Central Asia is dominated by the Himalayan massif. From that towering crown of the continent flow the great rivers, the Yellow and the Yangtze of China, the Mekong and the Salween of Southeast Asia. It is remarkable that the sources of all four are located within a narrowly circumscribed area of the Tibetan plateau. Other rivers, the Red, Chao Phraya, Chindwin, Sittang, and Irrawaddy, rise in the lofty highlands that form the southern approaches to the Himalayan crests.

Without venturing too far into the maze of theory and fact related to the origins of the peoples of the region, some brief discussion of this thoroughly controversial and clouded subject can be attempted. The soil of Java has yielded the remains of very early hominids, including *Pithecanthropus modjokertensis* or Java man from the Pleistocene. As it appears that Javanese specimens are closely related to *Sinanthropus pekinensis* or Peking man, overland wandering from the core of East Asia may have already begun as far back as 700,000 years ago. What may be the earliest skull of *Homo sapiens* ever discovered anywhere comes from Sarawak and dates from 40,000 years ago. Its owner is supposed to have been descended from advanced humans who seem to have originated in the northeastern quarter of Africa and spread from there to the outer rims of the African, European, and Asian continents, dislodging hapless hominids as they went.

The victorious first true humans in the region, who can be classified as Australoids, were followed by Veddoid or Negrito migrants, perhaps from the Indian subcontinent. From those two strains are supposed to have come the Melanesoids who are still represented in the eastern Lesser Sundas, the Moluccas, and New Guinea. Though the Australoid type has been virtually absorbed, Negrito pockets still struggle to survive in inaccessible parts of Malaya, Sumatra, Luzon, and a few other spots.

The three, presumably dark-skinned, types who are credited with having spread mesolithic culture through most of Southeast Asia were soon challenged by newcomers originally from the north, from that part of the Asian heartland that has since become China. According to theories now under attack, there were two waves of migration from that source: the first being that of the Proto-Malays, who were assumed to have brought neolithic technology in the fourth and third millennia B.C., and the second made up of Deutero-Malays, who were once thought to have introduced bronze and iron in the fourth and third centuries B.C. It has been argued, recently and quite convincingly, that no waves ever rolled south, that there was merely a gradual seepage of Malay peoples, possibly first coming by sea to the Philippines, and that great technological and cultural advances began in Southeast Asia, not in China. Of course, the likelihood that the movements of peoples and cultures were both southerly and northerly cannot be excluded, particularly if technological advances flowed from south to north. More treatment of cultural developments will be included in the next chapter.

In any case, the Malay peoples (ancestral to but not to be confused with the modern ethnolinguistic group of that name) were quite different in appearance from the Australoid and Veddoid pioneers. Their skin color was presumably much lighter; their facial features are believed to have combined both Caucasoid and Mongoloid characteristics. Whether or not the Malay influx stimulated technological progress in the region, one thing is certain: The Malay interlopers set out to dispossess their predecessors, and the process has continued down to the present. Today, as already noted, the Australoids have disappeared, while the Veddoids are isolated on remote hilltops or distant islands.

The Malay peoples were to enjoy lasting ethnic dominance over the maritime lands that have now become Malaysia, Indonesia, and the Philippines, but their hold on the continental parts of Southeast Asia to the north was soon endangered and ultimately broken by the arrival of more peoples on the move. From the highlands of western China and

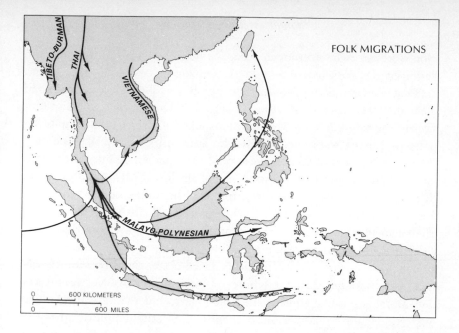

Map 2.

the marchlands of eastern Tibet, the spawning grounds of folk wanderings, came closely related peoples, generally referred to as the Mons
and Khmers. The linguistic affinity of those groups of speakers of
Austro-Asiatic languages permits the use of the hyphenated, collective
term, Mon-Khmer, for both. The Mons came south quite early and
were firmly rooted in the delta and coastal parts of Lower Burma by
the time of the Southeast Asian transition from prehistory into the historic period around the beginning of the Christian era. Other Mon settlers, more or less simultaneously, moved into the Chao Phraya delta
country to the east. The first political states of the region, built upon
the economic foundation of wet rice cultivation, came into existence at
Pegu in Lower Burma and near Lopburi in modern Thailand. The affluence of those Mon kingdoms stimulated trade and the development of
cultural contacts with India, a land of high civilization rather easily accessible from the Mon territories by sea and overland routes. It is en-
chanting to speculate on how different the course of history might have
been had outside cultural and political inspiration reached the Mons and
most other Southeast Asian peoples overland from China rather than
from India. But the difficulties of tapping the source of Sinic civiliza-

tion were not to be overcome, except by the Vietnamese and, to a much lesser degree, the Thais.

The Khmers, moving south from the Sino-Tibetan borderlands, did not initially menace their Mon cousins. The Khmer route of migration was to the east and led to the middle reaches of the Mekong, where the state of Chenla was founded. By the latter part of the sixth century A.D., the Khmers of Chenla were ready to open an assault on the state of Funan to the south, in the lowlands of the lower Mekong. It took the Khmers almost a century to triumph, but the momentum of their victory over Funan was to generate the conquest of the Mon territories of the Chao Phraya delta in the late ninth century and create the homeland of the great Angkorian civilization.

The Mons of the lower Irrawaddy fared better than those to the east who were conquered by the Khmers. Lower Burma was not subjugated by migrants pushing south until much later; and then the newcomers were not Khmer relatives but a wholly alien ethnolinguistic group of Tibeto-Burman speakers. The new intruders, the Pyu, appear to have moved down the Salween and the Mekong in the first two centuries of the Christian era. By the sixth century, while maintaining a hold on Upper Burma, the Pyu had begun the construction of their capital on the lower Irrawaddy, leaving the Mons in occupation of the territory to the east of the river. The ascendancy of the Pyu was brief, for by the eighth century the migration into central Burma of a people, possibly the ancestors of the Karens of today, had cut the Pyu domains in half, leaving the capital above the Irrawaddy delta area to wither. The remaining Pyu state in Upper Burma survived for a time, but was liquidated by the Tai[1] kingdom of Nan Chao, to be discussed shortly, in the first half of the ninth century.

The Burmans,[2] like their linguistic kin, the Pyu, originated in the Tibetan borderlands. They, too, flowed southward through the river gorges and, by the end of the ninth century, built a capital at Pagan, having conquered or pushed south the briefly resurgent Mons and begun the task of banishing the Karens to the east of the great river. It

---

[1] *Tai* describes a linguistic group; *Thai* refers to the main population of Tai speakers and the majority population of modern Thailand.

[2] *Burman* is used in referring to the people who became and remain the dominant population of Burma; *Burmese* refers to the chief language and the citizens, regardless of ethnicity, of Burma.

was at that point that the historical continuity of the Burman kingdoms began.

The Burmans appear to have had much to learn upon their arrival in central Burma. Their earlier, presumably semi-pastoral culture, developed under the rigorous conditions of the Tibetan highlands, was singularly ill-suited to the circumstances of a tropical, intensively cultivated land. Happily, teachers were at hand, for the Mons had been able to reconstitute themselves after the disintegration of the Pyu; and, lengthy contact with India had endowed the Mons with the cultural resources needed to transform their Burman overlords. The art of political control over an agrarian populace, the symbols of monarchy, literacy, artistic traditions, and Indic religious faiths were taught the victors by the vanquished. The culturally symbiotic relationship between the Mons and the Burmans was broadly like that between Greeks and Romans a thousand years earlier. The pace of Burman Indianization was clearly accelerated in the middle of the eleventh century, when the granary of the remnant state in Lower Burma fell to Pagan arms.

There is uncertainty over the date of the initial Tai movement into Southeast Asia, but there can be no doubt that the migration became one of a new kind and brought settlers in possession of a rich heritage. The Tai peoples originated in western China and seem to have moved from modern Szechwan into Yünnan in the face of Han Chinese expansion one or two centuries before the Christian era.

The power of the Han dynasty had brought many Tai communities under Chinese suzerainty by the start of the second century A.D., but only a hundred years later the Han imperial house was overthrown, and China sank into a prolonged state of disunion. There were Tai chieftains ready to grasp the opportunity presented by the ebbing of Chinese might. Armed with institutional and administrative resources of Chinese inspiration, Tai princelings began the construction of an order that was to evolve into the kingdom of Nan Chao. Centered on the plain of the Tali lake region in Yünnan, Nan Chao was to enjoy vigor and comparative security until the thirteenth century. Its economic foundations were stable; its geography provided natural protection against both Chinese and Tibetan attacks; trade routes led to both India and China. The Tai elite, governing an assortment of peoples, was not a coterie of savage chieftains. The kings of Nan Chao were invariably taken seriously by the Chinese, who first tried to subdue the Tai kingdom but eventually allied with it to curb Tibetan expansion. The formation of advantageous alliances appears to have remained ever since an honored tradition of Tai, later Thai, statecraft.

Nan Chao achieved the pinnacle of its strength in the ninth century when Tai troops overwhelmed the vestiges of the army of the Pyu of north Burma and were militarily effective as far from home as Tonkin. From that time on, however, a new historical course was to be opened to the Tai, and Nan Chao was moving toward extinction. The end came for the Tai kingdom in the mid-thirteenth century at the hands of the rightly feared Mongols. Yünnan was thus opened to full Chinese control when the Ming dynasty arose in the fourteenth century.

The Tai of the Nan Chao centuries had begun the classic southward push well before the Mongol victory. Tai princes and chiefs thus established in the border areas north of the Khmer and Burman kingdoms were seen by Mongol khans to be useful allies in keeping peace on the southern frontiers. Accordingly, though Nan Chao was eliminated as a state, the Tai who had already migrated into Southeast Asia were backed by the military and diplomatic power of the khans. The progress of those Tai who eventually built a homeland surrounding the Chao Phraya was not so much the panicky flight of refugees as it was the advance of conquerors in their own right. By the close of the thirteenth century, the Mon-Khmers of the Chao Phraya basin had been crushed and the Tai had founded a kingdom directly ancestral to modern Thailand. At that point in history, then, the Thai people and polity emerge to challenge Burmans to the west, Khmers to the east, and Malays to the south. The confrontation has waxed and waned ever since.

The Tai migrations were the final pre-modern massive folk movement; but the earliest great migratory and military push into Southeast Asia in historic times, the expansion of the Vietnamese, is still in progress after more than two millennia. Like the other major population shifts, that of the Vietnamese originated in what became China; but, in this instance, the southeastern coastal region, not the mountainous southwest, was the original homeland. The flooding tide of Chinese civilization submerged the Vietnamese by the second century B.C. and was to transform them during more than a thousand years of Chinese rule. The Sinification of the Vietnamese will be discussed in the next chapter; here it is appropriate only to consider the history of their southward push.

The eventual expulsion of Chinese authority from Tonkin and northern Annam in the tenth century A.D. left the Vietnamese to continue on their own to deal with traditional enemies to the south, the Chams and the Khmer, against whom Vietnamese pressure had been building up during the centuries of Chinese overlordship. The two enemy peoples obligingly often fought each other, yet it took 500 years, down to 1471, to obliterate Champa and extend Vietnamese settlement down the coastal strip south from the vicinity of present-day Hué to the edge of the Mekong delta. Once that victory was secured, it was Cambodia's turn to yield to the Vietnamese southward drive. Caught between a Thai suzerain too weak to provide protection and the aggressive Vietnamese, the Cambodian king was compelled to surrender the last of his Mekong delta lands by the mid-eighteenth century. The political frontiers of modern Vietnam had finally been drawn, but the flow of Vietnamese beyond them into adjacent areas continues today as it has for so long in the past.

LANGUAGE

The brevity of the treatment of early Southeast Asia attempted here precludes offering even a cursory inventory of the cultural baggage carried by the various peoples who moved from north to south. Folklore, religious beliefs and practices, kinship systems, material technology, and all the other things that constitute culture differed from one people to the next. Anthropological research in recent years has documented the enduring vitality and exuberant variety of much of the cultural legacy brought into the region by the folk wanderings; but, it would be impossible here to seek to synthesize the various conclusions of these studies. Language, however, is an aspect of culture that can be most conveniently discussed in order to illustrate the complexity of the Southeast Asian human mosaic.

Just as scholars have yet to achieve consensus on the history of the folk migrations, there is still no universally accepted system of classification for the languages of the region. While bearing in mind, therefore, that almost any point made can be debated and quite possibly refuted, a scheme of classification may be attempted.[3]

Four language families are dominant in the region: Sino-Tibetan, Austro-Asiatic, Tai-Kadai, Malayo-Polynesian. The four, as distinct from one another as the Indo-European is from the Semitic family, are of course divided into many languages and subdivided into innumerable dialects. It must always be kept in mind that membership in a language family hardly assures mutual comprehension among members. Just as a knowledge of English opens no doors to Latvian or Bengali, a speaker of Chinese has no measurable head start in seeking to master Sino-Tibetan languages, such as Burmese or Karen or dozens of lesser ones.

One cartographic phenomenon is worthy of notice in this context. Agricultural or food-gathering practices cause many upland peoples to live only at certain altitudes. As a result, patterns of settlement follow contour lines, twisting and weaving around the hills and mountains, so that an ethno-linguistic map of continental Southeast Asia resembles a geodetic survey.

The Tibeto-Burman lineage of the Sino-Tibetan macrofamily is dominated in Southeast Asia by Burmese, the language of the principal population of Burma. Other speakers of Tibeto-Burman languages, such as the Kachins and the Lolos, live in the hilly Sino-Southeast Asian border country that stretches across northern Burma, Thailand, Laos, and Vietnam and into southern China and northeastern India. Related to the Tibeto-Burman languages within the larger Sino-Tibetan family are Karen, the major minority language of Burma that also extends into northern Thailand, and the Miao and Yao tongues of southern China, Thailand, Laos, and Vietnam.

The languages of the Austro-Asiatic family are remarkably numerous, though most of them are used only by small, harassed hill populations in mainland Southeast Asia. An exception to this generalization is the Khmer tongue of Cambodia spoken by nearly six million people.

The thirty million speakers of Vietnamese may or may not also merit listing under the Austro-Asiatic label. Since their place is uncertain, a special word on Vietnamese is necessary. The language is, at most, a distant relative of those easily tagged as belonging to the Austro-Asiatic

[3] Based primarily on Frank M. Lebar, Gerald C. Hickey, and John K. Musgrave, *Ethnic Groups of Mainland Southeast Asia.* New Haven: Human Relations Area Files Press, 1964.

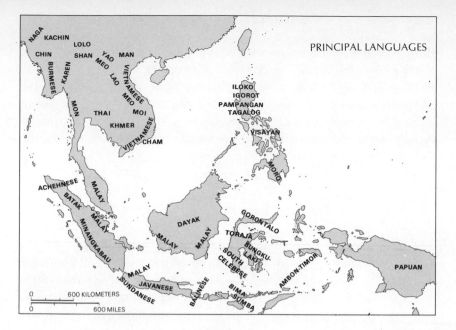

Map 3.

family. Indeed, Vietnamese has also been classified as a Tai-Kadai or Sino-Tibetan language. The fact that it is tonal and can seem mono-syllabic accounts in part for the confusion. The further fact that Vietnamese is heavily larded with loan words from Chinese adds to the uncertainty. The vocabulary of Vietnamese is largely Chinese in origin, in much the same way that English, a Germanic language, is massively indebted to Romance tongues. English obviously is not a Romance language; Vietnamese, rather less obviously, is not Sino-Tibetan. Possibly linguists will someday conclude that it is in a family of its own.

The Tai-Kadai languages include Thai, with perhaps thirty to thirty-five million speakers, Lao, Shan, and numerous lesser languages of scattered minority peoples in China, Burma, Thailand, Laos, and Vietnam. There are grounds for speculation that the Tai languages may not actually belong to a separate Tai-Kadai family but are remotely Sino-Tibetan. The difficulties of linguistic mapping in Southeast Asia are, thus, seen to be as formidable as those involved in labeling the other cultural manifestations of the area.

Malayo-Polynesian or Austronesian family members in Southeast Asia are located in seven of the nine present-day countries of the region; Laos and Burma are the two exceptions. The dispersed remnants of the Chams live in Malayo-Polynesian language pockets in Vietnam and Cambodia. Thailand, Malaysia, and Singapore all have ancient and substantial Malay communities; and in Indonesia, Malay and other Malayo-Polynesian tongues, such as Javanese and Balinese, are spoken by almost the entire population. The polyglot Philippine archipelago is also Malayo-Polynesian in language.

DEMOGRAPHIC PATTERNS

Southeast Asia, as a whole, is not overpopulated, but most of its people live packed together on the alluvial plains of the rivers and streams or on the fertile volcanic fields of Java. The bulk of the land of the region is unsuited to intensive agriculture due to thick jungle, impoverished soil, rugged terrain, or a combination of those handicaps. Beyond the bulging pockets of dense settlement there are only bands of slash-and-burn farmers or hunting and gathering peoples.

The concentrated farming peoples of the fertile enclaves, of course, constitute the majority populations of their countries. That demographic fact would not be especially noteworthy if it were not for the parallel ethnolinguistic and economic facts that the majorities are generally divided from the smaller populations by language and culture, as well as by living standards. Some random examples of the divisions are the Malays and the Sakai, the Lao and the Kha, the Vietnamese and the Moi. The nature of the separation between dominant and subordinate peoples is revealed by the fact that in the three examples just cited, as in countless others, the common name applied by the majority to the minority group is pejorative and means "slave" or "savage." Linguistic minorities are likely to be both despised and disadvantaged in Southeast Asia.

Bold efforts have been made to alter demographic imbalance and promote economic growth by bringing marginal or previously neglected land under intensive cultivation. Little success has been attained. Heavy demands for investment capital put such resettlement schemes beyond the reach of most. The progress of rural development and the opening of new lands in western Malaysia are atypical; only a relatively affluent country can afford such ventures. Successive governments in Indonesia for half a century have urged peasants to migrate from the central

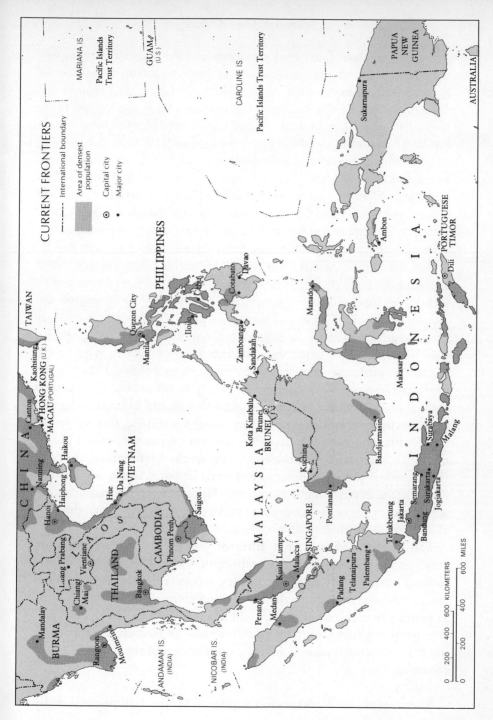

Map 4.

Javanese anthill to the virgin stretches of Sumatra; but, those who would be economically benefited have been reluctant to leave their home island. The inroads of land-hungry Christian Filipinos are fiercely resisted by the Muslims of Mindanao. All in all, it appears unlikely that population pressure in the heavily settled sections of Southeast Asia can ever be eased solely by outward migration.

The ethnolinguistic and economic gap between the concentrated farmers of the deltas and plains and the minorities of the hinterland are duplicated in part by the division that increasingly separates the peasant masses from the cities. Until not too long ago, Southeast Asian cities were few in number and functioned all but exclusively as places of residence for the elite and those who served them. The countryside supported the cities with taxes and food, but received little beyond rather capricious authoritarian rule in return. The old pattern of urban-rural dichotomy has lately been powerfully reinforced. Modernization obviously begins in the cities and spreads, usually with glacial slowness, to rural areas. Electricity, running water, and telephones are taken for granted in the major cities, with the exception of Jakarta, where daily life can be made adventurous by malfunctioning utilities. Villagers not far from the centers of modernity are likely to till the soil with ancient technology and to live in circumstances that would not seem odd to a ghostly visitor from Champa or Angkorian Cambodia. The chasm between cities and villages today is one of centuries as well as one of distance. To compound the problems of urban-rural bifurcation, many of the people of the cities today, most notably the Chinese, are alien to those of the countryside by ancestry. Moreover, acculturation to the values and habits of modernity can make even indigenous city dwellers almost equally alien in the eyes of rural compatriots.

The existence of two such different peoples, one urban, the other rural, might not be a threat to stability if the peasantry were wholly isolated from the city dwellers. In fact, however, the millions of country people who now go to the cities as temporary laborers or to settle as permanent residents of hideous slums are fully aware of the division. The great migrations of the present are those of landless peasants moving from the countryside to join the proletariat and the unemployed of the cities.

A survey of the fragmentation produced by the folk migrations, by patterns of settlement, and by current urbanization may suggest that Southeast Asia is simply too heterogeneous for analysis within a general framework. The suggestion would be unreasonable, for it is precisely in their individual and collective diversity that the states of the region manifest their similarity. Ethnolinguistic parochialism and economic imbalance afflict all the countries as they strive for nation-building. The states of today also share a set of common historical experiences that are due to their position at a crossroads of influences and pressures from outside. First came the impact of India and China; later Islam and Western imperialism arrived. It is to those great developments that attention must now be given.

READINGS

Burling, Robbins, *Hill Farms and Padi Fields: Life in Mainland Southeast Asia,* Englewood Cliffs, N.J.: Prentice-Hall, 1965.

Dobby, E. H. G., *Monsoon Asia,* 3rd ed., London: University of London Press, 1967.

———, *Southeast Asia,* 9th ed., London: University of London Press, 1966.

Fisher, Charles A., *Southeast Asia: A Social, Economic and Political Geography,* 2nd ed., New York: Dutton, 1966.

Fitzgerald, Charles Patrick, *The Southern Expansion of the Chinese People,* New York: Praeger, 1972.

Fryer, Donald W., *Emerging Southeast Asia: A Study in Growth and Stagnation,* New York: McGraw-Hill, 1970.

Geertz, Clifford, *Agricultural Involution: The Process of Ecological Change in Indonesia,* Berkeley: University of California Press, 1963.

Ginsburg, Norton, et al., *The Pattern of Asia,* Englewood Cliffs, N.J.: Prentice-Hall, 1959.

Hall, D. G. E., ed., *Atlas of Southeast Asia,* New York: St. Martin's, 1964.

Kunstadter, Peter, ed., *Southeast Asian Tribes, Minorities and Nations,* Princeton: Princeton University Press, 1967.

Lebar, Frank M., Gerald C. Hickey, and John K. Musgrave, *Ethnic Groups of Mainland Southeast Asia,* New Haven: Human Relations Area Files Press, 1964.

McGee, T. C., *The Southeast Asian City: A Study of the Primate Cities of Southeast Asia,* London: G. Bell and Sons, 1967.

Pelzer, Karl A., *Pioneer Settlement in the Asiatic Tropics,* New York: Institute of Pacific Relations, 1945.

Spencer, Joseph E., *Asia East by South: A Cultural Geography,* New York: John Wiley, 1954.

van Heekeren, H. R., *The Stone Age of Indonesia,* 2nd rev. ed., The Hague: Martinus Nijhoff, 1972.

Weins, Harold J., *China's March towards the Tropics,* Hamden, Conn.: Shoe String Press, 1954.

2
Cultural Crossroads

Southeast Asia is rightly known as a meeting ground of cultural forces. The history of the region has been largely interpreted in terms of the importation and adaptation of ideas and institutions from India, China, the Islamic world, and the West. To ignore the role of foreign influences in the shaping of Southeast Asia would be worse than unrealistic, but to seek to explain all or most of the region's evolution solely in terms of alien inspiration is indefensible. After all, Vietnam could adopt Chinese culture to its needs without sacrificing its sovereign pride. Indianization in other lands never eradicated indigenous foundations. Conversion to Islam did not transform Javanese or Malays into Arabs. And, nobody would argue that the Southeast Asians of today have been made into Europeans or Americans by the colonial experience. It has been precisely their power to absorb without being absorbed that has bound the various peoples together historically.

It of course saved analytical labor to divide pre-colonial Southeast Asia, like Gaul, into three parts: Farther India, the Vietnamese microcosm of China, and the relatively "untouched" Philippines. The approach, however, was dangerous, for it suggested that had the advanced

Indic and Sinic civilizations not bestowed their gifts on the region nothing would have happened there. Historians who subscribed to such theories necessarily had to assume that Southeast Asia had been a cultural blank slate until some two thousand years ago. There is growing and convincing evidence to the contrary.

Far from waiting in pitiful savagery for guidance from their cultural betters, prehistoric Southeast Asians attained an impressive technological level on their own initiative. Confidence at sea and productivity on land were largely the results of indigenous development. It now even seems quite possible that Southeast Asia was a Far Eastern site of early human progress comparable to the Fertile Cresent of Western Asia. Revolutionary archaeological finds in northern Thailand strongly indicate that agriculture was autonomously developed and was not an innovation brought by migrants. Dry rice farming, the cultivation of vegetables, the raising of domesticated cattle and possibly pigs, all were practiced in Southeast Asia as early as 5000 B.C., well before any great tide of civilization could have come from the north or the west. Metallurgy was similarly advanced; bronze was in use in northern Thailand in 3000 B.C., a thousand years before the ancient Chinese began casting the metal. In fact, the technologies of metal and agriculture may well have been carried to prehistoric China from advanced cultures to the south. The same could have been true for the diffusion of the technique of writing. At present, the entire subject of Southeast Asian prehistory is being brilliantly reworked on the basis of new discoveries and interpretations.[1]

Whatever the outcome of the present ferment in prehistory, it is certain that outsiders who first came from India and China to Southeast Asia were met by settled agricultural peoples living within established social orders, not by scattered bands of forest dwellers. Clearly, without the requisite material and institutional infrastructure, aspects of higher cultures could not have been so successfully transplanted to the region. Nor would so much that is neither Indian nor Chinese have endured had indigenous cultures not possessed vitality and been both receptive to enrichment and able to maintain distinctiveness.

[1] For an informative and illustrative example, see: Wilhelm G. Solheim, II, "The 'New Look' of Southeast Asian Prehistory," *Journal of the Siam Society*, 60 (January 1972), part I, 1-20.

Buddhist sculpture in Bangkok. The artistic legacy from India is clear. (Lea E. Williams)

THE INDIC HERITAGE

Having recorded reservations to the notion that Southeast Asian culture is simply the product of imported wisdom, it is possible to survey the enormous contributions that came from outside. Except for the Red River lowlands of northern Vietnam and the Philippines, the settled agricultural peoples were first and most decisively influenced by Indic civilization. In discussing the subject, it is essential to keep firmly in mind the fact that only impulses and examples from the subcontinent, not waves of Indian immigrants, were the sources of cultural evolution. Southeast Asia was never colonized, politically or through alien settlement, during the centuries of Indic cultural ascendancy. The region made brilliant and selective use of Indic models, but it was not obliged to accept, nor was it offered, administrative control or masses of migrants from India.

Three great achievements of human creativity on the Indian subcontinent were adapted to Southeast Asian needs. In the interrelated realms of government, religion, and the arts, the Indic impact was decisive. For a thousand years, much of the region was under the tutelage, direct and indirect, of men and ideas of Indian origin. Today, after centuries of virtual isolation from India, the heritage remains rich and pervasive.

During the flood tide of their influence, religious teachers and traders traveled across the seas or overland between the homeland and the outposts of Indic civilization. The traffic moved in two directions, the Indians going east perhaps being equaled or exceeded in number by Southeast Asians visiting India for commercial gain or religious enlightenment. There has never been a lengthier or more widespread process of cultural domination without the accompanying political subordination of the junior partner in the enterprise. The cultural resilience of Southeast Asia, thus, was forcefully demonstrated by the ability to import without surrendering autonomy. Of course, it must be acknowledged that political imperialism was not then part of the Indian tradition and that the subcontinent was hardly a unified nation-state capable of directing vast colonial conquests.

The extent and nature of the evolution of the arts, especially sculpture and architecture, have been the most fully studied of all the aspects of Indianization. The reason is simple: there is a wealth of tangible evidence available for investigation. Except for inscriptions, there is virtually no indigenous written record to document the history of Indic influence. The preoccupation of the Indians and their cultural clients with theological rather than secular concerns accounts for this state of affairs and, more than anything else, epitomizes the sharp difference between Sinic civilization, with its scrupulous concern for the maintenance of historical records, and the Indic tradition, with its more fragile interest in the affairs of this world. It is appropriate to note parenthetically that what scanty written documentation of early Southeast Asian history is to be found is largely of Chinese authorship.

Wherever Indic culture penetrated, new art forms and techniques were introduced as an essential part of new religious faiths. As most of the art was merely Indian in inspiration, not in execution, some have denounced it as synthetic art, impure and unorthodox. Others have praised the synthesis as the unique product of alien inspiration and what Quaritch Wales admiringly called "local genius."

The mysticism and magic of Indian religions appear to have been the chief attractions of the imported beliefs. The aura of supernatural power and vision assumed by the bearers of Indic culture was doubtless awesome to Southeast Asians steeped in animism. Buddhist monks, Brahmans, and Indianized laymen alike opened paths to greater emotional security on earth and the possibility of release from fear of what followed. Moreover, a cosmic explanation of the universe and of man's place in it was offered to supplant the patchwork of animist practice and belief. The promise of a more meaningful and worthy existence and a brighter future made the process of Indianization functionally comparable to other great cultural transformations from the Hellenization of the classical Mediterranean world to the industrialization of non-Western lands today.

Two points are to be kept in mind. First, the importation of Indic culture was not solely or, indeed, primarily the task of Brahmans and monks. Merchants could be fully qualified representatives of the higher civilization. They were surely more numerous and probably more mobile than their clerical partners in Indianization. Such men could be either Indians or Southeast Asians who had been to the source of Indian culture and returned, doubtless with the dedication and conviction of all converts. It is also more than likely that Indian merchants in such circumstances claimed loftier status in terms of education and enlightenment than was actually their due. The phenomenon of rising on the scale of social stratification by moving from the metropole* to the colonies, in this instance cultural colonies, may well be universal.

---

* The term *metropole,* recently borrowed by English from French, is far more precise than *mother country* or *home country* as a designation for a state in control of a colonial empire.

Frieze at Angkor Wat. Miles of such intricate carving cover the great complex of ruins. (Lea E. Williams)

The second consideration to emphasize is the adaptability of Indic religions to a new environment. On the one hand, Hinduism and Buddhism are understanding of heterodoxy; on the other, Southeast Asians, doubtless because of their diversity and their geographical location at the vortex of cultural currents, had tremendous absorptive and adaptive facility. There was no dogmatic rigidity in the Indic tradition to preclude the accommodation within Hinduism or Buddhism of local ideas and institutions. The comforts of the old animist ways were not denied the Indianized. Correspondingly, adding Vishnu or Maitreya to the pantheon enhanced rather than eclipsed the strength of familiar spirits. Syncretism and tolerance were the bases of Indianization in religion.

Given the awesome mystical potency of the leaders in Indianization, it was natural that a new form of political authority should emerge. Kings, their secular commands strengthened with religious weapons, replaced earlier local chieftains. The power of such monarchs was theoretically even greater than that of the "Caesaro-papist" Chinese emperors, to use the apt term of Max Weber. The Southeast Asian king was not proclaimed to be merely an intermediary between man and divine beings, he claimed to be an incarnation of a bodhisattva or a Hindu deity. One especially worthy Javanese ruler was honored as both a reincarnated Buddhist saint and a manifestation of Siva, thus demonstrating quite tidily the syncretic flexibility of the two great Indic religions in their Southeast Asian setting.[2]

The palaces and royal cities of the Indianized kings were designed as architectural symbols of regal divinity. The kingdom was conceived of as an earthly model of the universe; and, the capital city was designed as a microcosmic representation of the kingdom. Thus, just as the center of the universe in Indic imagination was Mount Meru, the center of the capital and of the country was the palace complex, invariably containing a peak, usually man-made, in which was incorporated a symbol of "the divine essence of kingship . . . embodied . . . in the actual king."[3]

The god-kings owed their people nothing. *Noblesse oblige* would have been a wholly meaningless concept to them. Theoretically, their rule was absolute, since their mandate was not of human origin. In practice, it can be assumed that for the bulk of the populace well beyond the capital the kings were like gods merely in the unintended sense of being feared from afar. The inadequacies of transportation and communication ensured that kings could exercise no close control over their peoples.

Royal absolutism was weakened in a more explosive fashion by usurpers and claimants to the throne, for whom regicide was the only sure way to power. The ritual and symbolic roles of the palace and the capital, together with regalia comprised of the crown, the royal sword, and that most serviceable of regal emblems under the tropical sun, the umbrella, made their physical seizure the *sine qua non* of the successful bid for power. Since the palace coup was the only means to topple the incumbent monarch, coup leaders had to have access to the palace, and

[2] H. G. Quaritch Wales, *The Making of Greater India*. London: Bernard Quaritch, 1971, 2nd ed., p. 131.
[3] Robert Heine-Geldern, *Conceptions of State and Kingship in Southeast Asia*, Data Paper no. 18, Southeast Asia Program, Cornell University, Ithaca, April 1956.

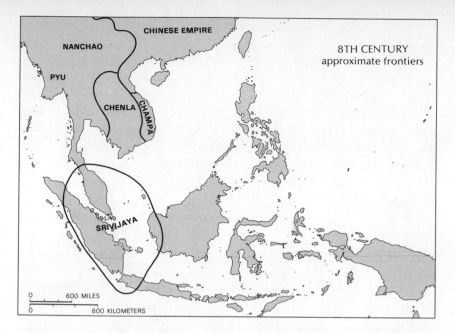

Map 5.

that requirement often limited their ranks to royal kinsmen. In consequence, kings frequently forestalled danger by exterminating close relatives.

The Hindu-Buddhist kings—the hyphenated designation conveniently implying that the two Indic religions were ascendant in different periods, places, and degrees—reigned over states of varied size and power. Inscriptions and other archaeological finds, together with Chinese dynastic records, establish the existence and extent of the major kingdoms and empires. Two basic types of states, agricultural and maritime, developed in response to the dictates of geography and economics. Some kingdoms were established primarily on a foundation of intensive agriculture in the rice-growing deltas and plains. Their populations were substantial; their territories were clearly defined. The surplus product of the paddy fields supported the royal edifice. Great public works in water conservancy and the construction of temples and palaces were undertaken by conscripted peasants and enslaved war captives, who had no doubt first entered military service as peasant conscripts themselves.

Continental Southeast Asia was, for the most part, the home of the agricultural kingdoms, though the productivity of Java permitted their

Colonnade at Angkor Wat. (Lea E. Williams)

establishment on a smaller scale on that island as well. Funan and Champa were the earliest major examples of these states. Established by the third century A.D. in what was to become southern Thailand, Cambodia, and Cochin China, the two were traditional enemies whose wars ultimately prepared them for convenient conquest, the rulers of Funan by the rising might of their close relatives the Khmer, and much later, Champa by the Vietnamese pushing south.

If monumental architecture and artistic creativity are measures of greatness, the Khmer kingdoms between the sixth and the fifteenth centuries tower in splendor over other Indianized states. Culminating in the grandeur of Angkorian civilization, Cambodia attained heights unapproached by her neighbors and never equaled subsequently. Angkor Wat and the lesser known Bayon and Banteay Srei still leave the visitor speechless in awed admiration. (One can merely hope that recent military occupants of the area have been similarly respectful.)

Angkorian greatness was threatened and, by the mid-fifteenth century, ended by the rise of the Thai. As reported in the previous chap-

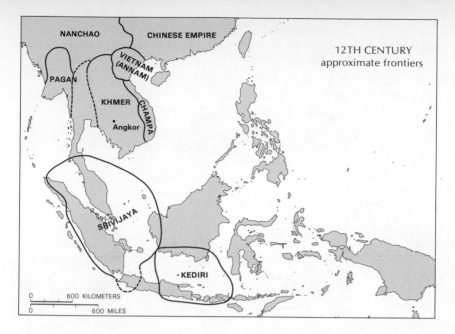

Map 6.

ter, centuries of migration from their southwest China homeland were greatly stimulated by the Mongols of the thirteenth and fourteenth centuries who both destroyed the vestiges of the kingdom of Nan Chao (in present-day Yünnan) and enlisted as allies those Tai princes already established along the upper and middle sections of the Salween and Mekong rivers. By 1347, with the founding of Ayutthaya on the agricultural base of the Chao Phraya delta, a Thai kingdom capable of challenging illustrious neighbors had come into being. The statecraft, religion, and art of Ayutthaya were largely derived from Khmer models, but no sense of cultural indebtedness impeded a Thai assault on Cambodia. The ancient enmity still smoulders, though mitigated since the eighteenth century by pressures on the Khmer from the Vietnamese.

Burma, as a land of sweeping agricultural plains, produced kingdoms roughly comparable to those of the Mekong and Chao Phraya deltas. Unification of much of the territory of modern Burma was finally achieved in the middle of the eleventh century with the conquest of the Mons of the lower Irrawaddy by the Burman ruler of Pagan. From that time on, the Burmans were in regular contact by sea with the South Indian and Ceylonese bastions of Buddhism that had withstood the spread of Hinduism. From those overseas sources, the Burmans,

33

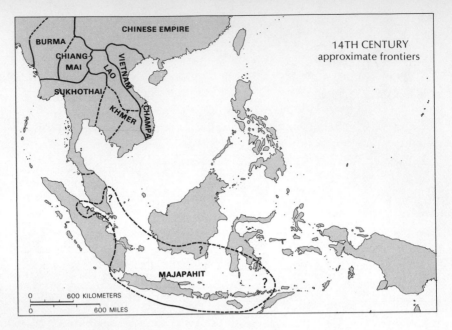

Map 7.

joined in due course by the Thai, the Lao, and the Khmer, were led to embrace Theravada Buddhism, now the chief religion of continental Southeast Asia, except in Vietnam, where the syncretic Mahayana Buddhism of the Sinic tradition prevails. The Pagan kingdom survived for two hundred years but in the late thirteenth century fell before the might of the Mongols and their Tai allies. It was well into the fifteenth century before Burma was reunited under a Burman dynasty, the Toungoo.

Maritime Southeast Asia, which includes the Malay Peninsula, did not give rise to Indianized kingdoms based on agriculture that compared in size to those of the continent. The reason was clearly geographic; only Java contained broad rice-producing areas. The maritime region, however, produced states of a different kind that rested on both farming and commerce and that, at least in claims, were territorially greater than Angkorian Cambodia. Two insular empires, Srivijaya and Majapahit, eventually dominated lesser kingdoms in the Indonesian archipelago.

Between the seventh century and the beginning of the thirteenth century, Srivijayan power was based on control over the Strait of Malacca from a capital at the southeastern end of Sumatra. The extent of the empire varied in response to the rise and fall of contending royal might on agricultural Java. From the late thirteenth century, after the tumult caused by a Mongol incursion into insular Southeast Asia, until the end of the fifteenth century, the Javanese kingdom of Majapahit sought with declining success to exercise authority over the sea routes and ports of most of what is now Indonesia and Malaysia. It may or may not be true that the kings of Majapahit did not rule the interiors of the islands and the Malay Peninsula, but the belief in a pre-colonial empire in effective command over much of maritime Southeast Asia has become a conspicuous component of the Indonesian nationalist faith in our own century.

The distinction between the continental Hindu-Buddhist kingdoms and the maritime states of Srivijaya and Majapahit was basically economic. The former were essentially "hydraulic societies," to use Wittfogel's term, supported by agriculture; the latter were enriched both by peasant toil and commercial profits. The sea routes of trade within the region and between southern and eastern Asia were commanded by the maritime rulers. Political mastery resting on a strategic geographical location was later to be won by the Malacca sultanate and eventually by Western imperialists.

The Indianized states in the long run were incapable of containing the spread of Islam in maritime lands and the invasion of Western conquerors throughout most of continental Southeast Asia, but their demise was gradual. Indeed, it can be argued that the survival of a rich Indic heritage in most of the region and the fact that Indianized Thailand was an absolute monarchy until 1932 and was never colonized are testimony to the enduring vitality of the old ways.

CHINA ON THE PERIPHERY

The role of China in the evolution of Southeast Asia is dwarfed when compared to that of India. Yet, China was surely not inferior to India in cultural attainment, material wealth, or population. Nor was she inaccessible, as is demonstrated by the maintenance of trade routes linking the Indian Ocean and the South China Sea since antiquity. The explanation of China's marginal involvement in the lands to her south is to be found in the very nature of traditional Chinese civilization and the Confucian state it supported and in the fact that the Chinese never attempted to export their culture beyond the frontiers of the Sinic world.

Religion is central to any discussion of the comparatively minor influence of Chinese culture on peoples to the south other than the Vietnamese. The picture becomes clear upon acceptance of the argument that "Hindu cultural influence had to do only with sacral rites and ritual, and also literature and government techniques, which had a consecrated magical character."[4]

The folk religion of ancient China, like all village traditions, was culture-bound and could not take root in foreign soil. The Confucian cult of the elite, even in its syncretic forms, was too austere or too recherché to have broad appeal even in its homeland. Moreover, the more orthodox Confucianists were inclined toward haughty agnosticism and held religion to be useful primarily as a means of soothing inferior beings, such as illiterates and women. The elite of old China was not a reservoir of Confucian evangelicals.

The Chinese emperor, unlike the Indic god-kings, laid no claim to divinity. The occupant of the imperial throne was believed to hold a heavenly mandate to rule, but he was still a mortal. His role was that of an intermediary between lesser beings and the powers of heaven. Though he could petition and serve the gods, he could not claim to be one of them. It is not reckless to imagine that the founders of the early kingdoms of Southeast Asia would have found the status of god-king more appealing than that of messenger between man and heaven had the choice been presented.

Finally, on the Chinese inability to export religion, two additional points can be made. First, the traders from China who dealt with overseas counterparts and customers were not cloaked in official or clerical garb. They were members of neither the secular nor the sectarian elites of their homeland. Indeed, at least within the idealized Confucian social scheme, merchants were lowly beings. Despite that fact, perhaps the Chinese traders abroad could have posed as upper-class representatives of a high civilization. To do so, however, the merchants would

[4] J. C. van Leur, *Indonesian Trade and Society,* The Hague: van Hoeve, 1955, p. 251.

have had to wish to convert strangers to their ways and beliefs. That raises a second and crucial point.

The phenomenon of Sinocentrism is known by all students of China. Not only did the Chinese believe their country to be central geographically, they were convinced that their civilization was pre-eminent. Barbarians could seek Sinification, but the Chinese were not inclined to lead them to it. It is only necessary to read the descriptions of foreigners left by Chinese travelers to recognize that, while barbarians could be seen as frightening, disgusting, quaint, or amusing, they were never held to be worthy of salvation. Missionary zeal, religious or cultural, never afflicted the Sinocentric.

The learning of China, like the religion, did not travel well. The writing system was probably the chief cause. Leaving aside the fact that the calligraphy of China was aesthetically admirable, it must be acknowledged that no other advanced civilization produced a system that approached that of the Chinese in cumbersomeness. The absence of an alphabet or syllabary obliged those seeking literacy to master thousands of ideographic and, with distressing rarity, pictographic characters. Outside China, only the Koreans and the Japanese, neither of whom had another model to study, and the Vietnamese, who were under Chinese rule for a millennium, adopted Chinese writing. For centuries thereafter, those three peoples struggled to bend the borrowed writing system to the needs of their own non-Sinic languages. First, the Vietnamese and, quite recently, the Koreans have traded the artistic joys of Chinese calligraphy for the efficiency of phonetic systems. The Japanese have not yet gone quite that far, but they have been moving in that direction for centuries.

Other neighbors of China who could tap Indic sources all developed writing systems based on Indian examples. Even the Mongols and the Tibetans, long in close contact with China, opted for Indic alphabets. It is not strange, therefore, that the more remote Southeast Asians followed a like course.

The matter of writing systems is stressed because literacy in Chinese was essential to extensive Sinification. The literature of the Confucian tradition was closed to those not literate in Chinese, yet command over the great books was indispensable to the development of a mandarinate of the Chinese type. Therefore, Chinese political institutions could be transplanted in recognizable form only to places where Confucian education had prepared the ground. (Japan managed to mesh feudal and Confucian patterns in government, but there is no need to consider that unique and intricate story in the present context.)

Two geopolitical points help explain the slight influence of China in most of the Far Eastern tropics. First, from the third century to the sixth century, precisely when currents from India were transforming much of Southeast Asia, China was divided as the result of the collapse of the Han dynasty. Chinese energies necessarily were channeled into coping with the internal difficulties of a fragmented country. It was no time for expansion into foreign lands. Significantly, it was during the three centuries of disunion that China herself came under the influence of Indian Buddhism. Second, while barbarian invasion was a periodic threat along the Inner Asian frontiers, the absence of a corresponding menace from the south quite properly led Chinese rulers to focus attention on lands to the north and northwest.

Despite the relative isolation of China from Southeast Asia, an imaginative argument has been devised to present China as passively responsible for the rise of the great kingdoms of the area beyond Vietnam. It has been suggested that, when there were vigorous Chinese dynasties able to pursue active policies abroad, nearby peoples were prevented from mobilizing their strength. Conversely, when China was internationally impotent due to domestic turmoil, neighboring states could expand in both size and power. The theory rests on the assumption that China could not tolerate challenges to her paramountcy. Although there is some chronological evidence to back this idea, there is nothing else of substance. Chinese political support, through the machinery of the tribute system, was doubtless welcomed, but outside Vietnam, China very rarely could put military force behind her diplomacy. Nevertheless, the Sinocentric interpretation of history retains some popularity, particularly among latter-day believers in a "domino theory," who hold the fate of Southeast Asia to be ultimately in the hands of the men in Peking.[5]

---

[5] One eminent Sinologist, for example, after citing chronological evidence in support of the theory of a Sinocentric East Asia, in which the rise and fall of Southeast Asian states is directly and causally linked to China, goes on to state: "This series is clearly no mere coincidence, but reflects a reality of power politics . . . which the later European conquests once obscured and made forgotten, but which is once more clear enough today." C. P. Fitzgerald, *A Concise History of East Asia,* London: Heineman, 1966, p. 229.

Having emphasized the essentially minor cultural role of China, it is necessary to record the fact that Chinese trade goods, merchants, and travelers eventually spread throughout the region. Finds of ceramics from the Han period confirm the early origin of commercial contacts. From that time on, Chinese products were sent south in exchange for tropical exports. It is more than likely, however, that most cargoes were carried in Southeast Asian, Indian, or Near Eastern vessels until a quite late date, possibly in the twelfth century. It is significant in this connection that two Chinese Buddhist pilgrims who sought learning in India and passed through the region, one in the fifth century and the other in the seventh century, reported sailing aboard non-Chinese ships. Similarly, the establishment of an Arab trading enclave in T'ang dynasty China indicates that ships and merchants from the western shores of the Indian Ocean had sailed out in strength by the eighth century. Later, Chinese shipbuilders and navigators were to excel, but their mastery was not achieved until the fourteenth and fifteenth centuries.

The historian concerned with early Sino-Southeast Asian contacts is distressed by the relative paucity of information on the subject. Since Chinese merchants and shippers did not enjoy the formal backing of the mandarinate, the official records all but ignore their private trade. Had imperial China sponsored quasi-official overseas commerce, as Holland and England, for example, were to do, the record would be far more bountiful. Even the most magnificent achievements in the maritime history of China and, possibly, the entire world, those of the Ming explorations, are thinly documented, for, though the voyages had imperial endorsement, the political and ethnocentric hostility of the men who finally drafted the dynastic history of the period precluded adequate and objective reporting.

Nevertheless, even sabotage by mandarin historians could not eclipse the brilliance of the early fifteenth-century Chinese seafarers. A series of seven voyages, from 1405 to 1431, took great fleets of up to sixty-two vessels, manned by as many as 37,000, to the ports of southeastern and southern Asia and to places as remote as Arabia and the east coast of Africa. It is even possible that a detached element of one armada rounded the Cape of Good Hope and entered the South Atlantic. The stately progress of Chinese ships of gargantuan proportions for the age of sail was reliably powered by the seasonal monsoons; the skill in dead reckoning of their sailing masters was reinforced by use of the compass and celestial navigation.

The most prominent commander in these historic enterprises was an imperial eunuch named Cheng Ho. His rise to authority inevitably was the result of court favor; and, just as inevitably, he thereby won the contempt of the literati-officialdom who held semi-educated eunuchs to be loathsome, venal creatures. It was such mandarin animosity that contributed in part to the abandonment of the exploratory endeavor once the original imperial patron was gone. China then pulled back into her complacent isolation, missing a chance to extend her might around the world. At that very moment, Europeans, feeble at sea though they were in comparison with the Chinese, were poised to burst upon the global scene. The one resource held by the West, but traditionally denied the Chinese, was the ambition to conquer distant lands.

THE SPECIAL CASE OF VIETNAM

A number of passing references to the Sinification of the Vietnamese have already been made; it is now appropriate to describe the bare essentials of the process. Long before the Chinese empire was unified, a great variety of peoples lived in the western and southern parts of what is now China. Chinese civilization, born along the Yellow River in the north, over time moved like a glacier to cover lands to the south. Also like a glacier, Chinese civilization did not reach some highland areas, leaving the peoples on the heights to continue in their old cultural patterns. Other non-Chinese, in the direct path of the invading civilization, were normally obliged to flee or to accept Sinification.

In a coastal arc of territory below the Yangtze River were a people known to the Chinese as the Yüeh. Those in the northern sections of their traditional homeland, who experienced early and massive cultural impact from their advancing Chinese neighbors, had been largely absorbed by the third century B.C. However, their kinsmen to the south, having been insulated by distance from the full force of Chinese expansion, had not lost their distinctiveness. Thus, when the first dynasty of China fell at the end of the third century B.C., a people calling themselves Nan Yüeh (southern Yüeh), as contrasted with their northern, Sinicized relatives, were formed into an independent kingdom, known to the Chinese as Nan Yüeh and, in the pronunciation of its inhabitants, as Nam Viet, later Vietnam.

The independence of Nam Viet was maintained for nearly a hundred years, but it was finally crushed in 111 B.C. by the power of the Chinese under a ruler of particular skill and determination, Han Wu-ti, whose reign title significantly means "Warrior Emperor of the Han." From that time on, until 939 A.D., the Vietnamese were without a country, living merely in a portion of the Chinese state called An-nan or Annam, the Pacified South, a name that appropriately suggests control through military conquest and occupation.

A thousand years ought to have been an ample period for the total absorption of the Vietnamese through Sinification, but, for reasons that are presumably destined to remain partially unclear, the people of the Pacified South resisted. The learning and the writing system of China were accepted, indeed embraced by the Vietnamese upper stratum. Confucianism and, in due course, Mahayana Buddhism transformed the religions of both the elite and the lowly. Administration by a mandarinate of classical education was imposed, with Vietnamese entering the prestigious ranks of the officialdom by the second century A.D. Logic and the precedents afforded by the numerous examples of other peoples ruled by China disappearing through Sinification suggest that Vietnamese separateness should have been impossible. So much for reasoning and a belief in the recurrence of historical patterns!

The key to the mystery of Vietnamese recalcitrance probably lies forever buried in the unrecorded history of countless villages. Speculation on the question offers clues but can never lead to certainty. For what it may be worth, an attempt can be made to offer an explanation for the unique resolution of the Vietnamese in the face of overpowering Chinese cultural domination for over a thousand years.

The continued use of the Vietnamese spoken language throughout the period of Chinese rule was surely the most conspicuous expression of ethnic distinctiveness. Every time a person spoke, Vietnamese identity was reaffirmed. Thousands of loan words and the writing system borrowed from China did not destroy the non-Sinitic foundation of Vietnamese. The world has produced so many instances of linguistic patriotism that it is not unreasonable to suppose that the people of China's Pacified South developed strong, emotional attachments to their language.

The folk culture, as manifested in mythology and village custom, survived the alien impact and remained patently non-Chinese. There is no cause for surprise in this, for members of the mandarin and gentry strata, both Chinese and indigenous, who were the agents of Sinification, were remote from the peasantry. In the case of Vietnam under Chinese control, the cultures of the elite and of the masses were characterized by differences of both economic station and national origin.

The centuries of intermittent warfare between the Vietnamese and the Chams, begun under Chinese auspices but continued from the tenth century to the fifteenth century by independent Vietnam, could only have served to heighten patriotic commitment and to instill military virtues. There is nothing like a foreign threat to stimulate an awareness of separate identity and the determination to defend the homeland. The Vietnamese emerged from ten centuries of Chinese occupation equipped with a warlike tradition and with probably the most keenly developed patriotism in Southeast Asia.

One last speculative point can be made. It was the custom in the Chinese mandarinate to assign officials with bad records or hostile superiors to remote posts where life was often hard and promotions were infrequent. Vietnam was such a place of banishment. There is evidence in the homesick, frustrated poetry composed by mandarins in exile that posting to Vietnam bred resentment and unhappiness that must have been reflected in arbitrary, even brutal, rule.

The centrifugal forces generated by the disintegration of an imperial dynasty, the T'ang, finally propelled the Vietnamese onto their own course in history. Earlier attempts to throw off Chinese rule, abortive though they were, indicate that restlessness had been growing for a long time. Once independence was established, the Vietnamese state was carefully modeled after that of China in a manner that suggests that the now familiar technique of defeating a colonial power by employing weapons and resources acquired from it had been mastered. There is also room for speculation that, since Vietnamese identity had been preserved most fully by villagers, the forces in the struggle against China represented the forerunners of peasant armies engaged in "wars of national liberation," to borrow a term from the Maoist lexicon.

The Chinese made periodic efforts to pacify the land to the south once again. All failed. The Mongols sent their troops to Vietnam, as did their successors, the Ming rulers, in the same period of expansionism that saw the voyages of Cheng Ho. In both the eighteenth and nineteenth centuries, the Ch'ing dynasty intervened, on the first occasion in an internal contest for the Vietnamese throne and on the second to check French aggression. Even our own century has produced Chinese involvement in Vietnam. In the 1920's, the Kuomintang of Chiang Kai-shek sponsored a Vietnamese puppet party to oppose French colonialism; at the end of the Second World War, Chinese Nationalist troops occupied Tonkin and the northern half of Annam. The People's Republic of China understandably has a close interest in its southern neighbor, though the Hanoi government has never displayed satellite obedience to Peking. The most enduring theme in Vietnamese history is that of the struggle to preserve independence from China.

THE TRIUMPH OF ISLAM

Possibly as a legacy from the medieval crusaders, Westerners appear to believe that Islam conquers solely by the sword. The Bedouin fanatic on his charger, armed with a cruel blade of Damascus steel, not the gentle teacher or the devout layman, is imagined to be the instrument for the propagation of the Islamic faith. Whatever may or may not have happened elsewhere, the spread of Islam in Southeast Asia was possibly one of the most peaceful processes of mass conversion in the history of religion. This is not to deny that wars between Muslim and infidel states took place, but it is difficult to blame religious zeal and bigotry in those cases. In any case, it is clear that no Arab forces swept into the region on a *jihad* with scimitars slashing at infidels. The most remarkable aspects of the Islamization of most of maritime Southeast Asia were the tranquility and the swiftness of the process.

Islam was represented in Southeast Asia from an unknown, but remote, time. Traders from the Near East at least passed through the region en route to T'ang dynasty China. An inscription on a Javanese tombstone of the early twelfth century establishes that at least one Muslim woman of unknown origins was on the island at the time. Presumably, another Muslim carved the inscription. There is no evidence of others, though their presence can be reasonably assumed. It appears that few, if any, local people had been converted at such an early date. Indeed, it was only at the end of the thirteenth century that Islam took root in the archipelago at its westernmost extremity.

Marco Polo sailed through Southeast Asian waters just as the first indigenous communities of Muslims were taking shape. He reported that by 1292 the people of the small state of Perlak at the northern end of Sumatra had been converted, whereas neighboring peoples remained outside the faith. Most would not do so for long.

The turning point seems to have come early in the fourteenth century, when in the Indian state of Gujarat, then just conquered by a Muslim sweep southward, many new followers of the Prophet were recruited. The extensive, long-established trading links maintained by Gujarati merchants with maritime Southeast Asia thereafter conveniently served as channels for conveying the Islamic message. Accordingly, the new religion was spread over the trade routes, affecting first the ports and their coastal environs. In little more than a century, the religion had begun its progress through the maritime region and was destined to reach as far as the southern Philippines.

It is clear that the Sufism, or mystical Islam, brought from India had a strong appeal. The magic and faith healing of the Sufi mystic *cum* traveling merchant who set out from Gujarat fitted in quite comfortably with the animist and Indic beliefs and expectations of Southeast Asians. The more austere, orthodox religion of the earlier Arab merchants had significantly made scant impression in the preceding centuries.

Reinforcing the attraction of Islam in its syncretic Sufi form were the direct simplicity of the Prophet's teachings and the ease of joining the faith. Once a person repeated the phrase that expresses the central belief of the religion, acknowledging Allah as the one divinity and Muhammad as Allah's messenger, he was a Muslim. The extent to which he became versed in the Koran and in the usages of Islam depended upon the availability of men who could instruct him. Conversion to Islam can be achieved in seconds; the attainment of theological sophistication and ritual purity can come later, even generations later.

The ease of conversion and the accommodation within Islam of followers with limited religious educations did not, of course, mean that

The National Mosque in Kuala Lumpur, symbolic of the vitality of Islam and the wealth of Malaysia. (Lea E. Williams)

Southeast Asian Muslims were ignorant of the "five pillars" of the religion that are basic guides to behavior and belief. Again, in discussing these five cardinal elements, the uncluttered directness of Islam is apparent.

First and fundamental, Muslims are required to make their confession of faith in the oneness of Allah and the prophecy of Muhammad. Second, prayer five times a day is obligatory, with the noon prayers on Friday ideally being said in assembly at a mosque. Third, the faithful are supposed to contribute a portion of their incomes to the religious and charitable work of their communities. Fourth, the strict observance of total fasting during the daylight hours of one month of the Arabic lunar year is to be endured. Finally, if possible, each Muslim ought to make the *haj* or pilgrimage to Mecca once in his lifetime. It is no doubt unnecessary to point out that, except in the case of the first requirement, a great deal of flexibility has existed in the observance of the regulations from place to place and from time to time.

45

It is significant that Islam, when it began its march through maritime Southeast Asia, represented a high civilization and offered ties with the outside world. It is also to be remembered that the egalitarian status of all men before Allah endowed the religion with democratic qualities that made it particularly attractive to the masses. The promise of salvation offered the Muslim is not dependent upon class or caste. There are no Brahmans; in fact, there is no clergy in the usual sense.

The appeal of Islam to the common people is not hard to imagine; but the willingness, indeed, the eagerness of their rulers to accept its teachings requires explanation. For one thing, the kings and princes of the trading countries must have seen Islam to be a useful link with the outside world. Further, the ruler who became a Muslim lost nothing of his earlier regal authority. He continued to hold the symbols of power of the Indic god-kings, as is still evident in the regalia and language of Malay courts today, and was able to reinforce his authority by becoming the spiritual leader of his people. Claims of illustrious ancestry tying the new sultans to figures in Muslim and Near Eastern history were often put forward to strengthen the legitimacy of their role.

When all the speculative paths have been explored, it seems that the chief reason for the victory of Islam must have been the Southeast Asians' ability to absorb external influences and bend them to their own purposes. Consequently, the Islam of the region is often syncretic and uniquely tolerant of actions that might be considered scandalous elsewhere in the Muslim world. Clifford Geertz has recorded the divine blessing invoked by a Javanese villager at a feast that tidily documents the relaxed nature of Islam in much of Indonesia. The prayer expressed reverence for an assortment of spirits, including the guardians of the village and of the principal figure at the feast, the household angel of the kitchen and the ancestors of the host, and all the guests. The spirits of the house, of a nearby volcano, of the fields and of the waters were equally honored, as were others, as well. The prayer ended piously with: "There is no god but Allah and Muhammad is His Prophet."[6]

Thus, Muslims in Southeast Asia can continue to enjoy the com-

6 Clifford Geertz, *The Religion of Java*, London: The Free Press of Glencoe, Crowell-Collier-Macmillan, 1960, pp. 40-41.

forts of their animist and Hindu-Buddhist heritages. The syncretic hospitality of Islam surely contributed decisively to the victory of the religion. The process of purifying the practices of Muslims can extend over centuries and, in the region, is still in progress.

THE RISE OF MALACCA

The state based on maritime commerce reached its fullest development after the establishment of Malacca around 1400. The models of Srivijaya and Majapahit clearly inspired the founder of the last pre-colonial trading empire, just as the example of Malacca was later to serve the Portuguese and their successors. Control over the shipping lanes was the key to power and prosperity. Malacca was built on the west coast of the Malay Peninsula overlooking the narrowest part of the strait that now carries its name. At a point where a river mouth offered anchorage to trading vessels and where a commanding hill loomed, the town was planted. Before long, patrol boats obliged passing ships to call at the new port and quickly established a prosperous pattern. Malacca became a great entrepôt where cloth from India and spices from the eastern archipelago, in particular, were exchanged.

The founder of Malacca remains a somewhat shadowy figure. It is generally accepted that he was a Sumatran princeling who had fled across the strait to avoid the uncertainties of life in the slowly declining Majapahit empire. He and his followers, many of whom were rough and ready seafarers, faced two threatening powers—Majapahit, still seeking to control the strait, and Siam, claiming sovereignty over the whole peninsula. Either of the two would have been delighted to see Malacca die in its infancy; Siam, especially, made substantial efforts to achieve that end. By happy coincidence, however, Malacca came into existence on the eve of the brief Ming expansionist era. Thus, the new state could profit from a Sino-Malaccan diplomatic alliance that was advantageous to China in that it helped keep the strait in friendly hands. A Chinese fleet first called at Malacca in 1403 and was followed by others over the next three decades. Formal tributary relations operated from 1405 until Malacca fell to the Portuguese over a century later. Even the founding ruler of the maritime state traveled north to the Chinese capital to demonstrate his respectful gratitude to the emperor. That royal gesture was repeated on a number of subsequent occasions.

The conversion of the Malaccan king to Islam may have been similarly prompted by the desire to enlist the support of diplomatic allies and trading partners. The threats from Majapahit and Siam clearly suggested the advantage of forging links with the small Muslim states at the northern end of the Sumatran side of the strait. The task was undertaken through diplomacy, including a reported marriage of political convenience, and the presentation of trading incentives. Despite those moves, Malacca eventually incurred the hostility of a rising Sumatran state, Acheh, which came to regard itself as a bastion of Islamic orthodoxy and became a commercial rival of Malacca.

Just when the Malaccan ruler assumed the Muslim designation Muhammad Iskander Shah to replace his original Indic name, Parameswara, is unclear. A Chinese delegation reported that the king had accepted the Prophet's teachings by 1409, though it appears that the effect and degree of conversion may have been slight. His two successors, perhaps significantly, were known by both Muslim and Indic names. Not until 1446 does Malacca appear to have become firmly and profoundly Islamic; but, from then on, the propagation of the faith gained momentum in the commercial centers of its far-flung trading empire.

The present state of historical scholarship does not permit more than speculation on the possibility that the first king of Malacca, in his eagerness to earn the support of the Ming emperor, may have considered the tactical desirability of entering the Muslim faith for that purpose as well as for winning Muslim friends in Sumatra. That Cheng Ho and some of his officers were Muslims could not have gone unnoticed in Malacca. Moreover, Chinese foreign policy in its Ming expansionist phase obviously was much concerned with establishing good relations with Islamic rulers, a circumstance that goes far to account for Cheng Ho's appointment to command the voyages across the Indian Ocean, by then a Muslim sea. After all, the Ming dynasty was still apprehensive over the possibility of a Mongol resurgence. It made sense to seek Muslim allies to check the Mongols in Inner Asia and the Hindu-Buddhist states of Southeast Asia, including Siam, known as a past friend of the Mongols.

The Malaccan kingdom eventually encompassed territories on both sides of the strait. The ports and, at least nominally, the hinterland of the central east coast of Sumatra came under Malaccan rule. On the Malay Peninsula, Siamese claims were successfully challenged in Perak, Selangor, Trengganu, Pahang, and Johore, thus establishing the frontiers of much of the land that now makes up West Malaysia, formerly Malaya. The islands off the coast of Sumatra, as well as Singapore and the Riau archipelago, were also brought into the kingdom. That last development helps account for the emergence in Malaccan times of the Malay language of sailors from the islands of the strait as the lingua franca of maritime Southeast Asia and eventually as the foundation of the national languages of both Malaysia and Indonesia in post-colonial times.

The profits of the Malacca trade invited jealousy. Throughout its century of existence, the kingdom was perennially threatened by covetous neighbors. The attacks were beaten back, but envy and bitterness persisted. The Portuguese assault that ultimately destroyed the kingdom was supported in part by old enemies of Malacca.

SOUTHEAST ASIA ON THE EVE OF THE PORTUGUESE ARRIVAL

The social and political outlines of modern Southeast Asia had already been roughly drawn by the time Western imperialism first struck. Despite profound changes, the broad picture of the area at the beginning of the sixteenth century does not seem strange when compared with the scene near the end of the twentieth. No one would claim that little happened in the intervening five hundred years, but the continuity of the region has been too often overlooked. Just as Indocentric historians have sought to portray the region as a cultural void before the glories of Indic civilization were bestowed upon it, Europocentric students of recent times have been inclined to suggest that Southeast Asia today is primarily, almost exclusively, the creation of foreigners. As the post-colonial period lengthens, it becomes increasingly evident that the Western presence changed far less than has been imagined.

At the opening of the sixteenth century, Theravada Buddhism dominated continental Southeast Asia, except for Sinicized Vietnam. Islam was well along on its march through the maritime countries. The great

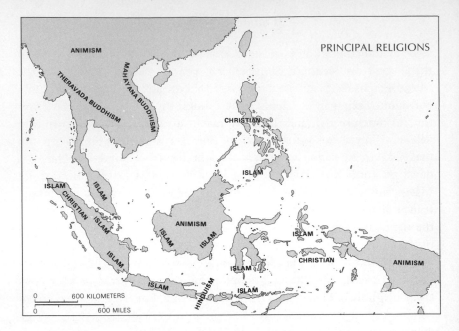

Map 8.

bulk of the people in the region were peasants toiling for subsistence. Rulers were answerable only to themselves or to rebellious contenders. Those conditions have not been much altered.

Five hundred years ago, a villager from one country, if transported to another, would generally not have found the way of life incomprehensible. Farming techniques, economic patterns, the structure of local political authority, artistic forms, folklore, animist beliefs, in other words most of the culture, would have seemed comfortably familiar. What was true then remains essentially true today. Peasant Filipinos, subject to the longest process of transformation under colonialism, even to the extent of mass Christianization, are no less Southeast Asian than the Lao on whom colonialism lay briefly and superficially. Indeed, it might be argued that the majority of Filipinos can be proud of a cultural tradition that owes but little to India, China, and Islam. In that sense, the Filipinos may be regarded as unique custodians of an ancient and indigenous heritage. It is certain that they are not aliens in the region.

The finest historian of Southeast Asia of an entire generation, the late Harry Benda, was especially interested in the process of decolonization, the casting aside of the superfluous residue of the period of for-

50

eign control. Recent history demonstrates that the toppling of nascent democratic institutions, the erosion of bureaucratic standards, the campaigns to replace Western with national languages in government and education, the expulsion of tens of thousands of foreigners and the attendant loss of their modern skills, the confiscation of much private and corporate capital, and all the other moves that have been made at various times and places to strengthen nationalism through attacks on the colonial legacy, have had astonishingly little effect on village life in Southeast Asia. To the masses, decolonization, like colonialism before it, is a remote phenomenon. There is no better proof of the endurance of the indigenous culture.

Moreover, the striking similarity in so many respects of the post-colonial countries suggests a regional uniformity that the Western intrusion could not shatter. It is not fanciful to foretell that, a century from now, the colonial experience will be seen as having merely disturbed, not diverted, the flow of Southeast Asian history. It is at least comfortably certain that no writer who now makes such a suggestion will be called to account if the prediction proves to be inaccurate.

READINGS

Audric, John, *Angkor and the Khmer Empire,* London: R. Hale, 1972.

Buttinger, Joseph, *The Smaller Dragon, a Political History of Vietnam,* New York: Praeger, 1958.

Coedès, George, *Angkor: An Introduction,* London: Oxford University Press, 1967.

———, *The Indianized States of Southeast Asia,* Honolulu: East–West Center, 1968.

———, *The Making of South East Asia,* Berkeley: University of California Press, 1966.

Firth, Raymond, *Malay Fishermen: Their Peasant Economy,* London: Kegan Paul, 1946.

Gibb, H. A. R., tr., *Ibn Battuta: Travels in Asia and Africa, 1325-54,* London: Routledge, 1953.

Giteau, Madeleine, *Khmer Sculpture and the Angkor Civilization,* London: Thames and Hudson, 1965.

Groslier, Bernard; Arthaud, Jacques, *Angkor: Art and Civilization,* New York: Praeger, 1966.

Landon, Kenneth B., *Southeast Asia: Crossroads of Religions,* Chicago: University of Chicago Press, 1949.

Le May, Reginald, *A Cultural History of South East Asia,* London: Allen and Unwin, 1954.

————, *The Culture of South-East Asia*, London: Allen and Unwin, 1954.

Ma Huan, *Ying-yai sheng-lau* (*The Overall Survey of the Ocean's Shores*, 1433), Cambridge: Hakluyt Society at the University Press, 1970.

MacDonald, Malcolm, *Angkor*, London: Jonathan Cape, 1958.

Mirsky, Jeannette, *The Great Chinese Travelers, an Anthology*, New York: Pantheon, 1964.

Phayre, Sir Arthur P., *History of Burma, from the Earliest Time to the First War with British India*, 2nd ed., London: Susil Gupta, 1967.

Schrieke, B. J. O., *Indonesian Sociological Studies*, The Hague: van Hoeve, 1955.

Sutterheim, W. F., *Studies in Indonesian Archeology*, The Hague: Martinus Nijhoff, 1956.

Wales, H. G. Quaritch, *Ancient South-East Asian Warfare*, London: B. Quaritch, 1952.

————, *Dvaravati: The Earliest Kingdom of Siam (6th to 11th Century A.D.)*, London: B. Quaritch, 1969.

————, *The Making of Greater India*, 2nd ed., London: B. Quaritch, 1961.

————, *The Mountain of God: A Study in Early Religion and Kingship*, London: B. Quaritch, 1953.

————, *Prehistory and Religion in Southeast Asia*, London: B. Quaritch, 1957.

Wheatley, Paul, *The Golden Kersonese*, Kuala Lumpur: University of Malaya Press, 1966.

Winstedt, Sir Richard, *The Malays: A Cultural History*, 4th ed., London: Routledge and Kegan Paul, 1956.

Wolters, O. W., *Early Indonesian Commerce: A Study of the Origins of Srivijaya*, Ithaca: Cornell University Press, 1967.

3
The First Wave of Imperialism: The Iberian Vanguard

Like Louis XVI, who observed in his diary on the day the Bastille was stormed that nothing of consequence had happened that day, the great majority of Southeast Asians were unmoved by the Portuguese capture of Malacca in 1511. Whereas the French king was speedily proven wrong, most Southeast Asians would continue in their complacency for a very long time. Western imperialism pried open the doors to tropical East Asia only with difficulty. Four centuries passed between the first Western attack and the final consolidation of colonialism in Mindanao, northern Malaya, and Acheh. As a result, the period of alien rule in the centuries after 1511 was brief for many peoples; and, even where colonial regimes were established, relatively few Southeast Asians ever saw their conquerors. The unevenness of the Western impact and the shallowness of alien penetration often seem to be obscured by the duration of the colonial era, but in fact the Western presence was remote for most villagers during those four and a half centuries.

To caution against assuming that history was drastically redirected by the first European interlopers is not to deny that a powerful new force was unleashed by the Portuguese who originally brought Southeast Asia into contact with the materialistic, aggressive civilization that was to set the direction of aspirations and apprehensions around the world. The Portuguese were the advance scouts of the conquerors who eventually burst onto the global stage armed with the might of industrialization; but that explosion came three hundred years after the initial probing sorties of the Westerners.

THE RISE OF THE PORTUGUESE

There is still no easy explanation for the astonishing rise of the Portuguese in the century after the death in 1460 of their patron of exploration, Prince Henry the Navigator. Reasons for the phenomenon can be discussed at length, but outstanding questions always remain. There is no simple accounting for the timing and the magnitude of the Portuguese triumph. That an impoverished corner of Europe should so swiftly emerge as the prototype of the modern great power, capable of shaping world events, could not have been anticipated nor can it, even now, be fully explained. In any case the Portuguese could soon declare with maudlin pride that, though God had given them a tiny birthplace, the world was their grave.

The very barrenness of Portugal, probably more than any other factor, stimulated the overseas thrust. History is replete with examples of poor, rugged peoples attacking vulnerable neighbors. With the reckless bravery of men with little to lose, Vandals, Huns, Bedouins, Mongols, and countless others have repeatedly lashed out in frenzies of conquest. The Portuguese seem to have been cast in the same mould, except for one important difference. Too feeble in number to challenge other Europeans, they mounted a new sort of offensive, one based on recent innovations in seafaring and naval warfare. That the improvements in ship design, especially in sail plans, and navigation were essentially of Eastern origin did not in the least deter the Portuguese from attacking those to whom they were technologically indebted. Like the Vikings, the Portuguese were a maritime horde; but, unlike the early Scandinavians, they possessed ships capable of transporting substantial armies and of being employed as floating fortresses. The Vikings could raid; the Portuguese could blockade and besiege. The developments in naval artillery and vessels in the fifteenth century, in terms of global impact, were comparable to the introduction of airborne weaponry in our own age.

Portugal's campaign of conquest was sustained by two unfailingly potent commitments, one to the service of God, the other to the winning of wealth. Seldom have men been so happily driven by lofty and base motives in tandem. The historical record establishes that the winning of commercial profits invariably took precedence over the saving of souls, but that fact does not diminish the role of religion as a source of justification for any action that seemed expedient. Slaving, piracy, torture, and killing all had their places in the Christian scheme of things in an age of savagery in the name of religion. Papal bulls of the mid-fifteenth century gave specific reassurance on that point.

The centuries of Moorish occupation in Iberia were drawing to a close as the Portuguese began their rise. Though the last European toehold of the Moors at Granada was not captured by the Spanish until 1492—a date not without other significance in the era of exploration—the Portuguese had freed themselves of Muslim rule two and a half centuries previously. That earlier victory, however, did not appreciably diminish the yearning for further triumphs of the Cross over the Crescent. Overseas expansion by the Portuguese can be said to have opened with their capture of the Moroccan port of Ceuta in 1415.

Their continuing crusade did not prevent the Portuguese from undertaking voyages of discovery that in no way contributed to the crushing of the Muslims. While fighting spasmodically in Morocco in the early fifteenth century, the Portuguese simultaneously pushed out into the Atlantic to find and colonize the Canaries, Madeira, the Azores, and the Cape Verde Islands, though only the last three were to remain under their sovereignty. Such deviation from the campaign against Islam suggests that striving to attain economic goals from the beginning at least equaled in weight dedication to the Christian God.

The odds against total victory over Islam were by no means unrecognized by the Portuguese. Expedient accommodations were often made with Muslims and other non-Christians in order to enlist allies and win trading partners. From the very start of their expansion, in similar acknowledgment of their own limitations, the Portuguese had hoped to find the Christian kingdom of the mythical Prester John somewhere to the east, so that a pincers offensive could be mounted against the Muslims. For a time, Coptic Ethiopia seemed to offer the promise of support by co-religionists, but the East African Christians remained isolated in their highland seclusion. In any case, the Portu-

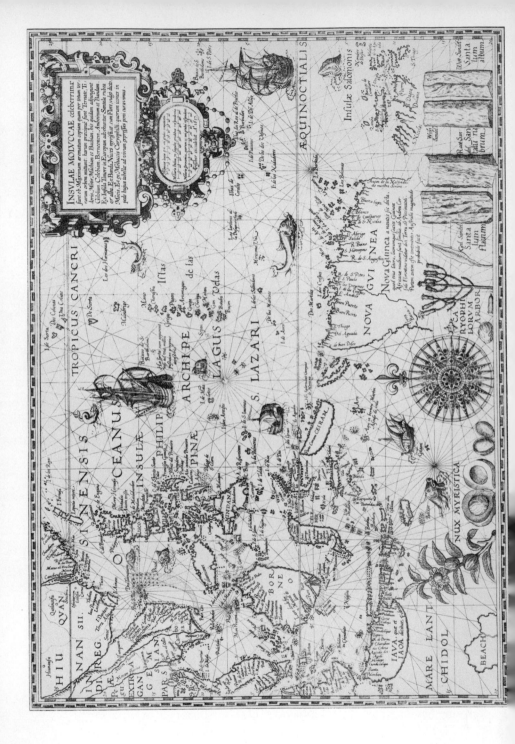

INSVLAE MOLVCCAE celeberrimæ

HIU

NAN SII.

QVAN

SINENSIS

TROPICUS CANCRI

OCEANUS

PHILIP

PINAE

INSVLAE

ARCHIPE

LAGUS

S. LAZARI

BOR
NE
O

IAVA

CHIDOL

MARE LANT

BEACH

NVX MYRISTICA

NOVA GVINEA

AQUINOCTIALIS

Insulæ Salomonis

CARYOPHY
LORVM
ARBOR

guese campaign was all but exclusively a maritime undertaking to which the Ethiopians could have contributed little. It is, in that connection, worth noting parenthetically that Western European attacks on Islamic countries made scant headway on land until the industrial revolution armed the imperialists with irresistible strength in the nineteenth century.

The first commercial profits won by the Portuguese were of West African origin. Gold from Guinea enabled Lisbon to play a leading role in the financial revolution that moved across Western Europe in the fifteenth and sixteenth centuries. The poverty of Portugal in natural resources and in agriculture was offset by the purchasing power of coins minted of gold acquired in Guinea. Dealing in slaves from the same general area of Africa also enriched Portugal, though the demand for slaves did not become insatiable until the opening of the Americas in the sixteenth century, well after the Portuguese had completed their sweep across the world's oceans.

The lure of Eastern products, notably spices, drew the Portuguese on once they had rounded the bulge of West Africa. A quarter of a century of southward probing finally brought a Portuguese ship under Bartolomeu Dias to the Cape of Good Hope and into the Indian Ocean in 1488. The sea route to the East was open; the means were at hand for the disruption of the spice trading monopoly of the Venetians and their Muslim partners. Vasco da Gama finally brought the first Indian cargo home from his voyage of 1497-99. Columbus died supposing he had found the way to India; the Portuguese knew they had done so.

The idea of entering into competition with Arab and Muslim Indian traders and shippers in the Indian Ocean was unappealing to the Portuguese, who regarded monopoly as the only foolproof basis for profitable commerce. Accordingly, once their strength was adequate, the Portuguese moved to secure fortified positions from which to dominate the sea routes. Under the leadership of the bold and imaginative Affonso de Albuquerque, Viceroy in the East from 1509 to 1515, a forti-

---

A late-16th-century map, variously attributed, depicting early cartographical knowledge and maritime technology and the tropical products that drew the Portuguese and their Anglo-Dutch heirs to Southeast Asia. A superb reproduction of this map can be found in *Portugaliae Monumenta Cartographica* (Lisbon, 1960).

fied trading center was built at Goa on the western shore of India in 1510, while other strategic points were occupied elsewhere on that Indian coast and along the rim of the African continent. With those positions secure, the Portuguese moved quickly to reach the great spice market to the east and to interdict the Arab sea lanes to the west. Malacca was seized in rather short order; but Ormuz, commanding the entrance to the Persian Gulf, was not captured until 1515.

The Malaccan sultanate had enjoyed a century of pre-eminence in Eastern trade when the Portuguese arrived in the waters it controlled. After the forceful and humiliating rejection of their diplomatic attempt in 1509 to win a place for themselves in the Malayan emporium, the Portuguese became convinced that an attack on the city was justified. Two years would pass before Albuquerque had developed a protected supply route and mobilized a striking force, a major proportion of which was composed of Indian manpower. In 1511 he was ready. The first of his assaults on Malacca was repulsed, but a month later vastly superior firepower and heedless bravery overcame the far more numerous defenders and gave victory to the Portuguese. Malacca was not to be restored to indigenous control until 1957.

Mastery over the strait that links the Indian Ocean, the waters of insular Southeast Asia, and the South China Sea did not automatically endow the Portuguese with monopoly control over Eastern trade. Co-operative indigenous merchants still had to be attracted to come to the Malaccan emporium; enemies of the Portuguese, including the remnants of the defeated sultan's forces, had to be kept at bay. Success was won without difficulty in the first endeavor, but the military security of Malacca never ceased to be menaced.

From the beginning of their rule over Malacca, the Portuguese welcomed Asian buyers and sellers who were prepared to trade on their terms. Non-Muslim Indians, some Sumatrans hostile to Acheh and the Chinese took immediate advantage of the opportunity. In fact, the Chinese on the scene appear to have been de facto allies of the Portuguese from the time of the 1511 battle for Malacca, when at least one Chinese junk was employed in the assault on the port. Muslim traders, on the other hand, had initially been chased away, though the Portuguese were soon ready to be more hospitable—especially to the Gujaratis, who had been the prime trading community under the sultans.

The monopolistic convictions of the Portuguese left them discontented even after the resumption of commerce at Malacca. The profits to be made solely from transporting Eastern products to Europe were deemed inadequate. Moreover, spices and other goods continued to be exchanged by Achehnese, Javanese, and Chinese merchants at ports outside Portuguese authority. The problem seemed to demand control over production at the source of supply. Hence, the Moluccas or, more descriptively and romantically, the Spice Islands, became targets of renewed Portuguese expansion. Ternate, Tidore, and Amboina, as well as other, lesser islands in the eastern part of the Indonesian archipelago, all came within the Portuguese orbit at various times in the sixteenth century. Cooperation with the Muslim rulers of some of the islands caused no obvious uneasiness among the Christian intruders, who were quite prepared to hold their own missionaries in check for the sake of good business. A combination of treaties with cooperative sultans, who generally sought Portuguese support against local enemies, and military incursions into producing areas not covered by treaties served to limit the production of spices for the sake of high price levels in the world market. The Portuguese monopoly was never total, but it was impressively profitable.

Crusading ardor and proselytizing zeal rarely overcame commercial acquisitiveness, as the complaints of the contemporary missionaries in the field testify. Nevertheless, the conversion of heathens was attempted where feasible. Relatively little was accomplished. Orphans were baptized; local wives embraced their husbands' faith; slaves and others helplessly subservient to the Portuguese might accept Christianity. Muslims and Hindus, with somewhat less firmness, were unswayed, despite rather strenuous efforts, particularly at Goa, to discourage the public practice of their religions. It is ironic that the Portuguese missionaries won their greatest victory in Japan, where up to 300,000 people accepted baptism in the second half of the sixteenth century, though the Portuguese had no colonial or military structures in the country. Sad to report, in the following century, the shoguns destroyed the Japanese Christians with a speed that at least equaled that of their conversion.

Statue of St. Francis Xavier at Malacca. Note that the figure has been garlanded in veneration by local Hindus. This is yet another example of religious syncretism in the area. (Lea E. Williams)

THE DECLINE OF THE PORTUGUESE

The first overseas European empire flourished for less than a hundred years before entering a decline that has gone on down to the present. It is frequently pointed out that the pioneers of Western imperialism are only now in final retreat from Africa and from Timor in the Indonesian archipelago. At Macao on the south coast of China, their colonial presence is tolerated solely because it serves the economic interests of the People's Republic. Possibly because Portugal never became an industrialized state, her colonies were not subjected to the pressures for change that ultimately emerged in the overseas holdings of the more affluent powers. There was no need in the Portuguese colonies to educate a large class of clerks and petty bureaucrats that could man extensive commercial and administrative structures and eventually constitute the nuclei of nationalist revolutionary movements. There were no great transfusions of capital into the Portuguese territories to disturb the traditional subsistence economies. There was surely little commitment in Lisbon to advancing colonial subjects toward modernity and autonomy, for such altruistic and politically subversive notions were necessarily a luxury to be afforded only in wealthy twentieth-century metropoles. The poverty of Portugal probably helped preserve the residue of her empire, just as it was once instrumental in the launching of her first campaign of conquest beyond the seas. Be all that as it may, it is also clear that a wealthier country would not have succumbed so swiftly in the contest for colonies that brought other European powers into Asia.

The population of Portugal was not much more than one million at the height of her imperial greatness in the sixteenth century. Manpower was always in a short supply, and the deficiency was compounded by the merciless toll taken by tropical diseases once men were sent to the colonies. So high was the death rate that it seems remarkable that volunteers for expatriation could have been found. In fact, relatively few were. A large proportion of the builders of empire were exiles who had somehow run afoul of the brutal laws of their homeland and suffered banishment.

The scarcity of men was especially acute in the professional seafaring ranks. Adventurous aristocrats could lead bodies of impressed sol-

Heraldic carving on a gate at Malacca, purported to be Portuguese. (Lea E. Williams)

diers, but the command and navigation of ships could not be left to amateurs. Partly for that reason, ships were perennially in short supply.

The deficiencies in manpower and shipping, it must be remembered, afflicted an imperial power with worldwide involvements. The Portuguese sought to maintain paramountcy along the African littoral, in Middle Eastern waters, on the western coast of India, as well as in maritime Southeast Asia. Major undertakings in trade took them to China and, far more profitably, to Japan. They also were obliged to worry over the security of a struggling venture in Brazil. From the Amazon to Kyushu, the Portuguese tried to stand guard. The burdens were too great. Portugal had to retreat from imperial grandeur.

In 1521 the sole surviving ship of the three commanded by Magellan in his rounding of the Horn and voyage across the Pacific reached the Spice Islands. The great explorer himself was not on board, as he had been killed in an affray with islanders in the Philippines. The Portuguese were anything but pleased to receive their Iberian cousins, for the Spanish had opened a new route from Europe to the Indies and thus threatened Portuguese domination over the marketing of spices in the West. Moreover, the Spanish quickly demonstrated their determination to do just what was most feared; more of their ships appeared in the islands in 1527 and 1528 and in the 1540's. In part because of the logistical shortcomings of the Spanish trans-Pacific route from Mexico and in part because the conquistadors were profitably preoccupied in the Americas, the Portuguese held a loose grip on the Spice Islands until 1574, when they were expelled from Ternate by islanders enflamed by Portuguese clumsiness and cruelty. The Spaniards immediately seized the chance afforded them in Ternate; but their move made little lasting difference due to developments halfway around the world.

In 1580 the Portuguese royal line died out and Philip II of Spain united the two crowns of the Iberian peninsula. For the next sixty years, Spain's Dutch and English enemies exploited the opportunity to shatter the Portuguese empire. It would be wrong, however, to regard the results of an accident of kingly succession as the principal cause of the ebbing of the Portuguese tide. Had Lisbon not been linked to Madrid, the pace of imperial disintegration might have been slowed; but, there is no reason to assume that the energies and ambitions of the two northern European states that so eagerly entered the imperial contest would have been held in check for long. The institutional, material, and human resources of Portugal simply could not have supported her global pretensions, once the determined opposition of superior powers was mounted against her.

A forewarning of impotence had actually come during the peak of expansionism in the first half of the sixteenth century, when the Chinese government brought the Portuguese firmly to heel, permitting them only the limited trading and tributary privileges customarily available to tractable barbarians. It is worth remembering that the establishment of the Portuguese on the tiny peninsula of Macao in the middle of the sixteenth century was, in the Chinese view, in keeping with a tradition that had long enabled barbarian traders to concentrate in their own ghettos. Legal sovereignty over Macao was not surrendered by China until late in the nineteenth century, when the dynasty was finally too weak to resist and too tired to care.

THE SPANISH IN EARLY MODERN EAST ASIA

The Spanish, despite a series of sorties into Southeast Asia, did not permanently establish themselves in the region until 1565, more than forty years after Magellan had led his ships westward across the Pacific. As observed previously, the lateness of the Spanish can be attributed primarily to the distractions of conquest and the lure of precious metals in the New World. There was no eagerness to leave known sources of wealth to engage in speculative ventures halfway around the globe. Furthermore, though it was to prove meaningless in Southeast Asia, a treaty between the Iberian states, concluded at Tordesillas in 1494, had confirmed the famous papal division of the world, under which the Portuguese claimed exclusive rights in Asia and Africa, while the Spanish were restricted to the Americas, except for the bulge of Brazil. If the treaty provisions had been faithfully honored, at least according to Portuguese interpretation, there could have been no Spanish offensive in the East.

The Philippine archipelago may indeed have been well within the zone of exclusive Portuguese treaty rights, but it was outside the primary area of Portuguese concern. The islands produced little for export; there was no great trading center comparable to Malacca that invited seizure and occupation. Hence, Spanish incursions into the Philippines caused no notable anxiety in Lisbon.

The archipelago had been named after Philip II while he was a young prince; under his kingship Spain undertook its conquest. In 1565 a small fleet from Mexico, commanded by Miguel Lopez de Legaspi and carrying some four hundred men, reached Cebu. The link between New Spain and the Philippines was to be maintained until the nineteenth century. Trade goods were carried in the galleons that crossed the Pacific to and from Acapulco; the islands were placed under the viceregal authority of Mexico City. The arrangements symbolized the Philippines' position as a remote appendage of the Spanish empire in the Western hemisphere.

Like the Portuguese, Spaniards went to the Orient in search of spices to market and souls to save. They largely failed in the first endeavor but were hugely successful in the second. Cloves, nutmeg, and pepper were not produced in quantity in the Philippines, nor were there other readily tapped sources of wealth. On balance, possession of the Philippines by Spain was economically unwise, for it was long necessary to draw on the treasury of the Mexican viceroy to subsidize the Asian colonial enterprise. Had it not been for the exchange of Mexican silver for silks and other Chinese goods that became centered on Manila, the galleons would have made their homeward passages in ballast.

It was, in fact, the trade in Chinese goods that caused the Spaniards to shift their main Philippine base from Cebu to Manila in 1571. The superb harbor at the new location had by then become the meeting place of junks from China and trading vessels from the southern parts of the Philippines. A flourishing bazaar had grown up for the exchange of silk and china for spices, sandalwood, and other tropical products from the south.

The Spanish saw a dual advantage in winning control over the great bay at Manila. The shippers from the southern islands were Muslims—Moors or, more accurately, Moros to Spaniards with long folk memories. Dislodging them would be consistent with the most compelling of crusading goals. Once the Moros were put to flight, the Chinese goods traded at Manila could be sold at substantial profit to the ladies and grandees of both New Spain and the mother country. Moreover, there was no doubt that the Chinese junk skippers were eager to trade delicate consumer goods for indestructible specie. So great did the trans-Pacific flow of silver become that the Mexican dollar was in due course established as the standard unit of commerce and accounting on the China coast and enjoyed that prestige until the eve of the Second World War.

Evicting the Moros at Manila and driving them back to the southern end of the archipelago has been customarily credited with having halted an Islamic spread that would have enveloped the Philippines and closed the islands to Christianity had the Spanish arrived on the scene a few decades later. There is room for speculation on the matter. Elsewhere in maritime Southeast Asia, Islam moved most swiftly along the trade routes and into the port cities and towns. Merchants and the rulers of trading centers were the principal agents in the process. When trade flourished—as it did with the coming of the Portuguese—Islam gained rapidly. Progress by the religion in areas little touched by commerce was slow or even impossible, as is demonstrated by the examples of the Bataks of Sumatra, the Dayaks of Borneo, and the Balinese. Moreover, acceptance of the Prophet's teachings, once they had been introduced into an area, normally moved down the social ladder from royal court to peasant village. The absence of elaborate and extensive political structures in the Philippines precluded conversion of the masses by royal example and encouragement. Therefore, it is likely that without a commercial web and without kings to guide the people, Islam could have made but creeping advances in the Philippines.

The political organization of the pre-colonial Philippines was as much a blessing to the Spanish as it was an obstacle to the propagation of Islam. There were no states in the agricultural lowlands and no extensive tribes in the mountainous regions. Kinship was the basis upon which the settled farming and fishing people formed each local, small polity or "barrangay." (The term was derived from the word for sailing canoe and referred to the craft that had brought the first settlers of an individual barrangay from lands to the south and west.) A barrangay, each headed by a senior clansman, might contain between 200 and 2000 people. There was no higher political or administrative authority than the headmen of the innumerable barrangays. No basis for ongoing cooperation among the tiny units was maintained; indeed, suspicion and enmity often existed among them. The decentralized, fragmented social and political structures of the Filipinos could not have better suited the Spaniards, both lay and clerical.

Though resistance, both passive and warlike, developed locally, the inability of the barrangays to mobilize for collective defense against the intruders enabled the Spanish to spread their rule and their religion with mercifully less bloodshed than in conquered American lands. Only the Muslims of the southernmost islands and inaccessible hill peoples escaped baptism and quasi-serfdom.

Drawing upon their experience in Mexico, the Spanish divided the conquered areas of the Philippines into administrative units called "encomiendas," each headed by a Spaniard established by royal order as the "encomendero." The people of the several peasant communities in an encomienda were obliged to pay an annual tribute in goods and render labor service to the encomendero, who for his part was charged with protecting those under his authority and serving as a lay missionary to instruct the people in the rudiments of Christianity in preparation for baptism. Encomiendas were generally awarded to veterans of the conquest or to other favored colonists, though a considerable number of districts were exploited as crown lands to help support the colonial regime. Despite official restrictions to minimize excesses, there were numerous opportunities for abuse and exploitation by encomenderos and their private bodyguards and agents. Moreover, the co-opted remnants of the pre-colonial barrangay headmen were reconfirmed in their positions and pressed into the service of encomenderos, often skimming off their own shares of peasant tribute in the process. Possibly the most burdensome provision of the system was that which enabled the encomendero to force the people to sell agricultural surpluses to him at fixed prices. It is presumably needless to add that the profits gained through the subsequent sale of such goods did not flow back to the peasants. "The good-humored Filipinos," as one of their most distinguished historians, Horacio de la Costa, observes, "had need of all the cheerfulness they could muster."[1]

The Christianization of the lowland and coastal peoples of Luzon and the Visayas moved ahead quite smoothly, once enough Spanish friars reached the islands. By the start of the seventeenth century the process had attained the proportions of an epidemic. The reasons for the success of the missionaries are refreshingly straightforward. There was, of course, no pre-colonial religious establishment to destroy; the animist tradition had been observed essentially on an individual or family basis without the need for an organized clergy. Equally important, the demands made on those who were drawn or coerced into Christian conversion were initially light. Only the memorization of a few religious formulas, the renunciation of paganism, and the acceptance of monogamy were obligatory. As plural marriage had not been general, even the third requirement was easily met by most. Divorce, on the other hand, was a conspicuous part of the indigenous culture and posed something of a problem to the friars. Possibly because of that circumstance, the missionaries were inclined to give their most active attention to instructing children who had not yet fallen into the wicked ways of their parents.

Once baptized, the new Christians could seek through study to qual-

---

[1] Horacio de la Costa, S. J., *The Jesuits in the Philippines, 1581-1768*, Cambridge: Harvard University Press, 1961, p. 151.

ify for reception of the Eucharist; but, in the early decades at least, relatively few converts were certified as qualified for confirmation. This pattern of Christianization in successive stages had been applied in Mexico and was deemed suitable for *Indios* on either side of the Pacific. Though the arrangement obviously helped overcome deficiencies in missionary strength, gradual Christianization also resulted in the survival of pre-Conquest beliefs and practices, or what has been called the "Philippinization of Spanish Catholicism."[2]

The Portuguese empire in Southeast Asia was shattered in the first half of the seventeenth century; that of the Spanish survived, though just barely. Both suffered from inadequacies born of imperial overexpansion. The Portuguese had spread over more of the world than they could defend against determined opposition. Spain remained a great power by the measures of the age, but the task of extracting wealth from her American holdings left little energy and generated even less incentive for economic construction in the Philippines. As a result the archipelago slumbered. The friars continued their spiritual endeavors and the Manila galleons made their annual crossings; but the masses of Filipino peasants remained in their villages, toiling to win subsistence for themselves and tribute for their encomenderos. Economic growth and political awakening lay centuries ahead. Despite increased demands for their labor and new burdens of conscience, the Filipinos largely continued in their traditional ways. The islands had become an outpost of empire, yet they would long remain, as they had when the tides from India and China and Islam had come to Southeast Asia, virtually isolated from the changing world outside.

The principle of royal monopoly upon which the Portuguese and Spanish based their imperial systems impeded colonial development in two costly ways. First, there were no inducements to attract private capital or stimulate its formation. Second, Iberian administrators were committed to policies that served home country interests but might not be productive in the colonies. The subsidization of the church and the absorption into overseas service of poorly qualified men who had to be accommodated because of noble birth or royal favor are examples of the latter liability. The Dutch and the English, to whom atten-

[2] John L. Phelan, *The Hispanization of the Philippines*, Madison: University of Wisconsin Press, 1967, pp. 72 ff.

tion must now be given, chose a course that was not merely different; it was revolutionary.

READINGS

Boxer, Charles R., *Fidalgos in the Far East, 1550-1770*, The Hague: Martinus Nijhoff, 1948.

Collis, Maurice S., *The Grand Peregrination, Being the Life and Adventures of Fernao Mendes Pinto*, London: Faber and Faber, 1949.

———, *Siamese White*, London: Faber and Faber, 1941.

Cortesao, A. Z., tr., *The Suma Oriental of Tome Pires*, London: The Hakluyt Society, 1944.

De la Costa, Horacio, S. J., *The Jesuits in the Philippines, 1581-1768*, Cambridge: Harvard University Press, 1961.

Lach, Donald F., *Asia in the Making of Europe*, Chicago: University of Chicago Press, 1965.

Meilink-Roelofsz, M. A. P., *Asian Trade and European Influence in the Indonesian Archipelago between 1500 and about 1630*, The Hague: Martinus Nijhoff, 1962.

Parry, J. H., *The Spanish Seaborne Empire*, London: Hutchinson, 1966.

Phelan, John L., *The Hispanization of the Philippines: Spanish Aims and Filipino Responses, 1565-1700*, Madison: University of Wisconsin Press, 1959.

Pigafetta, Antonio, *First Voyage around the World*, Manila: Filipiniana Book Guild, 1969.

Shurz, W. L., *The Manila Galleon*, New York: Dutton, 1959.

Van Leur, J. C., *Indonesian Trade and Society*, The Hague: van Hoeve, 1955.

4
The Second Wave of Imperialism: The Company Formula

THE DUTCH

In the light of subsequent history, it is sometimes difficult to recall that the close of the sixteenth century found the Dutch far better equipped than the English for the winning of an empire. Hence, Holland was able to establish and maintain hegemony in maritime Southeast Asia for nearly two hundred years, until the convulsions of the Napoleonic era. In population, the Dutch were as poorly endowed as the Portuguese, so their rise to imperial greatness should perhaps be regarded as equally remarkable. That is not the case, however, for Holland was able to exploit resources denied the Portuguese, resources that more than compensated for her weakness in numbers.

If the drive of the Iberians for empire was initiated and in part sustained by momentum built up in the centuries of struggle against the Moorish occupation of their peninsula, that of the Dutch was similarly generated by their rising in 1568 against rule over the northern Low Countries by the Hapsburg king of Spain, Philip II. The rebellion of the Hollanders against a ruling house installed over them by the peculiarities of dynastic succession and royal politics was decisively reinforced by the ardor of the Reformation. The war between the Protestant Dutch and the Catholic Spanish was no less religious in origin and bitterness than the earlier contest between Iberians and Muslims. Indeed, the later set of enemies appears to have been the less compromising. When Portugal was united with Spain under the single crown of Philip II in 1580, the holdings of both pioneers in overseas imperialism became prizes to be won in the fight for the independence of the Netherlands and the glory of Protestantism.

The war against the Spanish crown was carried to distant lands around the globe and continued until 1648, when Dutch independence was finally conceded in the Treaty of Münster. The Portuguese, already grievously weakened, had to battle on till 1663, when the Dutch won their final prizes on the Indian coast. The earlier restoration of Portuguese national sovereignty in 1640 had proved to be a mixed blessing that preceded over two decades of intermittent struggle against both Spaniards and Hollanders.

Portugal, not Spain, bore the brunt of the Dutch global offensive for the simple reason that she possessed more colonial prizes vulnerable to Dutch seapower. She was also the weaker partner in the ill-starred Iberian union. Though they fared better than the Portuguese, the Spanish were by no means immune to Dutch attack, as, for example, when efforts were made in the early seventeenth century to blockade Manila Bay in order to prevent Chinese and other Eastern shipping from bringing cargoes for the galleon trade. The Dutch were defeated in that undertaking by Spanish resolve, reinforced by the determination of Chinese junk skippers to keep the Manila emporium open. On one illustrative occasion, a Chinese crew sought to save their ship by pouring molten sugar on their attackers, "whereby," in the words of a contemporary Spanish priest, "they sent fourteen Dutchmen to hell in the form of candy."[1]

Holland was no newcomer to seafaring when her imperial adventure began. Her North Sea fishing fleets had long been a rugged school for sailors. The Baltic trade and other European coastal commerce had given the Dutch both technical skill and capital with which to move into greater ventures. It was, in fact, in capital accumulation and investment that Holland was supreme. Merchant wealth and bank loans at interest rates that were productively modest for the period were the chief sources of Dutch expansionist vigor. Her population deficiency

[1] De la Costa, *The Jesuits in the Philippines*, p. 341.

could be and easily was offset by hiring Scandinavians and Germans for marine and overseas service. Thus, functionally, Holland was like an industrialized city drawing labor from the rural hinterland. The poverty of Holland in materials for building and outfitting ships was similarly overcome by the purchasing power of her entrepreneurs. Relatively unencumbered by unbusinesslike passions and prejudices, the Dutch were also superbly equipped emotionally for the realization of their grand imperial dream.

The first ships to reach the East from Holland arrived in 1596. Though Dutch vessels had been active in the Atlantic for some years before that date, there had been no previous effort to reach the Indies partly because Dutch merchants, through arrangements with their Portuguese colleagues for the distribution of spices in northern Europe, had enjoyed a share of the profits of the Eastern trade. When Philip II finally succeeded in closing Lisbon to the Dutch in 1594, there was no further reason to avoid offending the Portuguese by competing with them in the Indies. Of equal importance, the navigational intelligence required for sailing to the East Indies had been unavailable to the Dutch earlier. It was only with the publication in the last decade of the sixteenth century of a geographical and cartographic work by a Hollander with lengthy experience in Asia that the route was opened. Even so, some ships from Holland first tried with dreadful results to sail westward to the Spice Islands, following the course of Magellan and using the strait named after the Spanish explorer.

Initial Dutch voyages were sponsored by a number of groups of merchants from various cities and towns in the Low Countries. The arrangement was hazardous, for the loss of a ship in the service of one group could bring bankruptcy to an entire town. The solution lay in sharing risks and centralizing capital formation within a single corporate enterprise. Accordingly, in 1602, the United East India Company—Vereenigde Oostindische Compagnie or V.O.C.—was constituted to bring the various Dutch investors into a monolithic corporate structure to insure against dangers and to divide profits. It soon became a brilliantly successful arrangement for the shareholders.

The V.O.C. was able to mobilize funds on an unprecedented scale, six and a half million guilders being the initial subscription of the investors. That enormous sum permitted the dispatch of thirty-eight armed and seaworthy ships to the East in the first three years of company operations. In human terms, the Dutch ships were manned by volunteers attracted by the promise of riches. To a significant degree, at least in comparison with Portuguese practice, the men were recruited on the basis of their skills, not their social standing or past difficulties with the criminal courts. Even the hazards of the voyage—gales and enemies, but above all disease—did not deter men from serving. Death claimed an average of one-fourth of each crew, but the profits on a single voyage could be several times the initial investment.

The charter of the V.O.C. bestowed upon the company all the powers of a sovereign state. The conclusion of treaties, the making of war, the dispensing of justice were all within V.O.C. authority. The company was, thus, a government controlled by the seventeen businessmen who were its directors. The republican government of Holland, having granted the charter, had no further immediate responsibilities. There was no sharing of authority by the V.O.C.; there were no distractions that might endanger profits. The royal monopolies of the Iberian empires were cumbersome by contrast, weighted down by court politics, involvement with the church, and European dynastic quarrels. The V.O.C. ultimately found ways to destroy itself; but, in its formative years, it was not weakened by outside meddling.

The vast corporate wealth of the V.O.C. enabled the Dutch to overcome the inability of their home economy to produce many goods for export to distant markets. It was reasonably obvious that cheeses and pickled herrings could not become the foundation of a flourishing Eastern trade; nor, incidentally, could the Dutch follow the Spanish example and pay for Asian goods with the mineral wealth of the New World. The first of the V.O.C. ships carried what seemed likely to fetch profitable prices in the Indies. Cutlery, cloth, glass, weapons, even toys, largely of German manufacture, were traded; but a more secure basis for exchange was required. After the first two experimental decades, the company directors shrewdly decided that the earning capacity of their ships was their chief asset. Domination over the carrying trade of the East would provide a steady income from local sources. A Dutch ship, for example, might take spices north to China, Chinese goods on to Japan, Japanese silver or copper back to the Indies for trans-shipment to India to purchase cloth to use in exchange for more spices to restart the cycle. Earnings on each transaction would be used to defray the expenses of the company.

The first captains from Holland were charged with the task of breaking into the spice trade to obtain cargoes for the northern European market. The timing of the operation was advantageous, for by the turn of the century the Portuguese and Spanish had stirred up considerable local animosity among Muslim islanders. Accordingly, the Dutch were greeted with hospitality in the hope that they would join in the struggle against mutual enemies. Through treaties with rulers in the Spice Islands and through the building of fortified outposts, Dutch paramountcy was gradually attained. Diversionary attacks on the Spanish at Manila were part of a general Dutch offensive aimed at driving Iberian power from the eastern islands of the Indonesian archipelago.

Even before the founding of the V.O.C., the Dutch had secured a toehold on Java to serve as both a trading center and a way station on the route to the Spice Islands. The port of Bantam, a small state at the western end of Java, was visited by the first Dutch expedition in 1596, when a trade agreement between the Hollanders and the local authorities was drawn up. That document was the first in a series of treaties that eventually enabled Holland to extend her rule over all Indonesia.

Bantam at the time was an active center of trade in pepper and welcomed foreign merchants from whom various port charges and fees could be collected. The port was also a convenient stopping place for Dutch ships that made unbroken voyages from the Cape of Good Hope, across the Indian Ocean and through the Sunda Strait between Java and Sumatra, following a course that avoided Malacca and other Portuguese bases. The Dutch maintained a factory or trading station at Bantam but were obliged to compete in the marketplace with the traders of several nations, including the English. Moreover, the inefficiency and corruption of the port authorities were growing irritants. Hence, the V.O.C. in 1619 established its own sovereign base on the north coast of western Java and called the place Batavia, using the name once applied by the Romans to Holland.

The site of Batavia was selected in part because no Indonesian ruler seemed immediately capable of expelling the Dutch intruders. Furthermore, a promising anchorage and a supply of fresh water carried by a river that ran down from the mountains were powerful attractions. That silting of the anchorage would close it to all but fishing boats in a later century and that the clear mountain stream would become overpoweringly fetid were unforeseen. Motivated in part by memories of home and in part by the challenge of swampy terrain, the Dutch built a system of canals to serve all conceivable urban and human needs. After 350 years, those waterways remain monuments to man's ability to befoul his environment. The housing of the early Dutch at Batavia was justified solely by nostalgia for the Low Countries. Narrow, airless structures with stepped gables, the early houses could hardly have been less appropriate to the equatorial climate. To make matters worse, windows were battened down at night to keep out the miasma that was indicted as the bearer of malaria. Architectural conventions that made life miserable and generally brief were supplemented by the refusal of the early Dutch to abandon habits of eating and drinking and modes of dress brought from their homeland.

From the beginning, Batavia attracted traders and skilled craftsmen of various origins, the Chinese forming the largest group. It can be said that the development of Batavia was a joint Sino-Dutch enterprise. In due course, substantial numbers of Portuguese Eurasians settled in the city and made their language the lingua franca of a polyglot community until the eighteenth century, when a Malay patois took over. The Portuguese also helped instruct the Dutch in the art of tropical survival. Ventilated housing and bathing reluctantly came to be accepted by even the most homesick Dutchman.

The founder of Batavia, Jan Pieterzoon Coen, typified his age, as Albuquerque had exemplified his a century earlier. Coen was singlemindedly committed to increasing the profits of the V.O.C. No personal entanglements, moral or otherwise, held him back. An imperious man, he was capable of writing the seventeen directors of the company to complain that their stupidity was the greatest obstacle in his path. Coen was appointed governor general of V.O.C. holdings in 1618, at the age of thirty-one, and served two terms in that capacity before his death in 1629. Though he established Batavia as the center of Dutch operations and though he led the Dutch to supremacy in Eastern shipping, his most ambitious plan for enriching the company was rejected by his employers. The scheme remains, nevertheless, worthy of consideration as a window into Coen's mind.

The governor general concluded in 1628 that the company was not operating profitably, and proposed a solution that was highly imaginative, though of dubious feasibility. The recommendation called for sweeping independent Asian shipping from the seas so that all cargoes would have to be carried in Dutch or Dutch-controlled vessels. Moreover, the production of spices would be brought totally under V.O.C. direction by establishing substantial numbers of colonists from the Netherlands as the overseers of a labor force of coolies and slaves. The colonists from Holland would also constitute garrisons to protect the spice-producing islands against both local rebellion and foreign attack. The thinking that prevailed in Amsterdam was more humane, or at least more businesslike. The directors concluded that Coen's plan would antagonize Asian producers and customers upon whom the company was ultimately dependent. Only an adaptation of the scheme for increased Dutch participation in Eastern shipping was authorized.

Native opposition to the aims of the V.O.C. disturbed Coen, though possibly not as much as the restraints imposed on him by the directors of the company. Acheh, at the northern end of Sumatra, threatened for a time to dominate the Strait of Malacca, but an alliance of the Portuguese with two Malay states, Johore and Patani, finally checked Acheh by sending ships to cripple her fleet in 1629. To the east, the V.O.C. dominated the Moluccas, though in the Bandas there was local resistance reinforced by support from the English. From Celebes, the forces of the Macassar sultanate also slowed Dutch expansion. The English and their Bandanese friends were subdued without prolonged effort; but for over sixty years, Macassar continued to thwart the V.O.C. in its drive for the total monopolization of the spice trade.

The base at Batavia was the keystone of the Dutch colonial structure. Threats to it endangered the entire position of the V.O.C. in the Indies and had to be contained as swiftly as possible. At the beginning, the ruler of Bantam had put forward a somewhat questionable claim of suzerainty over the land on which Batavia was to be built, and it was necessary for the Dutch to fight to clear the area of Bantamese and local forces, which were assisted by a few Englishmen from time to time. The scale of the struggle is revealed by the fact that the Dutch lost only one man in the final battle for Batavia's site. A subsequent Dutch blockade of Bantam so weakened that small state that it could make no further moves against the Dutch at Batavia. Bantam began to

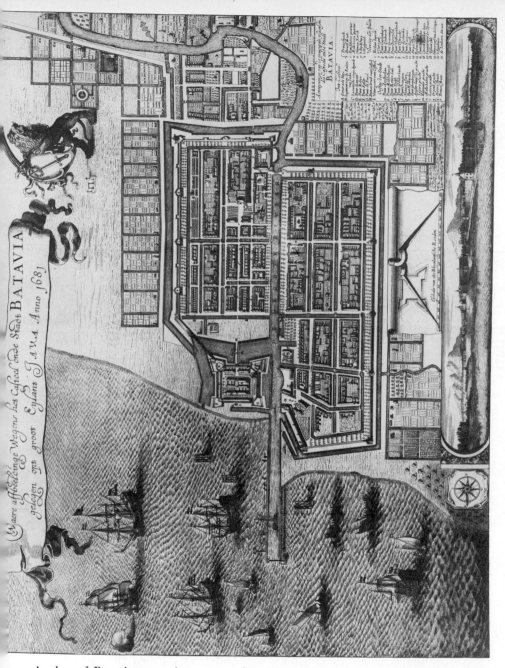

A plan of Batavia some sixty years after its establishment. The canals, the fortress, and the harbor are clearly shown. Less clear, though symbolic of the age and ruling style of early colonialism, is the gallows, outside the uppermost city wall in the picture. (From the author's private collection.)

77

retreat into obscurity. In time, the state was absorbed by the V.O.C., and its name came to refer only to the diminutive chickens that originated there.

Attack by a central Javanese ruler was to prove far more menacing to the company. Virtually from the day of his ascent to the throne of Mataram in 1613, Sultan Agung had battled to re-create a great Indonesian kingdom, based on the population and agricultural resources of inland central Java and claiming to be successor to the fallen Majapahit empire. The sultan's natural enemies were the small coastal states involved in maritime trade; and one by one they fell to his armies. After fifteen years, Mataram was master of all Java except its western and eastern tips, and the adjacent island of Madura. To complete his conquests, Sultan Agung opened a war against both the Dutch at Batavia and the declining Bantamese, thereby inducing the two to end their decade of enmity and cooperate against a mutual danger.

In 1628, using a new kind of Trojan horse especially designed to make the Dutch unwary, Sultan Agung dispatched a fleet to Batavia purportedly to trade, but actually to carry men to storm the V.O.C. fortress. The ruse failed, though by only a narrow margin. The next year, an army of many thousands was ordered to march along the coast from central Java and lay siege to Batavia. The sultan's men completed their march almost incapacitated by hunger, for their supplies had been shipped aboard coastal vessels that were helpless prey to Dutch warships. It was but another example of seapower and technological superiority winning over numbers in the history of Western imperial expansion. In due course, the army of Mataram was forced to break off the attack on Batavia and struggle toward home in retreat. Eventual mastery over all Java by the Dutch was virtually assured.

The occupation of territory had, of course, not been the original purpose of the V.O.C. Small islands rich in spices, trading centers, and fortified positions to protect the commercial empire were needed, but extensive colonial holdings producing little for export were held to have slight value. Indeed, winning and ruling large territories ate into profits. Needless to say, once the Dutch established themselves at a promising location and settled down to trade, concern arose over defense. Typically, pacification of the hinterland behind a factory or fort came to be regarded as essential. The momentum of territorial expan-

One of numerous surviving examples of Dutch architecture in Malacca, traditionally painted a delicate rose. (Lea E. Williams)

sion thus carried the Dutch across Java; by 1705, the entire island was under the direct or indirect rule of the V.O.C.

The Dutch focus on Java in the seventeenth century did not result in the neglect of other imperial interests. When the power of Macassar was finally shattered in 1668, the only remaining center of danger to the Dutch in the eastern half of the Indonesian island chain was eliminated. Of secondary significance, almost pathetically so, was the Dutch capture of Malacca in 1641. By then the Portuguese had fallen so far from greatness that the loss of their Malayan base brought no major changes to Southeast Asia. The Dutch simply found it comfortable to control the Malacca Strait in order to deny passage to others, while they themselves continued to be dependent upon the Sunda Strait. After its transfer to the Dutch, Malacca slid into a sleepy decline. Many of the town's residents moved to Batavia. The few Hollanders who settled in Malacca contented themselves with establishing a Protestant church and, as was frequently expedient, with robbing the old Portuguese cemetery of tombstones for thrifty reuse with freshly chiseled Dutch inscriptions.

THE ENGLISH

London had actually been ahead of Amsterdam in forming a company to develop Eastern commerce, although for almost two centuries that was the only lead the English could claim over the Dutch in Southeast Asia. The royal charter establishing the East India Company went into effect on the final day of the sixteenth century, December 31st, 1600, almost two years before the V.O.C. was born. The English company was granted autonomous powers comparable to those soon to be given the V.O.C. There was, however, a decisive difference between the English and Dutch in their corporate endeavors: The Dutch had about ten times as much working capital.

Elizabethan England had emerged onto the world stage rich in human and historical resources, but, compared with Spain, France, and Holland, economically disadvantaged. Her population of under six million was made up mostly of simple peasants. The coal and iron industries that would eventually support global predominance were in their infancy. She had little to sell the outside world except fine woolens—a singularly inappropriate trade good for export to the tropics. England stood at no central intersection of international commerce and had not, therefore, become a focal point of cosmopolitan merchant activity and capital accumulation. Clearly, no rational economic analysis would have hinted at the imperial future that lay ahead.

The island geography of England, on the other hand, had been instrumental in shaping the country's history and in providing the means for overseas expansion. Isolation from the Continent gave the English a certain immunity from involvement, except on her own terms, in the exhausting wars of European royalty; and, more important, no foreign invader had set foot on her shores since 1066. The growth of seafaring capability was obviously encouraged in an island kingdom; the sea dogs of sixteenth-century Devon were a legend in their own age. Insularity, perhaps most decisively, had contributed to the rise of a sense of English identity and distinctiveness that was translated under the Tudors into the world's earliest expression of modern nationalism. The triumph in 1588 over Philip's armada understandably gave tremendous impetus to the growth of national loyalty. The feeling of belonging to a nation that is held to be the guardian of the individual and collective well-being of all its members has become, as everybody recognizes, the supremely potent political force of our own century; and the English were the first to be enveloped by it. That intangible combination of convictions, loyalties, and hopes was the foundation of ultimate English success in the imperial contest. In seventeenth-century Southeast Asia, however, nationalism was not enough to give the English ascendancy over the wealthy Dutch.

It was, needless to say, the spice trade that attracted Englishmen to the Indies. Their task was to challenge the Spanish and Portuguese and compete with the Dutch. Too weak to attempt dislodging the other Westerners, the English were obliged to seek to outflank them. Cargoes were bought in the Spice Islands from local rulers who held grudges against the Iberians or who were swayed by the offer of prices well beyond the limits imposed by ineffectual monopolies. Wherever a hospitable king permitted the establishment of an East India Company factory, as at Bantam, the English arrived on the scene, much to the annoyance of the Dutch.

It was only a matter of time before superior force pushed the English out of the archipelago. The turning point was reached in 1623 on the island of Amboina, where the Dutch executed twenty-one of the thirty members of the East India Company staff, charging them with conspiracy, and expelled the survivors. Thereafter the English were largely restricted to the declining port of Bantam; and even that minor outpost had to be abandoned well before the end of the seventeenth century. The English were forced to retire westward and concentrate their growing, but still limited, resources on the achievement of imperial goals in India. At the time the Dutch could congratulate themselves for having won the more glittering prize.

THE SECOND CENTURY OF THE V.O.C.

The eighteenth century opened with the V.O.C. seemingly secure in its profitable pursuits; the century ended with the company bankrupt and dissolved. In 1700, the Dutch held comfortable control over all those parts of Indonesia that could be conveniently exploited. The tiny islands in the eastern part of the archipelago were fully dominated by the V.O.C. While only western Java was under direct company control, the rulers of the rest of that populous island were held accountable to Batavia. Elsewhere, Dutch authority was restricted to coastal enclaves or was expressed through diplomatic arrangements with Sumatran, Bornean, or other local princes. Only those places that lacked commercial attraction, such as Bali or the interior of Borneo, escaped Dutch interest.

Despite the unquestioned hegemony of the V.O.C., most Indonesians lived quietly in their accustomed village patterns. The earliest and most pervasive influence of the new overlords on the Indonesian peasantry was economic, and that was localized. Even where the Dutch kept the traditional ruling elite on a short leash or actually deposed it, the villagers were not directly touched. Government had never been answerable to those whose labor supported it. The affairs of kings were remote and unfathomable. Royal defeats could bring suffering to the villages; victories eventually might be immortalized in folklore. That was virtually the extent of peasant involvement.

The only tie with the larger world that had meaning to most of the humble people was religious. Unorthodox and syncretic though the Muslim practices of the Indonesians might have seemed by the more exacting standards of the Near East, Islam was a community that reached across seas and frontiers. As Muslims, the peasants of Java were, at least symbolically, freed from their isolation.

As a matter of fact, the eighteenth century saw the beginning of an Islamic revival that was later to become a pivotal force for change in Indonesia. Two elements in the process can be identified. First, the acceleration of commerce under the V.O.C. had attracted to Batavia and elsewhere a mounting, though relatively small, number of foreign Muslims, including merchants from southern Arabia. Among them were men who assumed roles as religious teachers; the machinery for the purification of Islamic belief and practice was thus set in motion by their coming. Second, advances in shipping encouraged some of the privileged minority to undertake the pilgrimage to Mecca. No peasants could dream of affording the *haj;* but the return of a *haji,* who had been to the sacred source of Islam, was likely to stimulate a religious awakening in his locality.

It was economic change, however, that most affected the rural population. The discovery by Europeans of the New World and, to a lesser degree, the Western penetration of Africa had a sweeping effect on Europe and on the lands of Asia. Around the world, the introduction of new crops transformed agriculture. Potatoes, yams, and peanuts, especially important as a source of oil, flourished in sandy soil that had been of little use earlier. Corn could be grown on hillsides where rice could be planted only after elaborate terracing and the construction of irrigation systems. Marginal land became productive; larger and larger harvests were won. The first green revolution had come to Asia.

Expanded agricultural productivity might have been expected to accelerate the accumulation of capital, leading to true economic development and higher standards of living. There is no evidence, however, that anything of the sort occurred, at least for the Asian peasantry. The multiplication of people, quite literally made possible by the increased yields, simply meant that a greater food supply was consumed by more mouths. The rural economies had to run to keep in their starting places. Only insofar as the agricultural innovations produced exportable surpluses was there net growth, but in Indonesia, few gains from the marketing abroad of cash crops reached village producers.

For the V.O.C., the introduction of all but one of the new crops was of less than minor concern. The diet of the peasants did not faintly interest the directors in Amsterdam. The one exception to their detachment from the agricultural and demographic changes that were shaping Indonesia resulted from the success of experiments by a company servant in the cultivation of coffee, originally a plant native to Arabia. There was no doubt that Javanese harvests of the bean could be bountiful; the problems lay in controlling supply and distribution.

The cession by beleaguered Mataram to Dutch authority of the Cheribon and Preanger districts, which together with Bantam comprised the western third of Java, had been secured in the latter half of the seventeenth century in order to provide Batavia with a shielding buffer zone. Defense concerns, not economic aspirations, originally made the Preanger districts worth holding. The company had not yet overcome its fear that territorial aggrandizement was commercially counterproductive, but hopes generated by the introduction of coffee soon gave Preanger and its peasants new value.

The administration of the Preanger districts was in the hands of local notables, known as regents. Their legitimacy might be based on heredity, but in all cases it had to be confirmed by the V.O.C. Thus, the regents were firmly subservient to Batavia. As Preanger coffee harvests grew, the regents were assigned assistants who were appointed by Batavia and charged with supervising the new production. That move was the start of direct administrative control over the hinterland by the company.

The V.O.C. had two purposes in the coffee trade: to preserve a monopoly and to adhere unswervingly to the honored practice of buying cheap and selling dear. Cracks in the monopoly—opened by smugglers and company men engaged in private trade—were never thoroughly sealed, but the exploitation of peasant labor in coffee cultivation was quite readily engineered. Villagers had traditionally been compelled to pay tribute, normally in rice, to their rulers. As the legal successor to the former regimes, the company felt that the tribute or an equivalent should now be channeled to Batavia. Rice was not then an exportable commodity and thus had little value to the V.O.C.; but coffee was different.

Using the regents and their staffs as agents, Batavia imposed regulations that established quotas for coffee production and obliged the districts to deliver the amounts specified for sale at prices set by the company. Tending the plants, picking the beans, and transporting the harvest to the V.O.C. capital were tasks borne by the peasants. The sums realized from the sales at Batavia went to the regents, who sensed little, if any, obligation to let the new income seep down to the village level, though they felt irrevocably tied to the company. For its own part, the V.O.C. profited from rising sales of coffee in Europe and America, where the popularity of the drink became a craze. Thus, under the Preanger system, feudalism and mercantilism were happily married. A Dutch scholar recently observed that "coffee culture no longer permitted the petty wars among the regents from which the poor peasants had suffered so much . . . and peace alone was a benefit for the people."[2] One could similarly argue that the great fire of mid-seventeenth-century London helped clear the slums.

The governors general in eighteenth-century Batavia were no longer heavily involved in directing conquests. Their chief tasks were to

[2] Bernard H. M. Vlekke, *Nusantare, a History of Indonesia*, The Hague: van Hoeve, 1965, p. 199.

preserve the military security of the V.O.C. and to keep its commercial system in operation. The suppression of internal rebellion was their prime military responsibility; the maintenance of monopoly control over the production and distribution of Indonesian products was their central economic duty. They were far more successful in the former than in the latter.

Vestigial Mataram and the enemies of that kingdom ceaselessly plotted and maneuvered against each other in the first half of the eighteenth century. Open fighting could not fail to draw in the Dutch, who were justifiably fearful of the reunification of central and eastern Java under a powerful ruler certain to challenge Batavian hegemony. The V.O.C. supported and, on occasion, installed pliable princes who were properly beholden to the Dutch. The armies of the company fought when necessary to preserve the fragmentation of Java, but intrigue and diplomacy were preferred over fighting as less costly. Nevertheless, Dutch fears of a popular rising were never far below the surface. At Batavia in 1740, fright assumed command over reason.

The considerable Chinese population at Batavia was indispensable economically, but it also seemed sinister. The specter of a joint Sino-Javanese rebellious attack terrified the Dutch. If Batavia were lost, all would be gone. For a number of years before 1740, rumors of Chinese plotting had swept the city. The presence of a substantial number of unemployed Chinese immigrants had come to seem particularly ominous. Resettlement in Ceylon or at the Cape of Good Hope appeared to be an attractive solution to the problem. The Chinese would be given work; the Dutch would feel safer. Furthermore, the interests of the company in two of its lesser territories would be served by the introduction of inventive and industrious immigrants.

Unfortunately, nobody consulted the Chinese to learn their views. When the first men were rounded up for deportation, resistance began and was soon intensified by rumors that the Dutch actually intended to throw their captives overboard once the ships reached open water. The Hollanders decided to strike before the Chinese could attack in force. Supported by a mob of Indonesians, the Dutch ran amok, killing every Chinese they found and driving the rest into flight. Actually, the massacre at Batavia was not the first of its kind in Southeast Asia; the Spanish at Manila in the grip of their own Sinophobia had pioneered in such mass murder. In further emulation of the Spanish, the Dutch soon found that, without the Chinese, commerce was stagnant. The feared immigrants had to be invited to return to Batavia.

Though occupied with violence and defense from time to time, the Dutch could never escape from their economic problems and the policing of the monopoly. Perhaps the most persistent violators of the V.O.C. monopoly were the company's own servants. The men had gone out from Holland to make money, but in the Indies they were paid miserable salaries. Moreover, they were at the mercy of fevers, plagues, and parasites that relentlessly thinned their ranks. Only through private trade could company servants hope to amass enough wealth for eventual retirement in the unlikely event that they survived their tropical labors. V.O.C. ships sailing for home normally carried vast quantities of contraband to be marketed in Europe to the profit of the smugglers and the detriment of the company. Periodic efforts to stop the private trade were never more than temporarily effective. Even such determined moves as the execution of twenty-six V.O.C. servants in 1706, and the dismissal in disgrace of the governor general and most of his senior aides in 1731, did no more than interrupt the lively illicit commerce.

Other smuggling channels led to Asian ports and were used by local or Chinese shipping. V.O.C. patrol vessels could never cope with the problem, just as they could not do much to quell endemic piracy in Indonesian waters. The archipelago was too rich in hidden anchorages and the coastlines were interminable. Moreover, as if the troubles of the V.O.C. were not sufficiently painful, competition from spices that had been successfully cultivated in India was a growing threat to the Dutch as the eighteenth century unfolded. The final blow to the monopoly, however, was struck far from the Indies.

The outbreak of the American Revolution prompted various European powers, notably France, to seek to settle old scores with Britain. The Netherlands made the mistake of backing the revolutionaries in a move that earned far more resentment from the British than gratitude from the Americans. When an Anglo-Dutch settlement was reached after the war, the V.O.C. monopoly over shipping in Indonesian seas had to be sacrificed as part of the price of the defeats suffered by the Dutch in their ill-considered support of the Americans. In the final fifteen years of the century, Indonesian ports were open to ships of any flag. British, Danish, and American vessels were especially active in exploiting the new opportunity. The V.O.C. had been mortally wounded; the coup de grace was soon administered by the directors themselves.

The eventual demise of the V.O.C. was not directly caused by Dutch smugglers, foreign competitors, or recalcitrant Asians: the company committed suicide. A combination of obfuscating methods of accountancy that bred confusion and deception and the insistence of the directors that dividends remain high regardless of realities led to bankruptcy. The debts of the company, largely incurred to permit the continuation of traditional dividend payments to shareholders, grew year by year. On the last day of 1799, the Netherlands government had to intervene, assuming a burden of debts that totaled 134 million guilders, a sum equal to more than twenty times the original capitalization of the company, and accepting responsibility for the administration of a colonial empire. No longer could the Dutch government and taxpayers remain insulated from developments halfway around the earth; and, with the rise of Napoleon, events were moving swiftly, even in Indonesia.

READINGS

Boxer, Charles R., *The Dutch Sea-borne Empire, 1600-1800*, London: Hutchinson, 1965.

——, *Francisco Vieira de Figueiredo: A Portuguese Merchant-Adventurer in South East Asia, 1624-1667*, The Hague: Martinus Nijhoff, 1967.

Foster, Sir William, ed., *The Voyage of Sir Henry Middleton to the Moluccas, 1604-1606*, London: The Hakluyt Society, 1943.

Glamann, Kristof, *Dutch–Asiastic Trade, 1620-1740*, The Hague: Martinus Nijhoff, 1958.

Masselman, George, *The Cradle of Colonialism*, New Haven: Yale University Press, 1963.

——, *The Money Trees: The Spice Trade*, New York: McGraw-Hill, 1967.

5

The Initial Impact
of Modern Colonialism
on Maritime Southeast Asia

It is both convenient and reasonable to regard the opening years of the nineteenth century as a time of transition in maritime Southeast Asia. Industrialization in the West led to the reshaping of international trading patterns; Western aspirations for economic growth began to replace faith in mercantilist protection. The enrichment of company shareholders or the replenishment of royal exchequers were no longer sufficient goals; colonies ought to be made to contribute to the economic might and politico-military prowess of the contending nation-states of the West. For a century, the new imperialism dominated world history, to recede only after the holocaust of 1914-18 that it so largely caused.

Just as the emergence of nation-states may be held responsible for the horror of total war, industrialization can be cited as the cause of intensified imperial drives and rivalry. The global scramble for colonies gained momentum as the nineteenth century went forward; and, more significant for immediate purposes, peoples and territories already under the Western shadow at the start of the century were subjected to unprecedented degrees of control and coercion.

THE INDIES

Indonesia was the first area to be engulfed by the rising colonialist flood. Java, particularly, became the scene of experimentation and change. In 1808 attempts were begun to harness the island to the Napoleonic struggle for world dominion. If it can be said that the French emperor launched the first modern campaign for global conquest, Indonesia can be called the first modern colony in Southeast Asia. The transformation was inaugurated by a Dutchman in the service of France and continued by the Englishman who succeeded him. Herman Willem Daendels and Thomas Stamford Raffles, in both similar and differing ways, worked to push Java into the new century.

Daendels was so steadfastly loyal to Napoleon and to the French cause that he had been elevated to the rank of marshal. With his exalted title, he arrived on Java at the beginning of 1808, determined to defend the island against the British enemies of the emperor and his brother, Louis Bonaparte, who had been perched on the Dutch throne.

The marshal was very much on his own. Not only was Java half a world removed from Europe, the British had established near ironclad control over the sea routes to the East. Whatever Daendels might seek to achieve in Java would have to be undertaken with the resources at hand. Equipped with little more than ruthless energy, the new governor general set out to make Java impregnable. He failed, but the island was never to be the same again.

The centralization of political control under his own authority was Daendels' chief administrative innovation. Indonesian notables who had enjoyed rank and power, in part hereditary, as quasi-autonomous auxiliaries of the Dutch were brought fully into the colonial officialdom to make them consciously and thoroughly subservient to their alien overlords. The costs of the bureaucratic reordering can be reckoned in terms of resentment on the part of the Indonesian elite and, possibly, an attendant decline in their prestige in the eyes of the common people.

Militarily, Daendels worked to raise an army of local recruits, for he could expect no reinforcements from Europe. Discipline and training, it was hoped, would make the Javanese levies equal to the task of meeting a British force that, after all, would also be largely colonial, Indian, in manpower. Though a small defense fleet was locally built, Daendels recognized that the impending battle would have to be decided on land. Adequate interior lines of communication for the swift movement of troops and supplies were appropriately seen to be essential. Hence, a Javanese highway system was constructed by corvée labor. The toll in human misery was huge, but the island was made more cohesive than ever before. Moreover, an unprecedented number of people were uprooted from their villages to serve in the colonial army and to labor, often to die, in the construction of ships, fortifications, and the great east-west highway. The shock waves generated by the partial disruption of the traditional village order would be felt for years.

The financing of his struggle to make Java a fortress never ceased to frustrate Daendels and burden the people. The earlier boom in the coffee trade had been ended by the vigilance of British patrol vessels. Nevertheless, production of the beans was enormously expanded and forced deliveries at reduced rates of payment were stepped up; but there was no way to market the growing hoard. Daendels was left with a vast stockpile of a commodity that is singularly worthless unless exported.

The sale of government holdings became the most effective means of raising emergency revenue. Two measures were adopted. First, claiming title to all lands other than those recognized as the property of royal and noble Indonesian treaty partners, the colonial government sold vast acreages to private, notably Chinese, capital. As a neo-feudal dividend, purchasers of government land gained the right to demand service and crop deliveries from peasant occupants.

The second source of revenue tapped by Daendels was found in the sale, again to Chinese, of licenses for the operation of various monopolies. The licensed retail distribution of opium was an especially lucrative producer of profits extracted from Chinese addicts and collected by Chinese monopolists. Licenses to run pawnshops, markets, abattoirs, and ferries were also sold to Chinese investors, and, in a long-term political sense, were even more devastating than the narcotic trade, since indigenous hostility toward the Chinese could only be increased by a system that installed them as the collectors of fees from the local populace.

Daendels' arduous efforts to make Java invulnerable were speedily shown to have been futile once the British attacked in 1811. A campaign lasting little more than a month opened with the peaceful abandonment of Batavia by the Dutch, who then, after a brief holding action outside the capital, broke off contact and began a retreat that took them to central Java and surrender. The Javanese conscripts seem to have been most martial when rising in mutiny against their officers. The princely allies of the Dutch, chafing under cavalier treatment, failed to rally to the defense of their island. Even among Dutch residents there was disaffection, for currency inflation had injured many and the raising of the French tricolor over Batavia after Napoleon finally deposed his brother and annexed the Netherlands had dismayed most. There was perhaps some mercy in the fact that Daendels was not obliged to witness the debacle, having already been ordered back to Europe before the British struck. He arrived home in time to join his emperor on the march into the Russian winter of 1812.

THE BRITISH INTERLUDE ON JAVA

The heir to command in Batavia was Raffles, one of the stellar figures in British imperial history. Just as Albuquerque and Coen had represented their own centuries, Raffles was a symbol of his. Ardently nationalist, he was fully convinced that the extension of British rule overseas was both a boon to the home country and a blessing for hitherto misruled and benighted peoples. He regarded the spread of imperial red across the map of the world as a measure of the pace of liberation from ignorance and cruelty. The altruism of his age, epitomized in the antislavery crusade led by Wilberforce, was enthusiastically embraced by Raffles. In his mind, colonial rule and good works were wedded. Almost a hundred years later, Cecil Rhodes would define this philosophy of empire as philanthropy plus a 5 per cent return on investments.

Beyond his eagerness to emancipate through imperialism, Raffles was a man of his era in another sense. He sought to promote his political cause and satisfy his own intellectual curiosity through study. Knowledge of the peoples and lands to be colonized was held by him to be the key to imperial success. Consequently Raffles eagerly responded to the scholarly challenges of Southeast Asia, mastering Malay, writing a history of Java that is still in service, collecting zoological and botanical specimens, exploring ancient ruins. That such study paid dividends would be demonstrated by the usefulness of political intelligence and cultural sensitivity in the service of British arms in the conquest of Java.

Raffles had reached Southeast Asia in 1805 as a junior servant of the East India Company assigned to Penang. The company had acquired that Malayan outpost in 1786 primarily to provide shelter for naval vessels or ships sailing in the China trade that might be caught by an adverse monsoon on the eastern shores of the Bay of Bengal. Successive agreements with the Sultan of Kedah, who encouraged the presence of a force that could—but never did—protect him from the Siamese, had permitted the establishment of company rule over the island of Penang and the mainland coastal area opposite it.

Possession of Penang had. proved disappointing. The naval stores required for the repair and maintenance of company ships were not locally available. The volume of trade remained low, for the island was too distant from the chief export-producing areas to make the lengthy and perilous voyage up the Strait of Malacca attractive to inter-island and coastal shippers. Nevertheless, the British toehold on the northern approaches to the strait provided a staging area for penetration southward into peninsular and insular Southeast Asia once the two decades of intermittent warfare against revolutionary and Napoleonic France were begun.

Malacca, the first prize won in the contest, had been taken without a shot by the British in 1795, when the Netherlands came under French occupation. The city had languished during a century and a half of Dutch rule; it was not rejuvenated during the ensuing period of British authority. Indeed, the initial plan of the British called for the destruction of Malacca's military and commercial usefulness so that the anticipated return of the port to the Dutch would not endanger freedom of passage through the strait or hamper the economic growth of Penang. Though the old Portuguese fort was blown up by army sappers, the razing of the residential and commercial parts of the town was prevented. Credit for Malacca's escape from obliteration is customarily given to Raffles, who visited the place in 1808 and wrote a plea that persuaded his superiors to halt further demolition. The rise to influence and authority of the youthful company servant had begun. In three years, just past thirty, he would be in command of the British experiment on Java.

The terms of Dutch capitulation on Java in 1811 provided that Hollanders were at liberty to enter the service of the British to help maintain administrative continuity. Accordingly, there was a high degree of cooperation between victors and vanquished, each side recognizing that the British interregnum would probably end once Napoleon had been brought to heel. The containment of France with the support of Continental allies, especially in the Low Countries, was of course the central pillar of Britain's European policy.

The exercise of British rule over Java and its dependencies was formally under the authority of the governor general at Calcutta, who relied on a deputy, designated a lieutenant governor, to implement his policies. The slowness of communications between India and Java, particularly in the face of contrary monsoons, encouraged independence of action and judgment by the lieutenant governor; the fact that command at Batavia was entrusted to Raffles ensured that the five years of the British presence would be a time of innovation. His superior at Calcutta endorsed the commission given Raffles with the injunction: "While we are in Java, let us do all the good we can." No order could have been more enthusiastically received by a man who saw himself above all as the architect of good works.

Challenges to British authority were initially offered by local rulers who, not without reason, felt that the destruction of Dutch power, achieved in part with their help, ought to have ended their vassalage to Batavia. The new lieutenant governor was quick to employ forceful political and military methods to depose such restless princes. His faith in the beneficence of British rule made independent stirrings intolerable; suppression was demanded and swiftly carried out. Once the Dutch returned, however, the lid temporarily clamped on local unrest would begin to slip off.

With pacification seemingly accomplished, Raffles set out to bring reform to Java. The eradication of social evils, notably gambling and slavery, and the restructuring of the fiscal foundations of the government were the two most absorbing tasks undertaken. Success was less than total in both endeavors.

There was a clear relationship between compulsive gambling, notably at the cockfight arena, and one form of bondage, for custom obliged bankrupt, powerless debtors to surrender themselves and their families into slavery to satisfy the demands of creditors. Manumission for debt slaves was virtually unattainable; unpaid for their labor, they had no way to meet financial obligations incurred in earlier years of freedom. Raffles struck dual blows at debt slavery by outlawing the practice and, with little lasting effect, banning cockfighting, surely the most widespread village sport in Southeast Asia.

To suppress the enslavement of animists by Muslims and Christians, who were prohibited from owning the bodies and descendants of co-religionists, the inter-island shipment of slaves was outlawed. Moreover, Batavia levied a special tax on slaveowners and decreed that government officers would no longer participate in the capture of runaways. These measures eroded the foundations of slavery and contributed to the eventual demise of the institution.

In fiscal reform, Raffles was equally eager to innovate; but, as in the anti-slavery campaign, only mixed results were achieved. He hoped to sweep away the inefficiency and end the abuses of state reliance on forced deliveries of agricultural products, the exploitation of corvée labor, and the operation of licensed monopolies that collected tolls from peasants who sought to market a portion of the yield of their fields. The collection of land rent, after the model in operation in British-ruled parts of India, appeared to promise both supportable burdens on the peasantry and a reliable flow of income for the government.

Once the notion that the state owned all land under its sovereignty was accepted—and there seems never to have been any doubt in Raffles' mind on the matter—all those who tilled the soil were obliged to pay rent in the form of a share of their harvests or a cash equivalent. The assessment of rents was scaled in accordance with the productivity of the fields; as much as half the harvest could be claimed by official collectors, though on the average the demands were somewhat more moderate.

Neither the realization of adequate revenues nor significant amelioration of the peasants' condition resulted from the introduction of the land rent system. The administrative machinery needed to appraise village fields and supervise collections did not exist, and Raffles' tenure on Java was too brief to permit its full development. The only easy path toward solvency had to be followed. Forced coffee collections continued; monopoly licenses were offered to investors; even land sales to private capital were authorized. In other words, Raffles was compelled to follow much of the course plotted by Daendels. Thus the first great opportunity to be an instrument of change was partially missed; the second chance would come with the colonization of Singapore.

THE FOUNDING OF SINGAPORE

Napoleon's banishment to St. Helena in 1815 was soon paralleled by the assignment of Raffles to exile as the lieutenant governor at Bencoolen, a drowsy town on the west coast of Sumatra where the East India Company had been permitted to maintain a minor trading station while the Dutch spread over the more profitable parts of the Indies. Predictably, personal restlessness and imperial dreams soon led Raffles to look beyond the confines of his tiny outpost. He concluded that Britain must acquire a base at the southern end of the strait to offset the temporary restoration of Dutch rule at Malacca, compensate for the disadvantages of Penang's remote location, and break the commercial grip on the archipelago maintained by the Dutch at Batavia. Once the governor general at Calcutta was persuaded to support the move, Raffles had merely to find a promising spot with a compliant local ruler willing to cede it. Singapore filled the bill superbly.

Singapore, an island off the tip of the Malay Peninsula, commands the narrowest portion of the sea lane between the Strait of Malacca and the South China Sea; thus, the shortest voyage to China from India and beyond brings vessels under its shadow. The anchorage was seen to be both spacious and secure. Equally important to Raffles, the island was inhabited by but a handful; and, better still, legal sovereignty was under dispute due to the internal quarrels and intrigue of the local Malay court. The British found it expedient to grant recognition and a small pension to an otherwise impotent and impoverished claimant to the throne of Johore in exchange for his signature on the document that effectively made Singapore a colony in 1819. The legality of the territorial transfer was verbally challenged by a Malay prince who had been bypassed—as well as by the Dutch who complained that the integrity of their sphere of paramountcy had been violated—but the British were to govern Singapore for nearly a century and a half. No Malay force could dislodge them; Dutch claims were surrendered under the Anglo-Netherlands Treaty of 1824 which traded Bencoolen for Malacca and established the boundaries that now divide West Malaysia and Singapore from Indonesia.

Singapore's meteoric rise to commercial dominance resulted directly from the institution of free trade at the port. For the first time, merchants in the region had access to an entrepôt where goods could be exchanged without restraint. As the news spread, people poured into the colony, Chinese always in the lead. The laissez-faire economic policy of the British and the industry of the Chinese soon transformed an obscure island into an emporium serving the world.

So rapid was the success of colonial Singapore in its first years that its founder—who was obliged to spend most of the period at dreary Bencoolen—could rightly feel a sense of accomplishment as he left the town after a final visit in 1823 to return to England and a premature death. The way to British pre-eminence in Southeast Asia had been opened by a combination of nineteenth-century liberal economics and the ancient technique of exploiting hegemony at sea that had served Srivajaya, Majapahit, Malacca, the Portuguese, and the Dutch in their turns. So committed to maritime imperialism were the British that over half a century passed after the acquisition of Singapore before territorial expansion into the Malay States of the peninsula was undertaken. There was simply no incentive to annex territory and submit to the burden of governing it while Singapore gave splendid returns on limited investments.

THE DUTCH RESTORATION

In sharp contrast to the prospering British, the Dutch found themselves obliged to secure economic viability for the colonial holdings returned to their rule in 1816 by the post-Napoleonic settlement that provided for the maintenance of a Netherlands counterweight to French ambitions. Before embarking on a new economic course in the Indies, however, the Batavian government was obliged to reimpose its authority over those Indonesians, both royal and common, who had been prompted by the spectacle of the Dutch collapse of 1811 to dream of liberation from colonialism. The task of pacification absorbed the energies and depleted the resources of the Hollanders for a decade and a half. The beginning of the period was punctuated by explosions of discontent in many parts of the Outer Islands; from 1825 to 1830, central Java was ignited by a great popular insurrection.

The conflagration that for a time seemed to promise the incineration of the Dutch in the middle section of the island is known in Western literature as the Java War. The name may suggest that the contest was decided by battles between contending armies, but that was by no means the case. The struggle matched the mobility and modern arms of the colonial army against a guerrilla force of ill-equipped peasants led by a prince of the Jogjakarta sultanate, Diponegoro.

The prince quite properly could feel that his legitimate claim to the Jogjakarta throne had been set aside through a combination of the complexities of dynastic succession and the machinations of the Dutch, who understandably preferred weak figures at the head of the Javanese state that historically and culturally merited pre-eminence. The installation in 1822 of an infant as sultan had been in direct violation of a previous promise to Diponegoro and served at the very least to demonstrate the perfidy of the overlords at Batavia.

Joined with any sense of personal disappointment that may have motivated Diponegoro were his profound Islamic devotion and his searching, introspective nature. To the Dutch, he was a religious fanatic who periodically hid in caves to seek divine guidance through meditation; to thousands of his countrymen, he appeared to promise emancipation from the burdens of life under infidel hegemony.

One by one, Diponegoro's lieutenants and his peasant volunteers were chased into the hills or subdued. By 1830 the prince was driven to parley with the Dutch commander, who took the opportunity presented by the meeting to seize his foe and have him transported to the Outer Islands to spend the twenty-five remaining years of his life in exile. The first attempt to break the alien grip on Java was thus crushed; the second, over a century later, armed with material and diplomatic resources beyond Diponegoro's imagination and made invulnerable by mass nationalism and effective leadership, would not fail.

Economic difficulties, even more than the central Javanese rising, made the early years of their restoration precarious and perplexing to the Dutch. The land rent system imposed by Raffles, by encouraging rice production, had led to a general reduction in the raising of crops for export. Moreover, the supremacy once enjoyed by Dutch shippers had been shattered by the appearance in Indies waters of growing numbers of British and American vessels. Revenues available to Batavia consistently fell short of meeting requirements for expenditures, including mounting military appropriations. By the time the Java War neared its end, the colonial regime was close to bankruptcy.

A new governor general, van den Bosch, arrived in 1830 with a new formula for fiscal salvation. Sharing the customary Dutch view that the Javanese peasantry was both indolent and ignorant of world market demands, he inaugurated a plan, the Culture System, designed to curb rural sloth and assure rich harvests and deliveries of products that commanded high prices abroad. One-fifth of cultivable village land would be planted in crops specified by the authorities and up to half the working days of peasants would have to be spent in tending the fields thus set aside. The rest of the land and half the time of the villagers could be invested as the country people saw fit. The scheme was hardly unprecedented, for it essentially represented a vast extension of the quasi-feudal pattern that had long been imposed on the peasantry of the coffee-producing areas of the Preanger districts of western Java. Under the Culture System, however, receipts from forced deliveries of coffee were enormously supplemented by revenue earned from government collections of sugar, tea, spices, cotton, and dyestuffs, all of which were marketed to the West by a giant trading monopoly nominally headed by the king of the Netherlands and of tremendous financial benefit to that monarch and his successors.

Using the Indonesian peasants as their part-time serfs, the Dutch squeezed nearly a billion guilders out of their distant colony. Paradoxically, the enrichment of the metropole had not in fact been the original purpose of the Culture System. Fiscal rescue of the colonial regime at Batavia had been the initial objective, but the system was so profitable that within three years Batavia was confronted with the problem, rare to any government, of disposing of a treasury surplus. Investment for the welfare of the colonized being unthinkable, funds began to be transferred home to erase the Dutch national debt—painfully increased in 1830 by the cost of an abortive military effort to deny independence to the Belgians—and to pay for the construction of the Netherlands railway system. Seldom, if ever, has colonial exploitation been so profitable. Beyond the grave, Raffles must have been reminded of his rhymed quip: "In matters of commerce, the fault of the Dutch/Is giving too little and asking too much."

A NEW COURSE FOR THE PHILIPPINES

Even the Philippines, at the far end of the arc of maritime Southeast Asia and long substantially insulated against the impact of outside events, could not be kept in permanent seclusion. Earlier attempts by the Dutch, on occasion abetted by the English, to take Manila had all been foiled, but in 1762 the city fell to the British as a prize in the Seven Years' War. The occupation lasted less than two years before the peace settlement obliged the British to retire. During that brief time, the Spanish and a loyal Filipino populace, the latter rallied as on earlier occasions by fear of a Protestant enemy, prevented the invaders from moving beyond the shores of Manila Bay and into the Luzon countryside. Nevertheless, the period of the British presence lastingly affected the islands.

For one thing, in part encouraged by the British and in larger part driven by deep-rooted hostility toward the Spanish and Catholic Filipinos, the Moros of the south intensified their campaign of almost two centuries' standing. Elsewhere in the islands, groups of Christian peasants rose in forlorn rebellion against those who exploited them. Of far greater historical magnitude, however, Philippine trade patterns were reshaped as the result of the mid-eighteenth-century alien penetration of the Spanish preserve. The commercial monopoly that for so long had rested on the security of the galleon trade was cracked. Foreign flags appeared in Philippine waters with growing frequency, drawn by opportunities for both legal trade and smuggling. The government at Madrid further weakened the galleon trade by ending the insistence that Acapulco be the only port of call for Spanish vessels clearing Manila. Direct seaborne contact with Europe was established, bringing metropole and colony half a world closer together and ultimately intensifying friction between the rulers and the ruled. Two centuries of exclusive economic dependence upon profits realized from the exchange of Mexican silver for Chinese luxuries were thus ended. Finally, in 1834, Manila was officially opened to foreign shipping. As the planting of crops for export then began to be increased, the Philippines made a halting debut onto the stage of world commerce and international involvement.

As global economic links were forged, internal political and social patterns started to change. The decisive domestic contest centered on the place of the church and its personnel and property. Without daring to go into the labyrinthian details of generations of infighting over the extent of episcopal authority over the friars, the rivalry between the religious orders, or the jurisdictional disputes that arose between state and church, it can be recorded that such issues were to be at the heart of Filipino political consciousness as it took shape. Decades of slowly mounting tension finally exploded in the late nineteenth century in the form of militant anticlericalism, more specifically anti-Spanish clericalism, and kindled modern Southeast Asia's first nationalist awakening. But that is a matter for later consideration; now it is appropriate to transfer attention northward from the maritime lands to consider the nature of the early Western assault on the continental countries.

READINGS

'Abd Allah ibn' Abd al-Kadir, Munshi, *The Hikayat Abdullah* (tr. by A. H. Hill), New York: Oxford University Press, 1970.

Anderson, Gerald H., ed., *Studies in Philippine Church History*, Ithaca: Cornell University Press, 1969.

Clodd, H. P., *Malaya's First British Pioneer: The Life of Francis Light*, London: Lujac, 1948.

Collis, Maurice, *Raffles*, New York: John Day, 1968.

Day, Clive, *The Policy and Administration of the Dutch in Java*, New Haven: Yale University Press, 1904; reprinted, Kuala Lumpur: Oxford University Press, 1966.

Hahn, Emily, *Raffles of Singapore*, London: Oxford University Press, 1968.

Marks, Harry J., *The First Contest for Singapore, 1819-1842*, The Hague: Martinus Nijhoff, 1959.

Tregonning, K. G., *The British in Malaya: The First Forty Years, 1786-1826*, Tucson: University of Arizona Press, 1965.

Wickberg, Edgar, *The Chinese in Philippine Life, 1850-1898*, New Haven: Yale University Press, 1965.

Wurtzburg, C. E., *Raffles on the Eastern Isles*, London: Hodder and Stoughton, 1954.

6
The First Centuries of Imperialism in Continental Southeast Asia

Geography gave the lands north of the Malay Peninsula three centuries of partial immunity to the imperialist onslaught. The penetration in force of the continental interior was beyond the capacity of the Westerners; moreover, trading opportunities on the mainland offered meager incentives in comparison to those of the maritime countries. In any event, the states of the continent, despite countless upheavals, were hardly insignificant principalities to be swallowed one by one as were so many of the petty sultanates of the islands.

Geographical protection, of course, was not total. Coastal areas were vulnerable from the sea. Merchants, missionaries, and adventurers managed to roam rather widely; but on the whole, the interlopers played a trifling, marginal role in Burma, Siam, and the Indochina states until well into the nineteenth century. These failures of early imperialism demonstrate the limitations and goals of the Westerners in the first three hundred years of their presence in East Asia and reveal something of the nature of the continental states and their societies.

CAMBODIA

In the late sixteenth century, there were Westerners who were eager to offer the mainland the technology and weapons of European warfare and the message of Christian salvation. Local rulers quickly recognized the usefulness of new military resources and initially were inclined to view the missionaries as harmless holy men. That combination of circumstances favored exploits by small numbers of ambitious foreigners.

One of the boldest schemes for the penetration of the mainland was that of the Spanish, who were drawn to Cambodia in the late sixteenth century by visions of the Christianization of the Khmers and the installation of a puppet monarchy at Phnom Penh. The constant threat posed by Siamese enmity had earlier prompted the Cambodian king to offer hospitality to Portuguese missionaries, expected to be accompanied by soldiers; but, at the time, the overextended Portuguese had already entered their long decline and had to ignore the summons. The Spanish at Manila, next approached by the desperate king, were more responsive.

Both Portuguese and Spanish missionaries and soldiers of fortune had already been at work in Cambodia, a land suited by its precarious situation to their opposing, though not necessarily antagonistic, purposes. Therefore Manila was aware of the possibilities of the country. There was even an expansionist faction among the Spaniards to champion the cause of intervention on the mainland. Consequently, Spanish agents were sent on a mission across the South China Sea and, after a tangled series of adventures, returned to Manila claiming to be empowered to conclude an agreement on behalf of the Cambodian king. The signing in 1595 of a dubious document resulted. Under the terms of what was purported to be a treaty, Spain was to exercise sovereignty over Cambodia, where Spanish troops, merchants, and missionaries would be established and where a grateful king would abandon Buddhism to become a Christian. Even though their puppet was installed on the Cambodian throne for a short while, Spain soon learned that it could not exercise control over a country aflame with internal struggles and subject to Siamese attack. By 1599, the Spanish game was ended by the massacre of most of their force by outraged Cambodians; their royal hireling soon became yet another of Southeast Asia's many victims of regicide. Four years later a fresh royal weakling in search of support made new overtures to Manila, but was speedily deposed for his pains. The Siamese had been annoyed once too often; the king at Ayutthaya installed his own man on the throne at Phnom Penh and put Cambodia under Siamese suzerainty.

SIAM

The relative might of Siam by no means assured that kingdom's security against alien plotters. Indeed, the most dramatic and bizarre chapter in the history of the first centuries of Western intrusion into the region was written by a Greek who tried near the end of the seventeenth century to transform Siam into a colony of Bourbon France. The man, known to history as Phaulkon, reached Ayutthaya in 1678 in the service of the English East India Company for which he had worked for some years at Bantam. His commercial and linguistic gifts enabled him to gain early prominence at court, where he functioned as the king's confidant and interpreter in diplomatic negotiations and as the chief official in charge of Siam's foreign trade.

A dispute with his English friends in due course led Phaulkon to link himself to the French, who at the time were welcome in Siam to counter the more powerful and, so it seemed, threatening Dutch. France had come onto the imperialist stage a bit late and had not yet been able to win prizes in the East. Especially frustrating were the objections and obstacles to French missionary endeavor raised by the Portuguese and the Spanish, based on Goa, Macao, and Manila. Entry into China and, for some years, Vietnam was denied priests of the *Société des Missions Etrangères*, founded in 1659 and blessed by Louis XIV. Understandably piqued, the subjects of the Sun King had to fall back on Siam as a more accessible field in which to sow seeds that might produce a harvest of Christian converts and commercial profits. An astonishing interlude of French meddling at Ayutthaya followed.

In response to the visit to France in 1684 of a Siamese mission, the first ever to travel to the West, diplomatic relations were established between the courts at Ayutthaya and Versailles. A large entourage of missionaries accompanied the French ambassador on his voyage to Siam, for the goal of bringing the king and people of the country to Christ was paramount. The ambassador, a convert from Protestantism, appears to have displayed the religious obsession so typical of the freshly enlightened, to have been, as his countrymen might well have said, *plus catholique que le pape*. He soon learned that the salvation of the Siamese would take time and ingenuity. In fact, it was recognized that missionaries would need substantial political and military backing for their sacred endeavor.

The year 1687 brought a small French fleet carrying over six hundred troops to Siam. Phaulkon at that point was obliged to commit himself to a dangerous gamble. It was his task to have the foreign soldiers enlisted in the service of the Siamese king and assigned to garrison Bangkok, near the mouth of the Chao Phraya, and Mergui, on the Tenasserim coast—then under Siamese control. It was hoped that alien mastery over access to the Gulf of Siam and the Bay of Bengal would force Ayutthaya to grant full license to French priests and traders. Phaulkon earned a Bourbon title for his manipulative services, but his glory was of short duration.

Within a few months, when the compliant Siamese king was incapacitated by a final illness, a counterattack was launched by the enemies Phaulkon had attracted through his efforts to increase his own power at the expense of Siamese sovereignty. He was seized in a palace coup and in due course publicly beheaded and disemboweled. The tiny French garrisons could not hold out for long and had to be evacuated. The end result was the confirmation of Siamese fears of Western imperialism. Almost two centuries would pass before Siam again opened its doors to the outside world.

Though imperialism was checked, Ayutthaya was far from secure against more traditional threats. Virtually from their establishment in force within the region in the thirteenth century, the Siamese and related Tai peoples had been regarded with hostility by their Burman neighbors. Interminable intrigue, countless raids and skirmishes, occasional wars characterized relations between the two populations. The finale came with the Burmese siege, capture, and leveling of Ayutthaya in 1767. Siam began to fall apart and might have done so had it not been for the reckless overextension of the Burmese and the assumption of command over Siamese resistance by a determined, youthful general, Taksin—half Chinese in ancestry, wholly Siamese in his loyalties.

By fighting the only successful holding action as the Burmese advanced, Taksin had already established his reputation before the enemy invested Ayutthaya. Soon convinced of the futility of fighting from a fixed position, he mustered some troops whose loyalty he commanded and broke out of the encircled capital, leaving the city and a feeble king to face destruction. The general speedily went from one victory to the next, attracting mounting numbers of recruits to the resistance at each favorable turn in his fortunes. The combination of Taksin's assault and the need to guard against increasingly ominous pressure from China soon compelled the Burmese to retire. Siam had been liberated. As his reward, Taksin had himself coronated at the site of Bangkok, where a new capital was to rise.

The warrior king's troubles were, however, far from ended. In the northern parts of the country, separatist attempts had to be crushed; moreover, the Burmese soon returned to seek vengeance once their own northern frontier was secure. Driven by the urge to reconstruct the imperial prowess once displayed by the kings of Ayutthaya, Taksin compounded his difficulties by sending expeditions into Laos and Cambodia. The fifteen years of his monarchy, a time of virtually uninterrupted warfare, took a cruel toll: Taksin slipped into hopeless insanity.

Just as military genius had elevated Taksin to the throne, his successor also came to power from the battlefield. When a usurper staged a coup at Bangkok, the ablest of the Siamese generals, Chakri, led a swift counterattack and engineered his own coronation. Before that ceremony, however, something had to be done about Taksin, then held in a monastery where he imagined himself to be a bodhisattva. The hero of 1767 was executed, reportedly with reluctance, which both cured the royal madness and removed a potential challenge to the Chakri dynasty that was inaugurated in 1782 and has continued down to the present.

BURMA

Strife among contending ethno-linguistic groups has been the central theme in the history of Burma; repeated fragmentation was the invariable result. In the middle of the eighteenth century, Burma was unified for the third time under a Burman, Alaungpaya, who rose from humble origins to found the dynasty that in the space of a century and a quarter flourished, faded, and ultimately was obliterated by British attack.

The military success that won Alaungpaya the throne also sowed the seeds of the dynasty's disintegration. Momentum born of victories in the campaign for reunification carried Burmese armies into neighboring lands, Siam, the Arakan coast, Assam, and brought large numbers of unassimilated, resentful Mons, Shans, Karens, and others under alien sovereignty.

The eight years of Alaungpaya's reign were a time of all but ceaseless warfare. No sooner had he pacified Lower Burma than he was obliged to send forces to Manipur, on the border of India, to eradicate a threat to his western flank, and into the Shan states to win the submission of their chieftains. Each time the army was dispatched to one area, the conquered peoples left behind were likely to rise in rebellion and have to be subdued anew. The human cost of the continuing campaigns was beyond calculation. Whole districts were stripped of population, entire communities being put to the sword or forced to flee.

It was, in fact, the exodus of Mon refugees seeking sanctuary in Siam that provided the king with an excuse to resume the tradition of war against Ayutthaya. The pursuit of fleeing Mons carried the Burmese army deep into Siam and to the siege of Ayutthaya. There, in 1760, Alaungpaya was mortally wounded, his impending death signaling a Burmese retreat to the homeland during which the king expired. The Siamese capital had been granted a reprieve from destruction; but, the next Burmese assault, in 1767, under a successor to Alaungpaya would be dreadfully successful.

The victory against Siam, as noted earlier, was rather handily transformed into defeat by Taksin and his army of resistance. In that endeavor, the Siamese leader was greatly assisted by the fact that the Burmese occupation forces had been depleted in response to an urgent call for reinforcements to defend the Shan states against Chinese incursions. The entire Sino-Burmese border region had become a maelstrom of unrest and banditry. Beginning in 1766, imperial Chinese troops were moved into the Shan country and beyond to protect chieftains, who were being forced to shift their tributary allegiance from Peking to Ava, and to restore order in a spawning ground of the raiding parties that had created growing turmoil in Yünnan Province. In all, three Chinese invasions pushed deep into Burmese territory. All ended in failure; two of the most distinguished commanders, one the viceroy of Yünnan, the other a son-in-law of the Manchu emperor, followed the customary practice of defeated Chinese generals by commiting suicide. Burma had been spared.

Driven out of most of Siam, but victorious over the imperial Chinese, the Burmese army turned once again against Manipur, driving the ruler into exile and implementing the forced resettlement of large numbers of Manipuris in Burma, where earlier wars had depopulated great parts of the country. The triumph in Manipur and the expansion of Burmese power into the Indian border region, like so many previous military successes, in reality led to eventual Burmese defeat—to be inflicted in this instance by the British.

Burma had been by no means untouched by the coming of Westerners. As was the case in other continental lands, European missionaries, adventurers, and traders had been arriving from the sixteenth century on, though there had been no sensational dramas like those staged by the Spanish in Cambodia and the French in Siam. One Portuguese attempt to seize a coastal enclave succeeded for a few years, but was ultimately defeated when the leader was executed by impalement and many of his soldiers were banished to the remote interior, where their Luso-Burmese descendants lived for generations. The English and Dutch companies struggled with slight result to forge profitable commercial links with Burma. The French and the British both tried to establish repair yards for their ships on the coast of the Bay of Bengal. All in all, however, Westerners were mere peripheral observers of the bloody contests that raged across Burma, until, as the eighteenth century neared its conclusion, a sharp change began to take place.

In 1784, when Arakan came under Burmese control, two belligerent powers were brought into direct confrontation along the border between Burma and Bengal. The tension was heightened by the escape of Arakanese refugees into territory under the sovereignty of the East India Company, where they were hunted down by Burmese troops from time to time. Worse, Arakanese bands, based in Bengal, periodically undertook guerrilla operations in their unhappy homeland. Anglo-Burmese relations were understandably strained, though for a surprisingly long time war was averted through bluff and diplomacy.

Peace, or at least the absence of full-scale conflict, was finally ended in 1824 by increasingly incendiary developments along the whole frontier from the coast north to Assam. Fearing a general Burmese offensive into Bengal, the British struck a pre-emptive blow, seizing Rangoon by surprise in the expectation that Burmese forces would have to be withdrawn from the border region to defend Lower Burma.

The plan worked, but just barely. Rangoon almost slipped from the grasp of the British, as the Burmese besieged the captured city and as disease made as many as nine out of every ten men in the Anglo-Indian force unfit for duty and killed one in three. Reinforcements and fresh supplies finally brought a turn in the tide. The British, by pressing northward into the Burmese heartland, mounted a threat to the royal capital that won the concessions for which the war had been fought. Burma renounced her claims to Arakan, Manipur, and Assam, ceded the Tenasserim coast—a traditional invasion route into Siam—and was compelled to pay an indemnity that left her government near bankruptcy. The British in 1826 had attained their immediate goals: protection for the Indian frontier, security for Siam—on which British commercial aspirations were beginning to focus—and the right to maintain a diplomatic presence at the Burmese court. Moreover, the cost of the colonial war, as was repeatedly the case in the nineteenth century, was conveniently borne by the defeated. A quarter-century of relative stability ensued, with the rulers of Burma obliged by British encirclement to contain their outrage. Once Burma came to be seen as a vulnerable target for attack in the second half of the nineteenth century, the British would resume the process of conquest.

VIETNAM

The same, rather forlorn, hope for the Christianization of East Asia that led the French to debacle in late seventeenth-century Siam brought them into Vietnam, but in the latter country the consequences of the alien intrusion would in time become historically decisive. Indeed, it is not unjustified to see the repercussions of French imperialism as continuing forces in the final third of the present century.

As was invariably the case throughout Southeast Asia, the Portuguese were the first Westerners to penetrate Vietnam; but, the lasting results of that initial contact were largely limited to showing the way to later visitors and to the development of the method of romanization for the

Vietnamese language, based on early modern Portuguese orthography, that is now the official writing system of the country.

In the seventeenth century various European traders attempted to open Vietnam to international commerce, but the country had little to sell for export and Western weaponry seemed to be the only import for which there was a market, due to endemic, internecine struggles for power between contending regional contestants. Accordingly, trading ventures, abandoned at the start of the eighteenth century, were not to be resumed for a hundred and fifty years. Hence, the Western penetration of Vietnam, prior to the second half of the nineteenth century, was led by missionaries.

Following in the footsteps of a few priests who had been sent out earlier by Portuguese or Spanish hierarchies, a Frenchman, whose religious name was Alexander of Rhodes, arrived early in the seventeenth century. From that time on, French missionary interest in Vietnam multiplied to culminate in prompting Louis XIV to support the founding of his society of foreign missions in mid-century. Thereafter, for a century and a half, French priests labored to overcome the disdain of the Confucian gentry and official hostility that frequently led to deportation and less often to martyrdom. Despite innumerable reverses the effort had produced viable Christian communities by the end of the eighteenth century. At that point, France was brought to political involvement in internal Vietnamese affairs.

A forceful, imaginative, and patently ambitious French bishop, Pigneau de Behaine, appeared on the Vietnamese scene precisely when opposing sides in the endless regional wars and rebellions were locked in battle to the death. The young heir to leadership of the side that by then found itself pressed into a corner of the south and seemed not far from final extinction was driven to turn to the bishop for support. More specifically, he sought protection from his enemies and was granted it, together with much more, by Pigneau. The rescue took place in 1777; twenty-five years later, the refugee prince, Nguyen Anh, would triumph to become emperor of all Vietnam. That victory would be won in part with French help obtained through Pigneau's good offices.

Throughout the years of his struggle, the fortunes of Nguyen Anh waxed and waned; victory over his enemies seemed unattainable. So harassed was the prince that he was prepared to seek help from any source: Siam, Cambodian mercenaries, the various European powers. Among the Westerners, only the French had an advocate at the princely headquarters, and it was Pigneau who finally persuaded Nguyen Anh to make a direct diplomatic overture to Versailles. Taking along the prince's infant son, as a living symbol of Nguyen Anh's good faith, the bishop returned to his homeland in 1787 to negotiate at the court of Louis XVI.

The fiscal illness that was soon to prove fatal to the Bourbon monarchy caused Pigneau's requests for French aid for his prince to be given a frosty reception. The Vietnamese royal child was a huge social success among blasé courtiers, but diplomacy fared badly. The best the bishop could get was a somewhat vague promise of French help, in exchange for which Pigneau, as Nguyen Anh's plenipotentiary, ceded to France an island off the southern tip of Cochin China and land for port development at Tourane, now known as Danang.

Equipped with no more than a hollow pledge of French backing, Pigneau sailed for the East, where he had to struggle for months against obstruction to his plan mounted by the authorities at Pondicherry, a colonial outpost maintained by France on the east coast of India. Through his unique powers of persuasion, the bishop eventually managed to solicit private funds from French merchants, who sensed that a commercial profit might be derived from the Vietnamese undertaking. Thus supplied, he hired, equipped, and dispatched to Vietnam a small and motley force of volunteers, most of whom were soon disillusioned by the slowness of Nguyen Anh's campaign and drifted away.

A few of the Frenchmen who remained with Pigneau ultimately rose to positions of power; but the bishop himself did not live to see the final victory of his prince, nor did he succeed in his primary endeavor by converting the heir apparent to Christianity. All of Vietnam was finally brought under Nguyen control in 1802 and the founding was proclaimed of the dynasty that was to preside over the dissolution of the country as the new century grew old. At its beginning, however, Vietnam seemed secure. Internal peace had been restored after long, bloody decades; for the next forty years France, preoccupied with the campaigns and consequences of the Napoleonic era, could make no effort to drive home the entering wedge that Pigneau had fashioned.

READINGS

Chakrabongse, Prince Chula, *Lords of Life: The Paternal Monarchy of Bangkok, 1782-1932*, New York: Taplinger, 1960.

Crawford, John, *Journal of an Embassy from the Governor-General of India to the Court of Ava in the Year 1827*, London: Henry Colburn, 1934.

Hall, D. G. E., *Burma*, 3rd ed., London: Hutchinson, 1960.

———, *Early English Intercourse with Burma, 1587-1743*, 2nd ed., London: Cass, 1968.

———, *Europe and Burma*, London: Oxford University Press, 1945.

Harvey, G. E., *History of Burma from the Earliest Times to 10 March 1824*, London: Longmans Green, 1925.

Hutchinson, E. W., *Adventures in Siam in the Seventeenth Century*, London: Royal Asiatic Society, 1940.

———, trans. and ed., *1688: Revolution in Siam, the Memoir of Father de Beze, S.J.*, Hong Kong: Hong Kong University Press, 1968.

Lamb, Alastair, *The Mandarin Road to Old Hué: Narratives of Anglo-Vietnamese Diplomacy from the Seventeenth Century to the Eve of the French Conquest*, London: Chatto and Windus, 1970.

Vella, Walter F., *Siam under Rama III, 1824-1851*, Locust Valley, N.Y.: J. J. Augustin, 1957.

Woodside, Alexander B., *Vietnam and the Chinese Model: A Comparative Study of Nguyen and Ch'ing Civil Government in the First Half of the Nineteenth Century*, Cambridge: Harvard University Press, 1971.

7
The Final Imperialist Conquests

Southeast Asians who looked around them as the second half of the nineteenth century began were likely to feel that the colonial presence in the area was peripheral. True, the Philippine and Indonesian archipelagoes were for the most part under alien rule; but, even there, colonialism had not shattered basic village patterns. Peasants still toiled to win subsistence for themselves and tribute for their masters. Though the burdens had no doubt grown more onerous, the path was familiar. Villages remained essentially isolated from the outside; the rural masses had yet to find the means for political expression. In the cities and larger towns foreign influence was pervasive, but that was of no real consequence to villagers who rarely traveled far from their birthplaces and seldom, if ever, encountered a European. As an illustration of the relative isolation of rustic areas, for many decades after its demise, the V.O.C. lived on in the memories of Javanese country folk, who continued to refer to the unseen alien authority remotely over them as the *kompeni*.

Beyond the island world imperialism had made but tentative inroads. Burmese enclaves and the three British settlements on the Strait of Malacca were firmly colonial, but the rest of the Southeast Asian mainland

spokesmen of expansionism exploited the findings of the great biologist. The material wealth of the West and the poverty of the rest of the world were held to constitute proof of white superiority. The repeated victories of imperialist armies were attributed more to genetic endowment than to possession of the Gatling gun. Even antediluvian Christians who clung to their curious convictions on the origins of man and were therefore horrified by much of Darwinism could subscribe to the belief that white was best; for them, the myths of Shem and Ham provided the rationale.

The smugness and viciousness of the white drive were repeatedly reinforced as one people after another fell before the tide. Some men ceased to be men and became "Fuzzy-wuzzies" or "Wogs." In the United States, death was the only path to goodness for the Indian. At the end of the nineteenth century, Kaiser Wilhelm made his only memorable contribution to the language of literature by coining a new term, "the yellow peril." Simultaneously, the kindest description of colonial peoples that came to Kipling was "half devil and half child."

Strangely enough, in the midst of the contempt and hatred, a corrupt form of altruism came into vogue. Raffles had been a precursor of the development with his faith in the beneficence of British rule. He and his Victorian heirs held that to subjugate exotic peoples was to liberate them, to sweep away ancient darkness and lift up lesser breeds to the light. The concept was appealing to the Western ego, for there was comfort in the belief that the hazards of pacification and the frustrations of control in faraway lands were endured in a spirit of sacrifice. Men naturally shy away from acknowledgment of their own base motives and selfish goals. As the closing decades of the previous century unfolded, growing numbers of conquerors were to suffer, even to die, in bearing "the white man's burden," in serving *la mission civilisatrice*, in defending *Kultur*.

The last great wave of Christian proselytism coincided with the final surge of Western conquest. Indeed, the two forces interacted in mutual support. Wherever no danger to colonial stability might arise, as would be the case in Muslim countries, the missionaries moved in with the gunboats. Emancipation from ignorance in this world and salvation in the next were the blessings offered. Once the natives wore trousers and led docile, devout lives, like the good working-class people at home, both God and the Colonial Office would be pleased.

The imperialist, as a man of his age, was committed to the cause of Progress. The world to him was destined to be improved infinitely by the material advances that had come to the West with the steam engine, the flying shuttle, and the Bessemer furnace. The Victorian was above all a materialist, as his appalling aesthetic sense so often demonstrated; and, within himself, there was generated a materialistic morality that made expansionism for greed a crusade for human betterment. No obstruction to the extraction of raw materials and the development of markets could be tolerated. Barriers to Progress around the globe had to be pushed aside, even if the cost in blood and treasure ran high.

Naturally enough, each Western nation saw its own brand of aggression as uniquely just; international rivalry was hardly a new invention. Yet the intensity of the late nineteenth-century contest reached unprecedented levels, fueled by the moral certainty of the combatants. Frenchmen and Germans challenged one another; and both raced to catch up with the British, while American latecomers to the sport felt duty-bound to evict the Spanish from their vestigial empire.

In a classic summation of the thoughts of an imperialist that is appropriately cited in most treatments of the subject, William McKinley explained how he concluded that the Philippine islands had to become American territory. Confidently suggesting that divine guidance had left him no choice, he had, the President reported,

> walked the floor of the White House night after night . . . and prayed Almighty God for light and guidance more than one night, and one night late it came to me this way—I don't know how it was, but it came: (1) that we could not give them back to Spain—that would be cowardly and dishonorable; (2) that we could not turn them over to France or Germany—our commercial rivals in the Orient—that would be bad business and discreditable; (3) that we could not leave them to themselves—they were unfit for self-government—and they would soon have anarchy and misrule over there worse than Spain's was; and (4) that there was nothing left for us to do but to take them all, and to educate the Filipinos, and uplift and civilize and Christianize them, and by God's grace do the very best we could by them, as our fellowmen for whom Christ also died, and then I went to bed, and went to sleep, and slept soundly. . . .[3]

[3] Charles Sumner Olcott, *William McKinley*, Boston: Houghton Mifflin, 1916, vol. 2, pp. 108-11.

There is no reason to assume that McKinley and his contemporaries who spoke in the same vein were evil cynics; on the contrary, the moralistic expansionist no doubt sincerely believed in the sanctity of his cause. Convinced self-righteousness, in fact, was the mainspring of the Western assault and stiffened the resolve of the colonialists once the battles ended. When the saintliness of the mission later came to seem less obvious, Western pretensions began to crumble, though the disintegration might be a protracted process, as has been so tragically demonstrated in three decades of post-World War II Vietnamese history.

BURMA

The first war between the British and the Burmese had been touched off by the inflammability of the border region adjacent to Bengal; the second came when the commercial opportunities and the prestige of the British appeared to be in jeopardy. Thus, the later conflict was a fitting prelude to the final campaigns for territorial conquest of the second half of the nineteenth century. The very triviality of the *casus belli* suggests the true state of affairs: by 1852, the survival of forceful, independent Asian states had become anachronistic in Western eyes.

One hundred pounds sterling might seem to be too trifling a sum to cause a war; but, when a Burmese governor levied fines in that amount against British merchant mariners at Rangoon, the act was interpreted as the flinging down of a gauntlet. Fearing that meekness in Burma would be misinterpreted by Asians elsewhere, especially in India, as symptomatic of British weakness, Calcutta dispatched a naval force to back up demands that the fines be waived and that the Burmese official involved in the case be removed. Both demands were speedily met, but the new governor seems to have been a poor choice. Implacably hostile to the British, he arrived in Rangoon with substantial reinforcements for the local garrison, and soon he injudiciously gave the enemy an excuse to attack by refusing to have his afternoon nap interrupted by the visit of a British delegation. The British reaction to what seemed an unthinkable insult was immediate. Rangoon was blockaded, the coastal batteries were silenced, and Burmese patrol craft were sunk by British naval gunfire. A war was begun for reasons that would have generated no more than testy notes of diplomatic protest had the states involved both been Western.

For the second time, Rangoon was occupied, as were important coastal points, in order to shock the Burmese court into conciliation, but the plan for an inexpensive victory did not succeed. Burmese unresponsiveness made the British feel compelled to advance northward to threaten the royal capital. The move served to give heart to a palace faction that favored peace. A coup deposed the old king and installed a new one, Mindon, who was genuinely eager to negotiate an end to Anglo-Burmese differences. He was not, however, willing to cede territory to attain his goal; on that, he stood firm and helpless.

By that point in the contest the British had unilaterally annexed all of coastal Burma and substantial portions of the hinterland. Mindon's pleas for the restoration of his territory were rejected; the peace talks broke down and a curious stalemate ensued. Formal hostilities were suspended, but formidable guerrilla resistance in British-occupied areas was not stamped out for three years, and restlessness went on much longer. Mindon never granted royal acquiescence to the loss of the southern part of his country, but he learned to live in grudging, tacit recognition of a *fait accompli* and, in fact, came to have remarkably friendly feelings toward the British, if not toward their policies.

One feature of Anglo-Burmese relations after 1852 grew increasingly irritating as time passed. The British, to impress upon Mindon that his kingdom was less than fully sovereign, required him to act in the manner of the heads of the Indian princely states and conduct diplomatic business with Britain through the viceroy of India rather than directly with London. In efforts to offset that purposeful insult, Mindon negotiated agreements with Italy and, far more importantly, France. By so doing, he sought to demonstrate his freedom to act, but he actually opened the way to the final destruction of Burmese independence.

In 1875, greatly adding to the climate of tension and suspicion, effective communication between the Burmese court and Calcutta was broken by the king's insistence that British envoys observe traditional etiquette by removing their shoes before entering into the royal presence. The British, on the crest of their imperialist surge, presumably could not bring themselves to make a conciliatory gesture to a dark-skinned ruler. Victorian hauteur collided with the determination of Mindon to preserve the symbols of royal dignity.

The king died in 1878 and was succeeded by an incompetent drunk-ard, Thibaw, under whom Anglo-Burmese disputes grew in bitterness. It would be wrong, however, to assume that a better king could have saved the country. Thibaw's personality merely helped the British to reach and justify the decision to add Upper Burma to their empire.

Commercial incentives, international anxieties, and, perhaps no less significantly, humanitarian pretense drew Britain into the final war against Burma. British merchants at Rangoon raised a mounting clamor for the annexation of Thibaw's state. Their conviction that renewed expansion in the country would open up profitable opportunities was reinforced by the arguments of industrialists at home who relentlessly pressed for wider, more secure markets, for beyond Burma lay the lure of China. It was hoped that the ancient trade route north into Yünnan could become an avenue leading to the millions of China's southwest who had not been reached by the foreign traders at Shanghai and other treaty ports.

As if to prod the British, France manifested similar interests. French diplomats, technicians, and commercial agents had grown active in Up-per Burma. Moreover, French moves into Tonkin in the '70's and '80's were in part aimed at opening the Chinese southwest via the Red River valley. Quite irrationally, a contest was begun to determine whether the Yünnanese would wear Lancashire cottons or drink the wines of Bordeaux.

Instability, scandal, and worse at the Burmese court were cited as further reasons for British intervention. There could be no doubt that the royal government was inefficient, weakened by plots and counter-plots. It was also true that periodic, gory palace upheavals and the cruel fates met by losers in the contests were shocking by contempo-rary Western standards. Britons had been chilled by the account of a queen executed under the trampling feet of elephants and horrified to learn of the murderous rebellion of two of Mindon's sons, who killed their uncle, the heir apparent. Even greater titillation was provided in the reign of Thibaw, who on one occasion ordered the execution of eight of his brothers in a single day, and the more leisurely dispatch of scores of other relatives. Surely, pious Britons told themselves, morality demanded action; it was the white man's duty to protect others against themselves.

The end for Burma came with surgical swiftness, once the danger of

French encroachment into the British sphere appeared to be close at hand. In 1884 renewed Franco-Burmese negotiations seemed especially ominous. Vietnam was coming under the tricolor, bringing French power close to the northeastern border of Burma. Also, a pretender to the Burmese throne was tucked under the French wing and ready for installation once circumstances became favorable. Britain felt compelled to move before the French.

The attack began in 1885 when Thibaw, as hoped, rejected an ultimatum demanding arbitration of a fine levied against a British firm in Upper Burma, the establishment at the Burmese capital of a permanent British political agent authorized to wear shoes at court, and the surrender to the Indian viceroy of full authority over Burmese diplomacy. It was not a dramatic war. In two weeks, Thibaw was captured, to be exiled to India, and his dynasty was extinguished. The Chinese imperial government protested that, as a tributary state, Burma was under the suzerainty of China; but the British refused to let Peking intervene. The rules of the game were set by the West, not by the diplomatic traditions of imperial China, a country grown too weak to defend even itself. The annexation of Upper Burma was proclaimed in 1886 and all the lands once ruled by Alaungpaya came under the authority of the viceroy at Calcutta.

BRITISH EXPANSION INTO THE MARITIME STATES

Possession of the three settlements on the Strait of Malacca satisfied the British for half a century. The booming port city of Singapore dominated commerce, while possession of Penang and Malacca ensured strategic mastery over the sea route leading to Singapore from the north. The development of trade, not territorial acquisition, was still the objective to be served. One rendered profits; the other was costly and troublesome. Hence, the peninsular Malay States were barely noticed by the British until the final quarter of the nineteenth century; and, even when alien power moved into the peninsula, a façade of indirect rule was devised in part to lighten the burdens of empire.

Events in the northern parts of Borneo similarly illustrated the official determination of the British to avoid costly entanglements. With the government at London playing a rather distant and auxiliary part in both developments, Sarawak became the private kingdom of an English adventurer, and North Borneo was made the preserve of a corporate enterprise.

Like Raffles, James Brooke has been a favorite subject of biographers. The story of his rise to royal rank to become the white rajah of Sarawak has captured the imagination of many. The tale is certainly unique, for it could not have unfolded in a different place or at another time.

Brooke came to the island where fame awaited him in 1839, aboard a large yacht purchased with the legacy left him by a father who had done well as a nabob in India. That the son would invest his inheritance in a search for adventure reveals a good deal of the young man's nature. He was presumably delighted to discover that at the time of his arrival Sarawak was boiling with rebellion against its overlord, the sultan of Brunei. The Englishman quickly enlisted his yacht and his experience from earlier army service in India in the cause of pacification, doing so well that by 1841 the uprising had been crushed, the local populace had been made loyal, and Brooke was the governor of Sarawak. Five years later, in payment for helping to save the sultan from enemies who had banded together in a coup against their ruler, he was proclaimed rajah of Sarawak and the state was ceded to him and his heirs in perpetuity.

The white rajah's climb had not been entirely unassisted, for the British navy had played a substantial part in the drama, drawn to Bornean waters in a campaign against the pirates who infested them and cruised as far as the seas near Singapore. As the rebellious force that had endangered the sultan of Brunei had been largely composed of pirates, Brooke's thirst for power and official British concern over the safety of seaborne trade had been complementary. To lend added support to shipping, Britain was also eager to acquire a coaling station on the northern coast of Borneo, and it was through Brooke's good offices that they succeeded, taking over the tiny island of Labuan in 1846.

For his services Brooke was knighted by Victoria and made governor of Labuan and British commissioner to the sultan of Brunei. Britain had won paramountcy in a vast area with little effort and even less investment. Over the years, Rajah Sir James and the nephew who succeeded him enlarged their kingdom at the expense of Brunei, which was ultimately reduced to a pair of coastal slivers.

The process that led to the inclusion of North Borneo within the

British sphere was as dull as the Sarawak story was romantic. The establishment of alien authority over the territory came about through a series of business deals and diplomatic agreements. In 1865, an American purchased a North Bornean leasehold, but his plan for economic exploitation was stillborn. Then, the sultan of Sulu in 1878 was compelled by military pressure to accept Spanish sovereignty over his lands, including by tradition the northeastern corner of Borneo. Meanwhile, the American claim had been transferred to a firm jointly headed by a British entrepreneur in Hong Kong and the Austro-Hungarian consul in that Crown Colony. To solidify its position the firm obtained ratification of its rights both from the sultan of Brunei, who had no legitimate stake in the question, and the enfeebled sultan of Sulu.

Spain quite ineffectually sought to assert authority over the Bornean area leased from the Sulu monarchy but in 1885 was finally obliged to sign a treaty with Britain acknowledging that Spanish jurisdiction did not extend south or west of the Sulu archipelago. As a consequence, a British chartered company ruled without hindrance in North Borneo until the Second World War. A tangled skein of ownership claims was to be brought out in the post-independence era to excite politicians and profit lawyers in the Philippines and annoy the government of Malaysia.

The small states of the Malay Peninsula, as observed earlier, invited scant attention until late in the nineteenth century. Thinly populated, they sold little and bought less in the world marketplace. Tin had been scratched from the red soil of Malaya from a remote and unrecorded date, but until the latter part of the nineteenth century the ancient mining endeavor was anemic in capitalization and primitive in technology. The rulers and villagers of the peninsular sultanates could not threaten the British in the Straits Settlements; no French or other Western force was poised to challenge Britain in a contest for control. Siam had long sought hegemony over the peninsula, but by the nineteenth century she was obliged to husband her resources to check the mounting foreign menace to her own survival. Placid and poor, the Malay States slumbered on.

Chinese economic drive ultimately was the motive power of the British push into the peninsula. The business community in the Straits Settlements, primarily composed of Chinese merchants, grew convinced that the hinterland was an untapped cornucopia of resources awaiting exploitation under stable and modern government, that is, colonial authority. As British trading firms were all but totally dependent upon their Chinese agents and customers, the clamor for expansion was carried to the home government.

The break came when endemic lawlessness and feuding in the Malay States got totally out of hand. Again, the Chinese were the prime movers, for the growth of tin mining after the middle of the century had attracted thousands of immigrant Chinese laborers, who banded together in fiercely contending secret societies. The tremendous influx of outsiders had been far more than the Malay rulers and chiefs could handle. Secret society clashes grew into battles, as each Chinese band, often with Malay allies, sought to defend its own mining concession while expanding territorially at the expense of enemies. The resultant drop in tin production hurt exporters in the Straits Settlements. More alarming, the explosion of violence on the peninsula seemed capable of endangering the three British colonial holdings and, in fact, secret society warfare did spill over into Penang.

The colonial government was finally persuaded to act. The leaders of the most troubled state, Perak, were brought together in 1874 in order that a peace settlement among them might be negotiated under British auspices. Once the establishment of order was pledged, the British granted recognition and support to a claimant to the throne of Perak. In exchange, the sultan agreed to the appointment at his court of a British resident, who would direct the monarch's political and administrative actions in all matters except those involving the Islamic religion or Malay custom. Thus was born the system that in due course and with modifications put nine Malay states under colonial control, while their rulers exercised nominal and symbolic kingship. The pattern established something less than full-fledged alien rule, and the legal fiction of Malay sovereignty was to serve as the foundation of political evolution in the twentieth century.

The first British resident in Perak was hacked to death in his bath by Malay courtiers who resented the foreign intrusion, but by and large the residential arrangement operated smoothly. In 1896 the four states of the middle portion of the peninsula were brought together in a centralized structure, the Federated Malay States, headed by a British resident general. The capital of the new entity was established at Kuala Lumpur, the site of a rough and raw Chinese mining camp in Selangor. The selection of a place built by Chinese capital and labor rather than a Malay royal town expressed the realities behind the British presence. The purpose of the federation was to protect and promote economic growth, while disturbing the indigenous people as little as possible.

In 1909 an Anglo-Siamese treaty permitted the extension of British authority over four northern peninsular states. Their four sultans were able to avoid accepting residents, as there was little economic promise in the states to attract aggressive outside interest. Accordingly, the northern sultans were obliged merely to listen to British advisers, who were supposed to convince rather than compel. The lands to which advisers were appointed were designated, somewhat unimaginatively, the Unfederated Malay States. In 1914, Johore, at the southern end of the peninsula and the most powerful of the sultanates, finally granted accommodation to an adviser and thus joined the unfederated states under formal British domination. Empire-building in Malaya had been completed. Memories of the general peacefulness of the process no doubt contributed to the relative absence of bitterness among those who led the Malay independence movement after the Second World War.

INDOCHINA

The original interest of the French in Vietnam as a missionary field was reinforced from the middle of the nineteenth century by political and commercial considerations not unlike those that led to the British conquest of Burma. Hence, there is a fair measure of similarity between the French and the British drives in continental Southeast Asia. Even the timing of the two major French military campaigns in Vietnam corresponded approximately to that of the two wars Britain fought to acquire the lower and upper portions of Burma in the second half of the century. On the other hand, the two conquests were dissimilar because the Vietnamese offered the more determined resistance to invasion, and the Chinese imperial government provided more than token support to her Vietnamese tributary.

The existence of a Christian community and the activities of the foreign priests who sought to serve it became increasingly imperiled under the emperors at Hué who succeeded the founder of the Nguyen dynasty after 1820. The last vestige of any sense of gratitude to Pigneau and his compatriots evaporated. Persecution grew in intensity and soon France felt justified in bringing force to bear on the Vietnamese imperial court. The protection of defenseless parishioners and the rescue of endangered priests were held to be sacred obligations. The vigorous anti-clericalism that had become a feature of French domestic politics was not generally allowed to diminish the ardor of French governments in protecting the faith overseas.

After the Opium War of 1839-42, when Britain broke open the southeastern doors to China, a French naval force of significance began to be assembled in Eastern seas. The fleet had been drawn there initially to back French claims for a share of the Chinese spoils but soon was charged with the additional task of menacing Vietnam. Repeatedly, French ships appeared off the coast of Annam to secure the release of imprisoned missionaries, many of whom were under capital sentences. The threat of naval bombardment was the usual device employed to convince the Vietnamese authorities of the wisdom of moderation.

Finally in 1847, when the French staged yet another naval show of force, the Vietnamese emperor wearied of the game and ordered his war junks to attack the intruders. The fireboats and other craft of the Vietnamese were predictably unable to stand up to European broadsides. France won a quick victory at sea, but little had really changed. A decade of stalemate ensued, and in fact the persecution of Christians was cruelly intensified. Thousands perished in a campaign launched by Hué to break up Christian villages by sending their inhabitants into banishment, each freshly branded on one cheek with characters meaning "infidel" and on the other with the name of the place of exile. Soon the addition of two priests to the ranks of the martyred brought French shells crashing into the fortifications of Danang.

Decisive action finally came in 1857. The execution of a Spanish monsignor in Tonkin that year had given France an ally in the Philippines. More important, French forces in eastern Asia had by then been substantially strengthened in preparation for a combined assault on China in collaboration with the British. The Vietnamese emperor, Tu Duc, had chosen an inauspicious time to display his xenophobia.

In 1858, after Tu Duc had rejected French demands for commercial opportunities and consular representation at Hué and after the first phase of the war against China had ended, a joint Franco-Spanish attack captured Danang. The ease with which the victory was won encouraged the invaders to plan moving north against the capital, but in that they were frustrated by local resistance and, with deadlier effect, tropical disease. An alternative to striking at the heart of the Vietnamese empire had to be found. Consequently, troops were sent down to Cochin China, the rice bowl of the country, to occupy the provincial town of Saigon in 1859.

Renewed hostilities in China soon compelled the French to withdraw a major portion of the Saigon garrison, leaving that body at a strength of less than a thousand to face a year of siege and sickness. When rescue eventually came in 1861, the French consolidated their hold on Saigon and began to fan out into the surrounding delta country to occupy three provinces. Their colonial bridgehead in Vietnam was secure. Only Tu Duc's formalization of the fact was needed and after some imperial procrastination that was grudgingly bestowed when rebelliousness in Tonkin rendered peace with the French militarily essential.

The French were soon carried into Cambodia where a harassed king, pressed by his Siamese suzerain on the one hand and by internal rebels on the other, was argued into placing his country under the protection of the colonial governor at Saigon in 1864. Bangkok complained as forcefully as non-military means allowed and, over the toothless protests of the puppet king at Phnom Penh, was able to frighten the French into transferring Battambang and Siem Reap provinces in western Cambodia to Siam. At the time, Tu Duc was far from subdued and France was eager to avoid a confrontation on two fronts. Moreover, restlessness in Cochin China had proven to be such a protracted annoyance that in 1866 the French had felt obliged to occupy the western part of the region and thereby reduce the Vietnamese empire to the territories of Annam and Tonkin.

Just as the British had futile dreams of penetrating western China via the overland route from Upper Burma, Frenchmen had begun to speculate on the feasibility of getting into China by way of the Indochinese rivers. When the Mekong was discovered to be unnavigable beyond a point well south of the Chinese frontier, attention was redirected to the Red in Tonkin, a river that ran through a chaotically disturbed part of Tu Duc's empire, where the authority of Hué was little more than nominal.

The central figure in the initial push into Tonkin was an enterprising, some might say criminal, merchant with the resoundingly bourgeois name of Jean Dupuis. Protected by a small private army of Filipino and Chinese mercenaries, Dupuis had done well selling arms to the imperial Chinese, then in the midst of putting down a Muslim rebellion in Yünnan, and delivering Yünnanese tin and copper to customers in Hanoi. In 1872, when the Frenchman sought to move into the salt business in Tonkin, the Vietnamese authorities cracked down, for in their country, as in China and many other pre-industrial lands, legal trade in salt was conducted exclusively under an official monopoly that produced crucial revenues for the state. Not to be barred from a lucrative endeavor, Dupuis ordered his men to occupy a portion of Hanoi and called on the governor at Saigon to send a relief force to protect the commercial interests and the life of a good French citizen.

In response, fewer than two hundred French regulars and a couple of dozen colonial soldiers were dispatched on a mission of rescue. The Saigon governor clearly hoped to achieve great results in Tonkin with a minimum of military effort. The hinterland beyond Haiphong and Hanoi was then in total chaos as the result of the depredations of bandits known collectively as the Black Flags. The origins of the brigands were thoroughly mixed. Some were Vietnamese outlaws; others were Vietnamese soldiers who had chosen to join in the pillage rather than suppress it. To add an international dimension, Chinese representation in the Black Flags was heavy. Many stragglers from the Taiping and Yünnanese rebellions had fled into Tonkin, and a goodly number of the Chinese imperial troops sent in pursuit had deserted their army for a life of banditry. Thus, while Dupuis was encircled at Hanoi, the mandarins in that city were themselves under siege. Under the circumstances the French were convinced that a small sacrifice could win them a pivotal position in Tonkin.

Francis Garnier, the commander of the French force sent in late 1873 to save Dupuis, was a reckless patriot who never doubted that swift victory in Tonkin was feasible and certain to help restore the prestige of his motherland, so recently pushed to its nadir by Prussian arms. Boldly capturing one Vietnamese position after another, the French overextended themselves and became vulnerable to the counterattack mounted against them by Black Flag units called into the contest by the desperate Tonkinese mandarins. When Garnier was killed, his superiors in Saigon lost heart and decided to negotiate an end to military intervention in the north. Dupuis, incidentally, was rescued to spend the next twenty-five years denouncing the French government for its faint-heartedness.

A treaty concluded with Tu Duc in 1874 provided that, in exchange for abandonment by the French of the Hanoi fortifications, the Vietnamese emperor would receive a French resident at Hué and permit the establishment of French consular and trading representation at three ports, including Danang and Hanoi. In addition, Tu Duc finally granted formal recognition of French sovereignty over all Cochin China and agreed to the opening of the Red River to foreign traffic. A customary and inevitably empty pledge of official Vietnamese toleration for Christians was tacked onto the treaty. In order to keep a foot in the Tonkinese door, the French promised military aid to support the destruction of the Black Flags. All in all, it was a poor settlement. Both sides, at least unconsciously, acted in bad faith. Tu Duc had underestimated the aggressiveness of the West; France was to be drawn more and more deeply into the whirlpool of global imperialism.

Because the Nguyen court had grown increasingly committed to Confucianism as the century ran on, it was hardly unexpected that the Vietnamese emperor would look to the homeland of that philosophy in his hour of need. Chinese intervention against the Black Flags was seen to be doubly appealing. The bandits might be defeated; more important, Sino-French confrontation in Tonkin could bog down both the most ancient and the newest of Vietnam's enemies. Tu Duc, in other words, sought to turn to his own advantage the Chinese international practice of using barbarians to control barbarians. At the time, expansionist sentiment in Paris was gaining strength just as the government at Peking, following a diplomatic triumph over the Russians, was growing belligerently self-confident.

French troops returned to Tonkin in 1882, allegedly to assist in exterminating the Black Flags, actually to seize the country. For the second time, a French commander fell in combat. His death touched off an outburst of jingoism at home that was highly welcome to Jules Ferry, the ferocious imperialist who headed the French government of the day. The occupation of Tonkin and the reduction of the Hué regime to subservience after the Cambodian model was ordered. The campaign was swift; Tu Duc's death just as it began generated a succession crisis in the palace that left the Vietnamese virtually leaderless.

When the French took the fortifications guarding the imperial capital, peace overtures were promptly extended to the invaders.

The treaty imposed on Vietnam in 1883 converted Annam and Tonkin into protectorates without power or dignity. The foreign relations of Vietnam were put under the control of Paris, her military forces were disbanded, and her civil administrators and customs service were brought under the strict authority of French officials. The Nguyen dynasty was preserved as a pitiful curiosity. For the first time since the tenth century, Vietnamese freedom seemed irretrievably lost.

All would then have gone smoothly for France if China had not decided to assert suzerainty over Vietnam. When troop reinforcements were sent south to block the French advance, war was begun in fact, if not in law. An effort by a peace faction in Peking to stop hostilities produced a Sino-French truce in 1884 that was supposed to lead to the evacuation of Chinese troops from Tonkin, but war fever ran too high. New clashes soon erupted, to be followed by open warfare.

The war went badly for the army of the French, but their navy saved the day. Humiliating reverses on land were offset by triumphs at sea. The sinking of China's tiny modern navy in a surprise attack at Foochow and the destruction of the naval yard in that port gave the French admiral license to take the main fortifications on Formosa and to occupy the Pescadores in the nearby strait. While those victories were being won, however, the French army in Tonkin was routed by imperial Chinese troops. There thus seemed to be no profit for either side in continuing the war. China could not regain the prizes lost at sea; France saw little hope of clearing Tonkin of Chinese soldiers. Peace advocates gained power in both Peking and Paris, led in the latter city by the young Georges Clemenceau. The Sino-French treaty of 1885 that resulted provided for the evacuation of Tonkin by the Chinese and the strongpoints of the Formosa Strait by the French. Thus ended the sole attempt by China to defend a Southeast Asian tributary state.

SIAM

It has become something of a cliché to observe that Siamese independence survived because the British and the French needed a buffer between them and because no bilateral agreement was achieved on how to divide the kingdom. There is partial truth in that interpretation, but it ignores two central points. First, Siam in fact lost significant parts of her territory and her sovereignty in the nineteenth century; second, the Bangkok monarchy proved to be both stable and perceptive in meeting the foreign threat.

The isolation from Westerners sought by Siam after Phaulkon's plot of the late seventeenth century was strictly maintained until the negotiations that preceded the conclusion of an Anglo-Siamese Treaty in 1826, and that agreement provided for little more than the neutralization of the northern Malay sultanates and the opening of a slight and ill-defined commercial opportunity in Siam for British merchants. The first meaningful break in the armor of seclusion was made only in 1855 with the signing of a new treaty that gave the British the right to reside and trade in Siam under generous and hospitable conditions. That development opened an era in which the Siamese were to be subjected to unprecedented pressures to accommodate themselves to a world shaped by its industrialized countries. The shift had by no means come inadvertently; it was carefully directed by Mongkut, a ruler who saw the futility of negative and reactionary policies in Burma and Vietnam and strove to save his land from their fate.

The man who reigned and ruled from 1851 to 1868 was a great and perceptive king. Coming to the throne in middle age, after almost three decades in a Buddhist monastery, Mongkut was the most sophisticated and learned monarch the Westerners had met in their imperialist advance. Much of his time as a monk had been invested in education, including training in English which Mongkut used effectively and enthusiastically, if somewhat individualistically.

The king was fully sensitive to the dangers inherent in depending upon the moderation of any Western power, on one occasion, comparing Britain's appetite to a whale's and France's to that of a crocodile.[4] Inviting as many powers as possible to develop interests in Siam seemed the best way to shield the country against the greed of any one. Therefore, after his initial sortie into global politics in 1855, Mongkut arranged for the early conclusion of treaties with numerous Western states, some powerful, some minor. The same pattern of internationali-

[4] Noel F. Busch, *Thailand: An Introduction to Modern Siam*, Princeton: Van Nostrand, 1964, p. 68.

zation was followed in recruiting foreign specialists to aid the Siamese in modernization.

Chulalongkorn, who inherited the throne in 1868, was the son of a king who had abandoned a life of monastic celibacy only seventeen years before his death. Thus, the new monarch was a minor under a regency for the first five years of his reign. Fortunately, the regents and, subsequently, the king and his advisers built wisely upon the foundation laid down by Mongkut, continuing and expanding established policies in diplomacy and modernization.

Study under foreign tutors and travel to nearby colonial countries had equipped Chulalongkorn with an understanding of the forces at work in the world that surpassed even that of his astute father. The dangers confronting an independent kingdom in a region swept by foreign conquest were clearly seen; and, as if to sharpen the king's vision, Britain and, more forcefully, France compelled Siam to contract her frontiers to accommodate imperial expansion. Under Mongkut, claims to suzerainty over Cambodia and some Malay states had already been surrendered; far more substantial losses were inflicted on Siam in the forty-two years of Chulalongkorn's reign.

Laos was the target of the most aggressive Western thrust. The fragmentation of the country and muddy confusion over questions of sovereignty there had invited French attention from the middle of the century. Once the French believed that they had established control in Tonkin in 1883, their westward push to the Mekong was begun in earnest. Rather dubious claims that parts of Laos had been tributary to the Vietnamese emperor gave the French their excuse to act. When the Siamese sought to defend their own position of suzerainty over Laos, a country populated in major part by close ethnolinguistic kinsmen, their first battle against Western powers was fought and promptly lost.

In 1893, after a decade of rising tension, France decided upon a display of force to awe Siam into submission. French gunboats, refusing to wait outside the entrance to the Chao Phraya, exchanged fire with coastal fortifications and steamed on to Bangkok. The Siamese were admirably and wisely moderate under the circumstances, but the French had no desire to be placated. An ultimatum was delivered to demand, *inter alia*, the withdrawal of Siamese troops to the west bank of the Mekong. At that point, Britain intervened diplomatically, seeking to check an advance that would bring French power to the borders of northern Burma, but it was an abortive effort.

When their ultimatum failed to produce humble acquiescence, the French imposed a naval blockade at the mouth of the Chao Phraya in order to paralyze Siam's international commerce. The obstruction to trade lasted only two days before Bangkok expressed willingness to bow to French demands. The speed of the Siamese capitulation encouraged Paris to tack additional demands onto the original list; most importantly, Siam was told to return to the original owner, and thereby place under French rule, the two western provinces of Battambang and Siem Reap taken from Cambodia in 1864. A few more days of blockade secured Siamese acceptance of the expanded claims. In a nearly bloodless campaign, France had succeeded in tearing great territorial bites from the Siamese kingdom. Moreover, the gains had been won over the timid objections of the British, whose pretended friendship for Siam had produced little more than advice to give in quickly lest French greed increase. Beyond that, Britain had her own plans for redrawing the borders of Siam.

The French attack had profoundly alarmed the British, who feared that momentum would carry it into the heart of Siam. In 1896 Britain happily exchanged empty assertions of a sovereign role in lost Laotian territories adjacent to Burma for French recognition of the inviolability of the Chao Phraya watershed. The Anglo-French rapprochement permitted further redefinition of Siam's frontiers. The French in 1904 and 1907 negotiated treaties with Siam that put the capstone on their gains in Laos and Cambodia.

The British, for their part, obtained territorial concessions on the eastern frontiers of Burma and, of far greater significance, on the peninsula pushed their political authority northward to encompass four Malay States that were traditionally, if vaguely, in vassalage to the Siamese monarchy. The Anglo-Siamese Treaty of 1909, by ending Bangkok's ineffectual efforts to dominate the four sultanates immediately to the north of the Federated Malay States, left the British free to extend colonialism up to the Kra Isthmus.

The extent of Siam had been greatly reduced; lands roughly equal in area to the United Kingdom had been lost to Siamese sovereignty and suzerainty. Furthermore, since Bangkok had been compelled to grant further concessions to the Westerners, such as the right of extraterritoriality, Siam had been pushed toward the semi-colonial status that had become China's lot. At a heavy price, then, the Siamese had bought the right to survive as a free people; but that in itself was no mean accomplishment in an era when most of the peoples of Africa and Asia were being colonized.

INDONESIA

Over three hundred years passed between the initial appearance of the Dutch in the archipelago and the total smothering of independence in the islands. For most of those years, considerable areas were bypassed as not economically worthy of conquest. The absence of Western challenges to their hegemony, after the post-Napoleonic settlement, permitted the Dutch the luxury of allowing many unconquered lands to continue under traditional authority. In the closing decades of the nineteenth century, however, political and economic developments in Holland and in the rest of the industrialized West revitalized Dutch imperialism and led directly to the final absorption of areas and peoples formerly spared.

In the middle of the century, in addition to occasional punitive forays against troublesome local rulers, Batavia sent troops into Bornean coastal regions, attracted by coal and gold deposits, and to the island of Billiton that rested invitingly on a foundation of unmined tin. However, only with the influx of private capital that came in later years was large-scale territorial expansion undertaken. Lombok and Bali were subdued without great difficulty, though on the second and very lovely island the Dutch were temporarily shocked by the spectacle of royal and aristocratic resistance that took the form of mass suicide. Far more painful experience was gained at the northern end of Sumatra, in Acheh, where from 1873 to 1908 one of the longest and bitterest of colonial wars was fought.

Acheh had been a force in the strait for centuries, since well before the coming of the Portuguese. The state's remote, yet strategic, location and the intensity of its Islamic devotion had provided the bases for widely respected military prowess. As the Dutch pushed northward, swallowing Sumatra piece by piece, conflict with the Achehnese grew inescapable. Reports of foreign, specifically American, designs on

Acheh finally jolted Batavia into action. The tiny Dutch force that was sent in 1873 to cow the sultan was quickly put to flight, and the war was on. It was to last thirty-five grim years.

The war was an indecisive, untidy affair during its first twenty-five years. The movement of colonial troops from a secure area to a trouble spot invariably touched off new resistance in the place abandoned. Guerrilla pressure on lines of communication was unrelieved and devastating. Fresh levies of troops, many of them Christian Amboinese, were fed into the contest; a series of Dutch commanders left for home in defeat. Finally, the talents of two gifted and strikingly different men, a soldier and a cultural anthropologist, were harnessed to break the impasse.

Van Heutsz, who eventually won the rank of general, devised and executed a plan for pacification that rested on the employment of mobile strike forces operating from impregnable, generously supplied bases. One by one, bands of Achehnese fighters were pursued and destroyed; undefeated pockets of resistance were gradually isolated from one another, reduced in size, and finally erased.

The general's partner in conquest was an improbable figure with, at least to English ears, an unlikely name, Snouck Hurgronje. He was an eminent Islamicist who had earlier acquired distinction by visiting the holy city of Mecca in disguise and writing an account of his observations. He later undertook a field study of Acheh that led to the publication of a monumental work on the customs, beliefs, and behavioral patterns of the people who had caused the Dutch such prolonged anguish. Snouck Hurgronje, in other words, provided the cultural intelligence that was to prove indispensable in bringing the Achehnese under control. He thereby established a precedent that gave anthropologists and other scholars a respected role in the making of policy in the Indies. No other colonial regime matched that of the Dutch in utilizing scholarly resources for administrative purposes. Consequently, the Indonesian islands became the best studied part of Southeast Asia.

There is a kind of poetic equilibrium in the fact that the year the Achehnese war ended, 1908, was the same as that which saw the first signs of modern Indonesian nationalism in Java. Just as the final embers of resistance to the alien invasion were crushed, a fresh flame began to rise, to consume, in little more than a generation, the colonial edifice that had been built over the span of three centuries.

THE PHILIPPINES

The Achehnese struggle was not the final gasp of organized resistance to alien invasion; that dying breath came in the southern Philippines, where the Moros made their stand against American newcomers to the scene. In assuming sovereignty over the islands, the Americans took on burdens for which they were singularly unprepared; crushing the Moros was merely one of them. Possibly there is some historical message in the fact that the last outside power to impose its rule in Southeast Asia in the final years of Western expansion until recently was engaged in a lone rearguard effort to employ military might to guide the destiny of the region in the post-colonial era.

Filipino nationalism was a vigorous force well before the United States dreamed of involvement in the archipelago. The movement was fueled by a combination of leadership from the elite and manpower from the masses. The class of landowners and notables, partly of mestizo ancestry, which had attached itself to the Spanish from the start of the colonial period, grew restless as the nineteenth century neared its end. The few Iberians in their midst treated them as colonial inferiors—decreeing, for example, that non-Spaniards could not affect dignity by wearing neckties. (The open-necked, embroidered shirt that is the national costume of men in the Philippines today was thus inadvertently invented.) More serious and especially galling was Spanish haughtiness in the area of church politics and administration.

During a liberal interlude in Spain that lasted from the deposition of the queen in 1868 to the restoration of authoritarianism in 1870, the growing class of literate Filipinos experienced unprecedented freedom of expression and thought. Much of the excitement centered on the enduring issue of the place of Filipino secular priests in relation to the Spanish friars. The church had become the avenue chosen by a rising number of sons of the Philippine middle and upper classes in a quest for advancement and service. Hence, the internal policy decisions of the church hierarchy directly touched the Filipino elite.

The destruction of liberalism in Spain was soon felt on the other side of the globe when a new, thoroughly reactionary governor general of the Philippines was sent out by the rightists who had taken power in Madrid. One of his first acts was to support a punitive measure aimed at the most respected element among the locally articulate, those priests who had spoken out for Filipino elevation. The offending clergymen were denied the right to conduct mass in public, and thus became little more than native houseboys within the church.

The sense of outrage generated by the humiliation of the priests contributed in ways yet to be adequately explained to the mutiny of a group of Filipino troops in 1872. Panic gripped the Spanish, long subject to colonialist paranoia. Fearful of a general uprising, the authorities opened a campaign of brutal police repression against Filipino liberalism. Some mutineers were shot; three innocent priests, as civilians, were slowly strangled by that ancient instrument of execution still in Spanish service, the garrote.

Filipino bitterness was smothered by Spanish severity for two decades after the horror of 1872, but in those years it grew in intensity. More important, formless expressions of discontent among the elite came to be channeled into a potent movement of protest. The turning point came with the publication in 1887 of one of those rare novels that shape history, in this instance, *Noli Me Tangere*, a pitiless exposé of the inequities of life in the colonial Philippines. The author was José Rizal, destined to be the great hero of his nation.

That Rizal has become the supreme and justly honored symbol of the Philippine fight for freedom tends to obscure the fact that he was a liberal reformer, never a nationalist revolutionary. His place in history was won not by leading a rebellion, but by giving voice to the longings and dissatisfactions of men like himself, members of the educated upper stratum who simply wanted their islands made a happy and progressive Spanish province. The stupidity and cruelty of the colonial government, by martyring Rizal, eventually drove enough liberal Filipinos toward the side of violence to give leadership to endemic peasant discontent. At that point, Spain had a revolution on its hands.

Rizal was a cosmopolitan, intellectual physician when his famous novel appeared. He was then twenty-six; in nine years, he would be dead. Almost as soon as his fictional attack on colonial injustices began to circulate with the liveliness that banned books enjoy, the young doctor was a celebrity. The printing of his second reformist novel in 1891 enhanced his fame but led the Spanish to retaliate against his family, obliging Rizal to return home from protracted residence abroad. He was immediately put under official surveillance. The subsequent founding of a society of moderate reformers, the Liga Filipina, by Rizal and likeminded patriots led almost instantly to his arrest and banishment to distant Mindanao. There, he would have vegetated had not a bizarre and tragic turn of events intervened.

The fateful year was 1896. Rizal, ever loyal to Spain, volunteered his medical skills in support of the campaign then in progress against revolutionaries in Cuba. Taken from the ship that was carrying him to military duty in the service of his king, Rizal was returned to the Philippines, tried for rebellion, and publicly executed in the grandest park of Manila, the Luneta. The Spaniards had struck once more in blind, pathological fear.

Though Rizal was blameless, as a matter of fact there was good reason for the Spanish to be frightened, for in 1896 a widespread insurrection had broken out. The patriotic struggle was led by Katipunan, a secret society that appealed powerfully to the common people. The use of a Tagalog rather than a Spanish name by the organization suggests both the nature of its nationalism and the basis of its support. The founder and director of the movement, Andres Bonifacio, significantly not a member of the comfortable classes, advocated total independence for the country; and the frustrations met by liberals had caused a number of educated members of the gentry to join him. Thus, when Katipunan was forced by Spanish terror to declare Philippine independence and strike prematurely, the rebellion united both men of privilege and the disadvantaged in its ranks.

After the founding of the Philippine Republic was proclaimed in 1896, factionalism within its leadership led to an attempt by Bonifacio to break away and set up his own rebellious headquarters. A brilliant young soldier, Emilio Aguinaldo, the best fielded in the contest, prevented the defection, had Bonifacio shot, and in 1897 became president of the new republic.

The Spanish were in fact far from military impotence at the time. Indeed, Aguinaldo was forced to accept a negotiated settlement. In return for a Spanish promise, sadly informal, that pledged sweeping liberalization and evolutionary political development for the Philippines, and in acknowledgment of the payment of part of a large amount of money, the Filipino general and a number of his officers went into exile in Hong Kong. Neither side to the agreement honored its terms. The Spaniards did not introduce meaningful political reforms nor did they pay the full sum owed the exiles; for his part, Aguinaldo used the money he had received to prepare for the next round in the struggle. Within a few months, rebellion flared anew. At that point, in an overseas campaign for empire that was alien to their most respected traditions, the Americans pushed themselves into the picture in a land that was known to few of them.

The conflict between Spain and the United States was, in John Hay's words, "a splendid little war,"[5] at least from the American perspective. Great power status was then measured in part by the extent of empire; and, in 1898, the United States won mastery from Spain over Puerto Rico, Guam, and the Philippines and annexed the islands that had been the Kingdom of Hawaii. If the hours of dusk were counted, the Americans, like the British, had an empire on which the sun always shone. Better still, the prizes had been gained at a most modest cost.

The presence of a United States fleet in East Asian waters when the war began was due to the foresight and spirit of imperial fun of the assistant secretary of the navy, Theodore Roosevelt, who one day had taken advantage of the absence from the office of his superior to order Commodore Dewey to stand ready to strike in the Philippines should hostilities with Spain begin. At the appropriate signal, Dewey took his ships into the bay at Manila and, with no fatalities among his crews, destroyed the ability of the Spaniards to defend the capital of their Asian colony against seaborne attack.

The naval victory was followed by many weeks of stalemate until enough American troops could be brought across the Pacific to effect a landing. The disembarkation took place on the day the Spanish-American war ended in armistice. The defenders of Manila by then had become more than willing to turn the city over to the Americans, but their commander insisted that his honor demanded a show of resistance. An understanding between the enemies provided for a brief flurry of fire before the 13,000 men of the garrison quit the fight. Forty-nine Spaniards and four Americans died in the charade; but that, surely, was a small price to pay for the preservation of a Spanish general's good name.

The reason for the eagerness of the Spaniards to surrender Manila to the *Yanquis* was quite simple; the place was encircled on land by Filipino insurgents. Permitting the Americans into the city gave the

---

[5] Frank Freidel, *The Splendid Little War*, Boston: Little, Brown, 1958, p. 3.

Spanish protection against a far more terrifying enemy. The Filipinos at that point were doing extremely well in freeing their country, virtually all of which was in their hands. Their drive had been sustained by patriotic fervor and by the expectation that the Americans had come to their islands as liberators. They then had good cause to take such a view of United States intentions.

During his period of exile, Aguinaldo had been courted by Americans. One of their consular officers, met during a trip to Singapore, assured the general that the United States, born in revolution herself, stood behind the cause of Philippine independence. Dewey had similarly encouraged Aguinaldo, for example, by carrying him home from Hong Kong aboard an American warship. Once Manila fell, however, the suspicions of Filipino patriots began to grow. Their allies day by day seemed to act more like conquerors and less like liberators. Soon, American intentions were unmistakable. The Filipinos had no choice but to fight.

The war that started early in 1899 was neither little nor splendid. It went on for over three bloody years. Far more Americans fell in subduing the Filipinos than had been lost against Spain. Altogether, 120,000 American troops were committed at one time or another. Generally referring to their opponents as "niggers," they often gave no quarter to wounded or surrendered Filipino soldiers.

In 1901 Aguinaldo was taken captive by a daring American officer who got into the Filipino camp disguised as a war prisoner. The general was led to Manila where he took an oath of allegiance to the United States and thus secured release. Aguinaldo then called upon his countrymen to lay down their arms. The response to his appeal was by no means universal, but in any event the war was petering out. Broken up into isolated and harassed pockets, Filipino resistance was gradually snuffed out and ended in 1902. For his part, Aguinaldo lived a long and prosperous life, dying in his mid-nineties in 1964.

After the defeat of the Christian Filipinos, there was still the problem of the Moros. Partially and temporarily pacified by the Spanish in the final years of their rule, the Muslims of the south wrongly interpreted Spain's defeat as a signal to rise. It took the Americans until 1915 to reimpose alien authority throughout Mindanao and neighboring islands. In the course of the struggle, an officer long in grade, John J. Pershing, won the fame that in due time catapulted him into command over American expeditionary forces in the First World War. The technology of the United States, as well as the skill of her soldiers, was pressed into service; the forty-five caliber automatic pistol was invented to meet the need for a weapon that could stop a charging Moro when lighter guns might fail.

By the time the West was engaged in its 1914-18 attempt at self-destruction, Southeast Asia was as thoroughly colonized as it was to become. Four centuries after Albuquerque, all but the Thais were under foreign flags. Less than three decades would pass before those flags would be pulled down, first by the Japanese, subsequently and permanently by the Southeast Asians themselves. But that is a matter for later consideration. At the moment, it is necessary to examine the changes wrought by colonialism.

READINGS

Agoncillo, Teodoro A., *The Revolt of the Masses: The Story of Bonifacio and the Katipunan*, Manila: University of the Philippines, 1956.

Blount, J. H., *The American Occupation of the Philippines, 1898-1912*, New York: Oriole, 1973.

Cady, John F., *A History of Modern Burma*, Ithaca: Cornell University Press, 1958.

———, *The Roots of French Imperialism in Eastern Asia*, Ithaca: Cornell University Press, 1954.

Comber, Leon, *Chinese Secret Societies in Malaya: A Survey of the Triad Society from 1800 to 1900*, New York: J. J. Augustin, 1959.

Cowan, C. D., *Nineteenth Century Malaya: The Origins of British Political Control*, London: Oxford University Press, 1961.

Crosthwaite, Sir Charles, H. T., *The Pacification of Burma*, London: Cass, 1968 (reprint of 1912 ed.).

Gullick, J. M., *Indigenous Political Systems of Western Malaya*, London: Athlone, 1958.

Hahn, Emily, *James Brooke of Sarawak*, London: Arthur Barker, 1953.

Majul, Cesar Adib, *The Political and Constitutional Ideas of the Philippine Revolution*, rev. ed., New York: Oriole, 1974.

McAleavy, John, *Black Flags in Vietnam: The Story of a Chinese Intervention*, New York: Macmillan, 1968.

Moffat, Abbot L., *Mongkut, the King of Siam*, Ithaca: Cornell University Press, 1968.

Palma, Rafael, *The Pride of the Malay Race: A Biography of Jose Rizal*, New York: Prentice-Hall, 1950.

Parkinson, C. Northcote, *British Intervention in Malaya, 1867-1877*, Kuala Lumpur: University of Malaya Press, 1964.

Pringle, Robert, *Rajahs and Rebels: The Ibans of Sarawak under Brooke Rule, 1841 to 1941*, Ithaca: Cornell University Press, 1970.

Runciman, Sir Steven, *The White Rajahs*, Cambridge: Cambridge University Press, 1960.

Sexton, William T., *Soldiers in the Sun: An Adventure in Imperialism*, Freeport, N.Y.: Books for Libraries, 1971.

Stanley, P. W. A., *Nation in the Making: The Philippines and the United States, 1899-1921*, Cambridge, Harvard University Press, 1973.

Stewart, Anthony T. Q., *The Pagoda War: Lord Dufferin and the Fall of the Kingdom of Ava, 1885-6*, London: Faber and Faber, 1972.

Storey, Moorfield, and Marcial P. Lichauco, *The Conquest of the Philippines by the United States, 1898-1925*, Freeport, N.Y.: Books for Libraries, 1971.

Tarling, Nicholas, *Britain, the Brookes and Brunei*, Kuala Lumpur: Oxford University Press, 1971.

——, *British Policy in the Malay Peninsula and Archipelago, 1824-1871*, London: Oxford University Press, 1969.

——, *Piracy and Politics in the Malay World: A Study of British Imperialism in Nineteenth Century South-East Asia*, London: University of London, 1963.

Truong-buu-Lam, *Patterns of Vietnamese Responses to Foreign Intervention, 1858-1900*, New Haven: Yale University Press, 1967.

Turnbull, Colin M., *The Straits Settlements, 1826-67: Indian Presidency to Crown Colony*, London: Athlone, 1972.

Winstedt, Sir Richard O., *Malaya and its History*, 7th ed., London: Hutchinson, 1966.

Wolff, Leon, *Little Brown Brother: How the United States Purchased and Pacified the Philippines at the Century's Turn*, New York: Doubleday, 1961.

Wright, Leigh R., *The Origins of British Borneo*, Hong Kong: Hong Kong University Press, 1970.

Wyatt, David K., *The Politics of Reform in Thailand: Education in the Reign of King Chulalongkorn*, New Haven: Yale University Press, 1969.

8
Colonialism in Its Prime

Armed with the certainty that immutable laws of man and nature had placed Westerners in authority over most of the world, the colonialists were committed to the task of benefiting from their position. The gains to be realized were by no means exclusively in the economic realm, though that is the most easily studied aspect of colonialism. There is no ambiguity over the tonnages of rubber and tin taken from Malaya, the volume of rice exports from Burma or Indochina, the flow of riches from Indonesia, or the growth of Philippine foreign trade. Whether or not economic changes under colonialism invariably enriched the rulers by depressing or stagnating the living standards of the ruled is a far cloudier issue, one that will be long debated.

Complex though the economic story becomes when serious analysis is attempted, the non-material dimensions of colonialism are perhaps even more awkward to measure. The conviction that mastery over colonies strengthened the metropole has been largely discredited by history. Not only are there several countries that have reached high levels of economic and political well-being without ever having engaged in territorial imperialism; the loss of overseas holdings has not necessarily brought ruin to former imperial states. Sweden and Switzerland are illustrations in the first category; Japan is a phenomenal example in the second. The costs of administering, policing and, most of all, defending empires may well have exceeded the profits of the venture. If the First World War is seen as primarily a struggle over imperial spoils, it is clear that colonialism did not pay. Profits from Vietnam could never cover the costs of Verdun; Ypres and Passchendaele were more expensive than India was profitable.

The particular psychological rewards enjoyed by the citizens of colonial powers must be presumed to be beyond definitive examination. Yet, the intensity of national pride apparent in the metropoles in the heyday of empire suggests that men were profoundly stirred by the fact that their segment of humanity had achieved mastery over distant lands and peoples. That many of the conquests had been won in competition with other imperial states, and that the global mission was seen as protecting the colonized from their base and primitive selves, enormously reinforced popular conceit.

National commitment and loyalty were only parts of the emotional baggage carried by those who went out to make colonialism work. For them, there was the reward of instant advance up the social ladder. The British product of a disadvantaged lineage and an unfashionable school was rocketed into the elite once he took up the burden history seemed to have imposed on whites. Servants, clubs, perquisites beyond the dreams of schoolmates who had stayed at home trapped in middle-class obscurity, were the due of the colonialist. There was, of course, class discrimination within the British community of a colony, but the lowest ranking member of the ruling group could always count on institutionalized supremacy over all natives. Promotions, home leaves, hill stations, and pensions were tangible rewards for the expatriate. No less real perhaps was the satisfaction of being a *sahib* or a *tuan*, while his wife, emancipated and elevated, was a *mem*.

The French and the Dutch in their colonies were less rigid than the British in the matter of racial exclusiveness, especially toward Eurasians, but of course the maintenance of unique privileges for whites was jealously preserved and understandably relished by the beneficiaries of the system. It is doubtless significant that the metropolitan French and Dutch used the terms *petit blanc* and *tropenadel* (tropical nobleman) in reference to the haughtiness of a man who rose far above his station through a career in the colonies. Naturally, Americans created their own colonial aristocracy when their country came to govern part of Southeast Asia.

Variety in administrative policy and practice distinguished the colonial powers from one another, but their basic similarities were more meaningful than their differences. All righteously believed in the purity and inevitability of their missions. The conviction that colonial rule had been thrust upon them by history and genetics was uniform. The assurance that peoples under colonialism would be bettered by the system was general. The determination to defend their holdings against foreign rivals or domestic troublemakers was powerful and unrelenting.

THE DUTCH EAST INDIES

The basically feudal nature of the Culture System made it vulnerable to attack by many of the same late nineteenth-century forces that powered the expansionist drive of the time. Forced deliveries of exportable agricultural goods by peasants whose only reimbursement was the right to subsist began to appear exploitative. Growing numbers of Dutch humanitarians, in unison with abolitionists and reformers throughout most of Christendom, condemned peonage in the colonies and called for freeing the serfs.

Complementary to the drive of the moralists was the rising clamor of contemporary economic liberals. Made possible in no small measure by the attainment of state solvency through the Culture System, capital accumulation in the Netherlands had generated investable funds in need of an outlet. Official monopolization of the riches and opportunities offered by Indonesia was contrary to the most sacred principles of the laissez-faire faith. In consequence, Hollanders who wanted to do good joined with those who wanted to do well. Public opinion and political resources were mobilized in an accelerating campaign that led bit by bit to parliamentary victory and the formal inauguration in 1870 of a fresh program for the Indies, sometimes called the Forward Movement.

Free enterprise made rapid advances, though the withering away of the Culture System was a most leisurely process. Full liquidation of colonial feudalism took fifty-five years, from 1862 when the first small blow was struck to 1917 when the last forced delivery of coffee was squeezed out of the Indonesian peasantry. Caution was clearly the watchword of the administrators who directed reform. Progress was ideologically enshrined, but pragmatically it was restricted to areas where change cost little or, better still, nothing.

As investors channeled more and more money into the Indies, the private sector of the economy came to equal and soon to eclipse state enterprise. Great acreages were taken over under long-term leases for the commercial production of export crops. Peasants, rescued from the Culture System, could choose between subsistence farming and plantation labor. Whether the transformation of village folk into rural proletarians was beneficial in human terms is perhaps conjectural, but there is no doubt that exports were enormously expanded. Fortunes were made by Dutchmen in producing, shipping, and marketing Indies goods.

The objections of the laissez-faire liberals to governmental participation in commerce were matched in volume by their demands for official generosity in the construction of the infrastructure upon which free enterprise would prosper. Roads, irrigation systems, railways, and harbors were required; law and order had to be preserved; more land had to be conquered. In consequence, government expenditures and personnel multiplied. An identity of interests happily linked the men in political authority with those who headed the banks and the corporations.

The impact of the new colonialism on the Dutch was unprecedented. The number of Hollanders who reached the Indies in the final decades of the nineteenth century was considerably greater than that of all those who had made the trip from the days of Coen down to that time. Not only were careers in the colony more numerous and inviting, the restful voyage by steamship via the recently cut Suez Canal was far more appealing than sailing around the Cape of Good Hope had ever been. New thousands of Dutchmen, many accompanied by their wives and children, headed for the tropics. Europeans and their ways were no longer known only to a handful of Indonesians in Batavia and a few lesser towns. As many as a fourth of the Dutch at home would eventually be somehow tied to the colony in the earning of their livelihoods. Perhaps only the British connection with India approached equaling that between Holland and Indonesia in emotional terms.

The number of Dutchmen who entered the Indies in the years of economic expansion after 1870 was tiny in comparison to that of a more enduring body of transients and settlers, the Chinese. Bringing raw lands into commercial cultivation, for example, for the raising of tobacco in Sumatra, opening up tin mines on Bangka and Billiton, and countless other endeavors created a demand for labor that was quite insatiable while world market prices remained high. Displaying the conservatism that is customarily expected of peasants, most rural Javanese were not lured away from the impoverished security of familiar villages. In southeastern China, however, millions of men were prepared to follow routes that had been laid out for many years by Chinese merchants and seafarers traveling to Southeast Asia. In the second half of the nineteenth century, the southward seepage of Chinese became a torrent. Both in magnitude and in its nature the emigration was of a new sort. There were not merely vastly increased numbers of Chinese; the bulk of the migrants were unskilled illiterates with only sweat to sell.

A substantial proportion of Chinese laborers eventually returned to their homeland once doing so became financially feasible, for repatriation was the ultimate goal of most. However, thousands stayed on in tropical exile to take advantage of the openings that were invitingly available in a growing economy. Separated from their own villages, the immigrants were perforce inclined toward economic boldness. A few worked their way to wealth; most simply worked. But, compared to Indonesian peasants, the Chinese were conspicuously successful. A myth of exploitation and of usurpation of opportunity by the Chinese at indigenous expense took root and grew to become a poisonous weed in our own age.

Of course, some Indonesians were also drawn to the centers of commercial development, where most went to work in unskilled jobs and a minority entered clerical or similar careers. Certain parts of the archipelago contributed disproportionately to the development. Christian Amboinese identified closely with the colonial regime, particularly its army; Minangkabau men wandered far from their Sumatran homes, possibly driven abroad by the anomaly of life as Muslims in a matrilineal society. In consequence of both such internal population movements and immigration, the age of economic expansion was also one of urbanization. Tens of thousands of people, who a short time earlier would have been cut off from one another by oceans or by village isolation, were brought together. The implications of the change would ultimately prove to be politically decisive, for the nationalist movements that toppled colonialism in our own century were born in the cities and towns.

1901 brought the proclamation of a new era for the Indies. The colonial administration, seemingly oblivious to the embarrassment of unflattering reflections on the nature of Dutch activities in the preceding three centuries, announced the start of a reform effort proudly named the Ethical Policy. The emphasis was on improving the lot of the native peoples, but the pace of advance was to be controlled and leisurely. Borrowing a Malay folk expression, it can be said that Dutch colonial reformers set about their task with the cautious timidity of "a mouse-deer entering a village." In the four decades that elapsed before the Japanese engulfed the Indies, little substantive progress was made.

The Ethical Policy rested on two thoroughly reasonable assumptions. First, laissez-faire liberalism had not been a blessing to the village masses and never would be; second, guidance and support by the government were needed for the success of a program of reform. That the effort must be judged a failure is not to be blamed on insincerity among those who launched it. Faulty perception, not cynicism, defeated the new policy from the start.

Administrative decentralization and political devolution were thought to hold great promise. Though direction from above would initially be unavoidable, it should be withdrawn at the earliest possible time. It was reasoned that bringing Indonesians into deliberative and administrative roles could contribute to the acceptability and viability of the Ethical Policy. Difficulties lay ahead, however. The paternalistic nature of the progressive attempt obliged the Dutch to keep an unyielding grasp on the reins of authority. The conviction that a benevolent bureaucracy was the only proper instrument to work change was deeply rooted, if unvoiced. Furthermore, the officers of the colonial regime were human in their reluctance to see so much power slip to Indonesian hands that they themselves would become superfluous.

Those circumstances prevented the establishment of meaningful participation in government by Indonesians. Some local talent was attached to the bureaucracy, essentially in apprenticeship capacities. At the pace set by the Dutch, the rise to journeyman status would have taken the Indonesians a generation or two longer than Japanese ambitions were to permit; the rank of master craftsman in government might never have been granted. The outstanding example of the emptiness of talk about shifting power to Indonesians was to be seen in the creation of 1918 of the *Volksraad*, a pseudo-parliamentary body always under the thumb of the Dutch governor general and never permitted to seat a clear voting majority of Indonesians. A wit, who merits identification but whose name appears to be lost, cuttingly dismissed the *Volksraad* as the only successful multi-racial club in prewar Southeast Asia.

Carefully selected welfare measures to rescue the peasantry from poverty and ignorance formed the core of the new program. Only mixed results were achieved. Again, it must be acknowledged that sins of omission, not of commission, were chiefly responsible. Public health programs were singularly successful. Indeed, to a coldly detached Malthusian, medical innovations would seem to have accomplished far too much and therefore to have been counterproductive. Population increased at a runaway rate—particularly on Java where the number of souls rose from 28 million in 1900 to some 45 million in 1940. It is to the lasting credit of those who engineered modernization in irrigation and transportation that a doubling of population in less than two generations did not seem to be accompanied by a decline in village living standards. Progress, however, is not made by running faster and faster to keep in one spot. Evidence of the classical costs of a demographic explosion sparked by elementary improvements in health and technology is seen in the fact that, despite a campaign for village education under the Ethical Policy, there were substantially more illiterates in the Indies when the labors of the reformers were ended than when they began.

Dutch colonial reformers held a little learning to be useful rather than dangerous. Local participation in the processes of government and modernization was seen to be partially dependent upon the ability of the populace to read and do simple sums and on the training of indigenous elites. Rudimentary literacy for the masses and, in due time, highly sophisticated training for an elitist minority were therefore among the objectives of the Ethical Policy. In practice, so slow was the introduction of higher education that the founding of the first university in the Indies came just on the eve of Japanese conquest and, even then, only a mere handful of Indonesians qualified for matriculation. Nevertheless, those few Indonesians who somehow had managed to complete secondary or technical educations at home or university programs in the Netherlands in the prewar years ultimately formed the nucleus of revolution against colonialism. A little education proved to be unsafe after all.

FRENCH INDOCHINA

In their islands, the Dutch looked vaguely toward distant partnership with an indigenous elite; the French in their territories sometimes spoke in terms of assimilation rather than symbiosis, and at other times of "association," a euphemism for domination. Presumably, there would be no point in seeking to rank colonial powers in terms of beneficence toward subject peoples, for too many variables would demand assessment. However, it is not particularly difficult to conclude that the record of the French in Indochina is not one to inspire admiration.

Isolated examples of conscientious administrators could be found among the French, but the general quality of their personnel was low. Political influence, not professional quality, was often the decisive factor in winning bureaucratic appointment. The pattern extended over the entire apparatus to include the office of the governor general. To make matters worse, the occupant of that high post normally enjoyed but brief tenure due to the mercurial processes of politics in Paris that caused cabinet after cabinet to fall. The colonial portfolio was usually handed to a fresh minister at the end of each *crise*, and often a new governor general would then have to be designated.

To compound the costs of instability and ineptitude in the French hierarchy, the myth of indirect protective rule over Tonkin and Annam and over the royal backwaters of Cambodia and Laos required the maintenance of a façade of indigenous administration in those territories. There, the public bore the double burden of supporting two bureaucracies, one generally ruthless and insensitive, the other ceremonial and impotent.

Villagers were unlikely to be aware of organizational weaknesses in the officialdom, but they were daily reminded of the rapaciousness of the tax gatherers. French ingenuity in the art of milking the populace was little short of monumental. The principle that the costs of material progress in Indochina had to be borne locally dictated the imposition of mounting financial demands on an agrarian land. The construction of a rail system, harbors, and paved roads, all built primarily to serve the needs of the overlords, was financed by peasant toil. No one escaped the head tax; customs levies and a multiplicity of excise taxes were almost as widely felt. The regime profitably monopolized the retail distribution of opium, though that concerned few Indochinese. For the most part, addicts of the pipe were found only among the Chinese minority and, to a surprising extent, the French.

Control over the distribution of alcoholic drinks was doubly desirable from an official viewpoint. It would not merely serve as a further source of revenue; if the traditional taste for rice wine could be replaced by preference for the yield of the grape, the clamorous lobby of vintners in France would be soothed. Bizarre as it may seem, the colonial authorities even went to the extent of setting consumption quotas for Indochinese localities. Failure to buy and drink enough brought penalties.

Of all the sources of revenue, the salt monopoly was the most foolproof. No one, no matter how destitute, can ignore the biological fact that the saltiness of the human bloodstream must be kept the same as that of the seas which spawned our primordial ancestors. State control over the production and distribution of the indispensable mineral puts a tax on every meal, however miserable; and, in Indochina, the French set the highest charges the public could bear, doubling and redoubling the price of the commodity within a few years. In fairness, it must be recorded that the salt monopoly was not a colonial innovation. The Vietnamese emperors had long ago borrowed the institution from their Chinese models. Indeed, the usefulness of salt in state finance has been widely recognized in traditional societies. Paradoxically, the *gabelle*, as the Bourbon salt monopoly was called, had served as a prime target of the frenzy of the French revolutionaries of 1789.

The transformation of the Mekong delta into a granary capable of exporting huge tonnages of rice was not designed by the French to benefit the peasantry. Improvements in transportation and water conservancy greatly stimulated agricultural productivity, but profits flowed to landlords, moneylenders, millers and others, including the officialdom, who treated the rice harvests as resources to be tapped.

A conspicuous feature of the process was the rise of absentee land-lordism. Mounting tax burdens compelled thousands of peasants to borrow at usurious rates more than could be repaid. The end result was the foreclosure of countless mortgages and a steady flow of conscripts to tenantry.

One writer has succinctly described the results of French colonialism in Indochina as the "progressive pauperization of the countryside."[1] Clear statistical support for that view is contained in the fact that in the first four decades of the twentieth century, as Indochinese rice exports earned fortunes, Vietnamese per capita consumption of the grain fell by over a third. In other words, hunger in the villages was painful to many but rewarding to the few.

Except for officials, Frenchmen played a peripheral role in the rice trade; but the story was quite different in the production of coffee, tea, and—most importantly—rubber. European-managed estates, where gangs of wage laborers tended the bushes and trees, spread over the countryside. The French never approached the success of the British in Malaya in large-scale agriculture, but Indochina was introduced to the production of crops for the world market and to the proletarianization of peasants. As in estate agriculture, French capital monopolized the extraction of mineral wealth, notably in coal mining.

These economic developments of course served some Asians. A local middle class, composed largely of Vietnamese landlords and the Chinese commercial stratum, did quite well. Those segments of colonial society appreciated the imposition of general law and order that the French brought along with their most awesome instrument of penal authority, the guillotine. No doubt, the Vietnamese bourgeoisie also welcomed the decree, ineffectual though it proved to be, of an early twentieth-century governor general who sought to prohibit his countrymen from striking Vietnamese with impunity and abandon.

The tiny Vietnamese elite nursed one major grievance against their rulers. The grudging reluctance of the French in extending educational opportunities to their Indochinese subjects was resented with special bitterness in a land of Sinic civilization where learning had traditionally been esteemed. A handful of the children of the indigenous privileged class was permitted schooling as a means of buying the

---

[1] Donald Lancaster, *The Emancipation of French Indochina*, London: Oxford University Press, 1961, p. 65.

loyalty of their parents, though there were never enough places to satisfy more than a splinter of the ambitious. The regime in general shared the conviction of the French *colons* that by educating a native you lose a coolie. Moreover, the official fear that learning stimulated political restlessness was perennial and pervasive. Such a view was in fact realistic, for the few Vietnamese who acquired educations were rarely able to obtain employment commensurate with their training and might turn to rebellion in frustration. Ho Chi Minh, the graduate of a good *lycée*, began his working life as a galley hand aboard a French steamship.

BURMA

The consequences of colonialism in Burma, while manifesting distinctive features, were actually quite similar to many of the results of alien rule in Indochina. The phenomenon could most easily be observed in the economic sphere. In both colonies, increases in production profited a minority at the expense of the peasantry. The two countries were similarly obliged to support from internal resources development in transportation and other areas of economic modernization that were primarily designed to serve outsiders.

The delta of the Irrawaddy, like that of the Mekong, was transformed into a great granary. Rice exports multiplied to meet food deficit needs elsewhere, especially in nearby Bengal. However, relatively few Burmese gained from the expansion. Extensive new lands were brought under cultivation by means of irrigation and flood control projects, but the peasants who tilled them faced cruel hazards in their efforts to win and retain title to the fields. Working small paddies with agricultural tools that would have seemed quite familiar during the ancient Pagan dynasty, the men of the delta waged an endless, Sisyphean struggle against the most universal of rural afflictions, indebtedness. Borrowing against the next harvest in time of need is endemic in peasant societies; foreclosure is often the result.

Absentee landlordism swallowed vast acreages in Lower Burma, particularly after plunging prices for rice bankrupted tens of thousands of peasants during the world depression. Land not only passed to remote men who had it worked by tenants or hired hands; most was transferred to foreign ownership. British Burma, until shortly before the Second World War, was administered as a province of India—as the colony of a colony. One consequence of that odd arrangement was an influx of untold numbers of immigrants who fled the uncertainties of their native India to seek security elsewhere. One group of Indians, the Chettyars, the traditional moneylenders of their own stratified society, found Burma a land of unimagined opportunity, for farming Irrawaddy delta lands was ultimately dependent upon peasant access to credit sources. The Chettyars made funds available, collected interest at fat rates, and in due time took over the fields of peasant defaulters. Land alienation multiplied the costs of absentee ownership and eventually added the fuel of ethnic animosity to the flames of economic discontent. The combination was predictably explosive.

Indian immigrants aroused hostility in other ways as well. Alien shopkeepers, who routinely encouraged buying on credit and thereby became moneylenders themselves; trained personnel from India, who monopolized so many jobs in the modern sectors of the economy and in the bureaucracy; and unskilled immigrants, who competed with the Burmese proletariat for pitiful wages, all came to be seen as instruments of colonial exploitation. From the British perspective, Indians were regarded as docile and dependent, as indeed they generally were. Accordingly, the contest for employment was heavily weighted against the Burmese. A price would ultimately be exacted when the colonial grasp was broken.

Rice exports were the mainstay of the economy. Other forms of development were largely restricted to the tapping of petroleum reserves and the exploitation of forest resources. Burma never became a major supplier of oil in comparison to some Arab areas, and almost all production was marketed locally or in India by a British corporation. Teakwood and other riches from the jungle found customers throughout the world, and taxes on lumbering made up a substantial proportion of state revenues. Thus, the natural wealth of the country was used for the benefit of foreign shareholders and colonial masters, just as profits from agricultural production primarily served outsiders.

The incorporation of Burma within India created unfortunate results in addition to those caused by unrestricted immigration from the subcontinent. In the realm of local administration, the pattern that had evolved in India for the control from above of village functionaries was substituted for a customary Burmese arrangement that had endowed rural leaders with a measure of quasi-feudal autonomy. The dignity and power of the traditional village notables were not enjoyed by those who were appointed to take their places under commissions granted by a remote and alien central government. The sundering of the old bonds of respect and mutual responsibility inevitably generated lawlessness and administrative lethargy.

Far more serious than the mistake made in local government was the British decision to disestablish the Buddhist church. Again, theories based on Indian patterns and advocated by veterans of the Indian administration were to blame. In view of the religious passions of a population divided between Hinduism and Islam, with smaller Sikh, Jain, Parsee, Christian, and other communities to add spice, India was a country where only a madman would forge official links with a single faith. Hence, the divorce of church and state was a cardinal doctrine of the British *raj* in India.

In the land of the Burmans, however, circumstances were diametrically different. There, Buddhism was the religion of virtually all and its hierarchy had long been involved in the governance of the country. To sever the church-state connection in Burma, as the British felt compelled to do, could only diminish the authority of the regime. Moreover, denying the clergy their traditional political role created a body of disaffected men around whom popular rebelliousness might coalesce. That is in part what happened once the campaign for independence gained momentum.

The connection with India was not an unqualified liability. As the *raj* began to undergo evolutionary changes that brought about a measure of Indian participation in government, Burma profited. In 1909, when parliamentary experimentation began in India, the Burma Legislative Council had seated a majority of members who were not part of the official establishment. Eleven years later, in delayed response to developments that had come in India in 1919, the membership of the legislative body at Rangoon came to have roughly three-fourths of its members chosen by a widely enfranchised electorate. More significant, the principle of dyarchy was applied to the country. The resultant sharing of ministerial authority by Britons and Burmese eventually led to the transfer to local hands of responsibility for most domestic legislation, though the British kept their hold on the portfolios covering defense, justice, foreign relations, currency, and the affairs of the non-Burman minorities. When separation from India, duly approved at Westminster, finally came in 1937, Burma was well along the road toward dominion status. Her people had undergone more schooling in participatory democracy than any other in Southeast Asia, except the Filipinos. More than a generation later, there is room to doubt whether it made any substantive difference.

In discussing colonialism in Burma, a final word must be added on the subject of the special place of indigenous non-Burmans in the scheme of things. The several minority peoples, Karen, Kachin, Shan, and others, had long folk memories of mistreatment at the hands of Burmans. Much of that sad legacy had been produced by rivalry arising from the clash of cultures, particularly where there was competition for land between settled peasants and semi-migratory swidden farmers. Imperial conquest by no means brought the various peoples of Burma together in resistance to a common enemy. On the contrary, the British, acting in the best tradition of *divide et impera*, exploited ancient fears and resentments. Furthermore, Christian missionaries discovered that their labors were most fruitful in non-Burman vineyards. Hence, a new wedge, Christianity, was driven between many members of the minority communities and the Burman majority.

Reinforcing the colonial logic of control through fragmentation was the patronizing posture of administrators who saw the protection and favoring of minorities as especially noble. The view was not uniquely British; in fact, it may have been characteristic of most colonialists. Nevertheless, Britons seem to have treasured the paternalistic image with particular pride. The result was often condescending affection for the least advanced inhabitants of a colony. The attitude was clearly and typically revealed by a British officer whose report on the Shan states, after expressing disapproval of some troublesome peoples, went on to say that "most of the other tribes are decent enough, some of them perfectly charming."[2]

[2] G. E. Harvey, *British Rule in Burma, 1824-1942*, London: Faber and Faber, 1946, p. 85.

THE PHILIPPINES

The experience of the Philippines under American rule was unique in two ways. First, from the beginning of their presence, the Americans displayed a certain ambivalence toward their colonial role. The gradual transfer of power to Filipinos was begun even before the last shots were heard in the suppression of the uprising against American successors to the Spanish. Internal self-government and eventual independence were the declared goals of the Americans, though such advances were to be patterned quite strictly after United States models. The hope was that, once sovereign, the archipelago would remain tied to the departed rulers by common political habits and shared constitutional principles. The country was expected to become free in the manner of a dutiful son who in due time matures and goes into the world, cast in his father's philosophical and moral image.

. In the second place, the economic impact of the American period did bring significant rewards to a colonial elite. Of course, profits also flowed to Americans and immigrant Chinese, but the Filipino landowning class that had come into being under the Spanish continued gaining in strength and wealth under the new masters. No other colony in Southeast Asia produced a comparable local concentration of property and power. It is to be noted, however, that the peasantry of the Philippines fared about as poorly as most of their fellows in other colonies. Furthermore, when independence came after the Second World War, the United States attempted to maintain economic ascendancy in the Philippines, while simultaneously seeking to retain political influence through American institutions transplanted to a distant island country.

During a protracted debate, in many ways like that over Vietnam policy three generations later, Americans agonized over the acquisition of the Philippines. Many condemned overseas imperialism as a violation of the principles that had inspired thirteen American colonies to break with their king a century and a quarter earlier. It was more than a little awkward to reconcile the self-evident truth of the equality of the creation of all men with the imposition of foreign authority over a reluctant people. Moreover, annexation of the Philippines came precisely when Americans were obsessed by morbid fears of being submerged under a tide of Oriental immigrants. The menace to the nation's viability, especially to its living standards, seemed so ominous that Chinese immigration had been halted. Suddenly, it appeared that victory in war would enable millions of Filipinos to cross the Pacific and undercut the American working classes. In terms of the American political faith, much of the guilt and embarrassment generated by seeming apostasy was eased by pledging freedom to the Philippines after a transitional period of benign tutelage. So far as the threat of a massive trans-Pacific migration went, the danger was overcome by the denial of American citizenship to Filipinos. The "little brown brothers" became mere wards of the United States, obliged to owe allegiance to a land they could not reach.

As the Philippine fight for independence began to peter out, the Americans set about substituting civil government for military rule. The appointment of William Howard Taft as governor general in 1901 was followed by the establishment of a legislative advisory body, the Philippine Commission, that contained Filipino members from the beginning. In 1907 a national assembly, representative of the literate and the propertied, was elected and seated as the lower house of a bicameral body. Though an American majority in the upper chamber, the Philippine Commission, continued to hold veto power over legislation passed by the lower house, the march toward republican sovereignty had begun.

The inauguration of Woodrow Wilson in 1913 was the signal to accelerate the process of legislative devolution, for the Democratic party had in general assumed an anti-imperialist stance in competition with the Republicans who had ruled the Philippines up to that year. Early independence for the islands was not approved by the United States Congress, as Wilson had urged, but in 1916 a law was passed liquidating the Philippine Commission and establishing in its stead a senate composed almost entirely of legislators elected by the literate male population of the colony. (Two of the total of twenty-four senators were appointed by the governor general to speak for the non-Christian minorities.) The governor general and the President in Washington still retained the right to veto bills passed by the two Philippine houses, but that authority was not exercised during the years to 1921, while a Democrat sat in the White House. Under the Republicans who followed in the Presidency, however, the American executive veto power was employed on occasion.

With the election of another Democratic President in 1932, the advance toward Philippine independence picked up speed, propelled in considerable measure by American pressure groups. The lobbyists representing domestic beet sugar producers were notably active champions of a cause that promised to end or reduce marketplace competition with Philippine sugar. The archipelago ceased to be a full colony late in 1934, when the office of the American governor general was abolished. The islands then became an autonomous commonwealth under a Philippine President and Congress. The chief representative of the United States in Manila was given the title of high commissioner, a designation chosen to underscore the fact that the office was primarily diplomatic. In the years of the commonwealth, until the final and full transfer of sovereignty, the American government held responsibility for the international relations and defense of the Philippines and retained the right to intervene should the constitutional integrity of the country be threatened. As it worked out, Washington never felt obliged to resort to its ultimate veto power in the few years before the commonwealth was overrun by the Japanese.

Equal in significance to the legislative and executive withdrawal of the Americans were the steps taken to fill judicial and bureaucratic posts with Filipinos. The Supreme Court was headed by a local jurist from its establishment in 1899. Lower court benches similarly came to be occupied by Filipinos. Very quickly Americans became a shrinking minority in the judicial ranks; and, after a quarter of a century of American rule, they were a vanishing breed. In a parallel process, the civil service was rapidly made the preserve of indigenous officers. That was particularly true during the years of Wilson's Presidency when "Filipinization" was the watchword. The percentage of Americans in civil service posts had fallen to about six by the early 1920's and was down to one when the commonwealth was created. As will later be demonstrated, such liberalization was not an unmixed blessing.

Educational development was the source of great American pride. The belief that mass literacy would serve to promote wise popular participation in politics led the Americans to invest openhandedly in public schooling. As the echoes of the insurrection subsided, teachers from the United States began to take up classroom duties throughout the islands. Those pioneers were soon joined by the numerous products of local normal schools. The eve of the Second World War found the Philippines far above other colonies in the region in terms of literacy. About half the population could read and write; and, English fluency was enjoyed by a small majority of the literate. In fact, the number of people at home in English came to be greater than the number of speakers of any one of the many local tongues. For the first time in their history, the people of the Philippines were served by a lingua franca that was not the monopoly of a privileged few.

Constitutional democracy, an independent judiciary and a reasonably well-educated public ought to have been the bases of economic and social progress; in reality, there was pitifully little improvement in the lives of most Filipinos. The reasons are not difficult to find. The transfer of executive, legislative, and judicial authority to Filipino hands simply strengthened the old elite and fattened their purses. Political parties contested elections but the voice of the voters was never decisive in comparison to that of the small leadership clique of men from the upper classes who ran the parties. The proportion of landlords and professional men, mostly lawyers, in the Congress ran to about nine-tenths. The same power elite produced the judges and the senior bureaucrats who controlled the judicial and administrative arms of the government. Native oligarchy in the Philippines was not demonstrably less exploitative than direct alien rule in neighboring colonies.

The economic record of the United States in the country distressingly counterbalances satisfaction over gains in education. The security of profits to be earned in the American market through the sale of traditional export products discouraged Philippine investment in innovative ventures. The proportion of exports made up of sugar, copra, and hemp was not appreciably altered in the American era despite official programs to sponsor industrialization and diversification. Worse still was the failure of the United States to deal with the problem of tenancy. Peasant proprietorship in newly opened frontier areas was encouraged, but official corruption and mismanagement joined with peasant undercapitalization to defeat the scheme. Similarly, the disposition of extensive acreages that had been purchased by the government in 1904 from the Roman Catholic religious orders did not put much land under the ownership of those who tilled the fields. The former haciendas were generally divided among the local gentry. In the few decades of American rule, the percentage of peasants who labored for their landlords more than doubled. Such circumstances were certain to thwart colonial experimentation in Jeffersonian democracy.

THE MALAYSIAN TERRITORIES

Judged on the basis of cost accounting, the British record in maritime Southeast Asia was enviable. No other colonial enterprise gave greater returns on investments. The extraction of tin from peninsular deposits was brought to high levels of efficiency and productivity with the introduction of giant dredges that wallowed like mechanical dinosaurs in the mining pools that were their feeding grounds. Smelting operations were likewise modernized to speed the export of ingots to industrialized countries.

Tin, however, was not the sole source of wealth. Late in the nineteenth century, inspired by the promising experiments of a British botanist who had brought strange saplings from Brazil to learn if they might grow in equatorial Asia, entrepreneurs began clearing jungle tracts for the planting of rubber trees. Climate and soil were perfectly suited to the endeavor; the timing of the breakthrough was equally fortunate. Just as rubber was established as a reliable crop, the automobile was perfected and the race was on. Much of the western side of the Malay Peninsula came to be covered by rubber estates.

The demographic consequences of Malayan economic expansion were unprecedented in human history. Within a few years, the indigenous peoples became a minority. The country had been a thinly populated land of littoral and riverine settlements of Malay farmers and fishermen and interior camps of wandering slash-and-burn aborigines. The demand for labor in tin-mining and, more greedily, rubber-tapping, a notoriously labor intensive operation, could not be met locally. Hence, immigrant workers had to be recruited in swelling numbers. South Indians were brought across the Bay of Bengal by the shipload; but, for every new arrival from Madras, there were four or five from China. Tin-mining was primarily a Chinese occupation; rubber-tapping was especially attractive to Indians. Both immigrant groups were of course heavily represented in the mushrooming cities and towns of the

A Chinese temple in Penang reflects the affluence and tastes of its clientele. (Lea E. Williams)

peninsula and in the Straits Settlements. Malay villagers remained confined to pockets on the western side of the peninsula and to the economically underdeveloped sultanates of the east coast. Moreover, the Malays experienced the disillusionment of staying poor as their native land grew ever richer. The emotional impact of that painful experience is still the prime driving force of politics in Malaysia today.

Parenthetical clarification of one aspect of the situation of the Malays is needed here. A substantial proportion of present-day Malays are in fact of rather recent immigrant origin themselves. As more Malayan lands were cleared for agriculture, thousands of Indonesians left home to settle in British territories. Linguistic affinity and adherence to Islam enabled the Indonesian newcomers to achieve full-fledged status as Malays virtually as they disembarked from the ships that brought them. Though custom and law provided instant naturalization for Indonesians, permanent alien labels were reserved for Chinese and Indians because only Muslims could be subjects of the various sultans under British guardianship. To increase the complication, all those born in the Straits settlements, regardless of ancestry, were British nationals. The complexities of the laws of citizenship and the disabilities of aliens were to cause considerable political anguish when Malaya eventually approached independence.

Across the South China Sea, the British dominated three portions of Borneo: Sarawak, Brunei, and North Borneo, now Sabah. The general pattern in those territories was a small-scale replica of that created in Malaya. Immigrants, almost all Chinese, moved into occupations generated by expansion in mining, the pumping of petroleum, lumbering, and the production of export crops. The indigenous peoples and the coastal Malays for the most part remained tied to their traditional ways of life.

Ruling the British parts of maritime Southeast Asia in the twentieth century was really not very demanding. The Malay sultans were normally docile protégés, content with their symbols of royal dignity, invariably including Rolls-Royce limousines, and delighted with the new affluence afforded by the efficient collection of expanding revenues. In the Straits Settlements, Sarawak, and North Borneo the quality of administration was generally high and the public was quite peaceful. The one real worry of the British in the interwar years of this century was the politicization of the Chinese, especially in Singapore, where they made up about three-fourths of the population. In response to the fear that belligerent Chinese nationalism might disturb tranquility and endanger prosperity, the government in 1925 felt compelled to ban the Kuomintang, the party of Sun Yat-sen and Chiang Kai-shek. That only an outside, hardly revolutionary threat was deemed worthy of major concern was a measure of the comfortable authority enjoyed by the British. Everybody seemed to agree that a multinational country could best be run by a corps of conscientious and able colonial officers. As no Asian elite seemed capable of keeping the peace where three incompatible ethnic groups lived in mutual suspicion, the British were held to be indispensable. The marriage of colonial convenience thus appeared destined for enduring happiness. Besides, the great island fortress of Singapore stood guard over all.

AN OVERVIEW OF THE COLONIAL IMPACT

Considered as a whole, the nations of Southeast Asia in the decades of full colonialism underwent processes of change that were remarkably alike, nearly uniform. Even Thailand, at one remove from direct foreign manipulation, went through most of the experiences that came to her colonized neighbors. As the Thai record ought properly to be considered as part of the treatment of the nationalist awakening that has transformed the region in this century, it will be presented in the next chapter. Here, it is appropriate merely to observe that the striking similarity between Thailand and the colonies during the flood tide of Western dominance helps to establish that Southeast Asian history has its own momentum and follows its own course and is not exclusively the product of alien forces. Just as it is absurd to imagine that the premodern societies of the region were microcosmic facsimiles imported from India, China, and the Islamic world, it is false to see the independent countries of today as the stepchildren of the capitalist West or, in the case of the Indochinese states, the communist East.

The demographic, economic, and political changes in the years of high colonialism were interwoven in complex patterns of causality. Population growth was general throughout the region, especially in areas where agricultural productivity or the extraction of natural bounty were expanded. The deltas of the Irrawaddy, the Chao Phraya, and the Mekong became mosaics of paddy fields and canals stretching from one horizon to the other. Elsewhere, lands that had supported only jungle were opened by miners and planters. The periodic estimates and tallies of the population of Java in particular rose by successive quantum jumps. While the demographic explosions were of course most spectacular where economic growth was greatest, the developmental wastelands—for example, the Burmese Shan states, the Bornean interior, or Laos—experienced little to disturb their stagnant population pools.

Although the Dutch became alarmed over the runaway growth of population on Java, the colonialists for the most part were intensely proud of the human multiplication. The imposition of peace where war had been a recurrent horror was rightly seen as life-saving. Innovations in public health, even the most rudimentary, stimulated population expansion. That was particularly true insofar as the lowered infant mortality rates permitted more of the young to mature and marry.

Burgeoning numbers of colonial subjects were seen not only as indices of Western efficiency and humanitarianism, they seemed to promise a reliable supply of cheap labor. The expectation, however, was not altogether solidly grounded, for, as noted earlier, peasants were inclined to cling to their villages rather than run risks in the unknown outside. That circumstances of course dictated the importation of foreign workers and created substantial alien minorities in all the countries of the region, including Thailand. The Chinese were ubiquitous; the Indians concentrated in Burma, Malaya, and the Straits Settlements; the Vietnamese moved into Cambodia and, in lesser numbers, Laos. When the colonialists ultimately retreated, the alien Asians and their unassimilated descendants for the most part remained behind to swell population further and, in part innocently, to add to the difficulties of national integration.

A final demographic point must be made. The economic growth and administrative centralization that characterized the late colonial decades inevitably stimulated rapid urbanization. Saigon rose on the site of a drowsy provincial town; Bankgok and Rangoon grew where once there had only been villages; Kuala Lumpur sprang from a rude and lawless mining camp; Singapore, Batavia, and Manila became great cities where none had existed before. Hué, Mandalay, Jogjakarta, and other pre-colonial centers tended to slip into quaint obscurity. Since the new metropolitan concentrations were especially attractive to Asian immigrants, the rising cities were separated from the village hinterland by both their relative modernity and their ethnic distinctiveness.

The emergence of new middle classes, largely products of the cities, was phenomenal in a region that had earlier known only princes and peasants. Their wealth and role further widened the urban-rural cleavage, particularly as so many of the bourgeoisie were of immigrant origin. The material benefits of modernization, coming first and most pervasively to the cities, rapidly eroded pre-conquest traditions. The people of the countryside, customarily poor, came to be backwards as well. The old feudal and royal links between the men in political power and those who tilled the land were smashed as the traditional elites decayed or disappeared.

The consequences of the decline of the old ruling classes can partially be measured in terms of the post-colonial stability of the countries of Southeast Asia. Wherever the pre-conquest elites were destroyed, downgraded, or discredited, as in Burma, Vietnam, and much of Indonesia, moves toward political viability have been painful and slow. The survival of the top strata in Malaya and Thailand, on the other hand, clearly has had a steadying effect, though the rising middle classes now seek to challenge the established order. The largely mestizo upper crust of the Philippines succeeded to power early in the American period and has remained in command ever since. The royal authority in Cambodia, until toppled by external forces, was the fountainhead of national stability. What there was of a ruling caste in Laos was unable to transform a geographical expression into a nation-state and accordingly split into contending segments.

It has been observed earlier that one common consequence of colonial rule was an intensification of rivalries between majority peoples and indigenous minorities. Administrative convenience often prompted foreign rulers to exploit ethnic fragmentation in order to win support from at least a portion of the population. Even without such purposeful division, however, new animosities were stirred and old ones strengthened by the increasing pressure of people on the land. As the minorities were typically the last to experience population growth sustained by economic advance or improved health standards, the threat from majority peoples seemed to grow in direct proportion to their rising numbers. Smouldering resentments of long standing became pressing fears. In further exacerbation of tension, the imperialists had drawn frontiers around their conquests with little regard for human geography. Political boundaries, especially those of the continental countries, were established for territorial, not ethnolinguistic, reasons. The fates of minorities divided in the process were to become international issues.

Accelerated tapping of the region's sources of wealth pushed Southeast Asia onto the world stage in new and powerful ways. With developments in shipping that permitted the handling of bulk cargoes, the entire pattern of trade changed. In earlier times, sailing vessels could profitably carry only small quantities of goods of high value, notably spices, on voyages that took months. With the advent of steam navigation and steel hulls and with the cutting of the Suez Canal, however, great tonnages of tin, rubber, rice, oil, sugar, and other riches began to be moved across the seas. The global patterns of trade that developed put Southeast Asia vulnerably in the center of international political and military contests.

The political costs of the forging of the commercial chains that bound tropical East Asia to distant markets were matched by economic liabilities. Dominant foreigners, guided by rational self-interest, channeled their investments and energies into the maximization of profits in a classical exercise of colonialism. Primary products were taken from the region in exchange for imported manufactures. All the countries touched by the process were put at the mercy of world price fluctuations, and their susceptibility was increased where there was reliance on only one or two chief export products. A drop on the London exchange in tin or rubber quotations was quickly reflected in Malayan living standards; unusually bountiful rice harvests that depressed world prices hurt peasants across the continental deltas. Monocultures can be sensationally profitable when all goes well, but they carry no insurance against future economic perils. For this reason, the governments of post-colonial Southeast Asia have recognized the desirability of economic diversification, though it now must be acknowledged that attaining economic autonomy has not proved to be as easy as winning political freedom. This may be partly due to the fact that, while it was possible to enlist mass support for movements to overthrow alien rule, the realization of economic independence has not been made similarly popular or comprehensible. If such an appraisal is valid, it helps substantiate the belief that nationalism, the next subject to introduce, is invariably most forceful when combat is joined against a concrete enemy rather than in support of an intangible objective.

READINGS

Allen, G. C., and Donnithorne, Audrey G., *Western Enterprise in Indonesia and Malaya: A Study in Economic Development*, London: Allen and Unwin, 1957.

Allen, Sir Richard H. S., *Malaysia: Prospect and Retrospect: The Impact and Aftermath of Colonial Rule*, London: Oxford University Press, 1968.

Bernstein, David, *The Philippine Story*, New York: Farrar, Straus, 1947.

Blythe, Wilfred, *The Impact of Chinese Secret Societies in Malaya*, London: Oxford University Press, 1969.

Brock, J. O. M., *Economic Development of the Netherlands Indies*, New York: Russell and Russell, 1971.

Chai Hon-chan, *The Development of British Malaya, 1896-1909*, 2nd ed., London: Oxford University Press, 1967.

Emerson, Rupert, *Malaysia: A Study in Direct and Indirect Rule*, New York: Macmillan, 1937.

Ennis, T. E., *French Policy and Developments in Indochina*, New York: Russell and Russell, 1973.

Forbes, William Cameron, *The Philippine Islands*, Cambridge: Harvard University Press, 1945.

Furnivall, John S., *Colonial Policy and Practice: A Comparative Study of Burma and Netherlands India*, New York: New York University Press, 1956.

———, *Netherlands India: A Study of Plural Economy*, London: Cambridge University Press, 1967.

Harvey, G. E., *British Rule in Burma, 1824-1942*, London: Faber and Faber, 1946.

Larkin, John A., *The Pampangans; Colonial Society in a Philippine Province*, Berkeley: University of California Press, 1972.

Legge, J. D., *Indonesia*, Englewood Cliffs, N.J.: Prentice-Hall, 1964.

Long, N. V., *Before the Revolution: The Vietnamese Peasants under the French*, Cambridge: Massachusetts Institute of Technology Press, 1973.

Osborne, Milton E., *The French Presence in Cochinchina and Cambodia: Rule and Response (1859-1905)*, Ithaca: Cornell University Press, 1969.

Palmer, J. Norman, *Colonial Labor Policy and Administration: A History of Labor in the Rubber Plantation Industry of Malaya, c. 1910-1941*, New York: J. J. Augustin, 1960.

Pannikar, K. M., *Asia and Western Dominance: A Survey of the Vasco da Gama Epoch of Asian History, 1498-1945*, London: Allen and Unwin, 1953.

Quezon, Manuel L., *The Good Fight*, New York: Appleton-Century, 1946.

Rizal y Alfonso, José, *The Lost Eden (Noli Me Tangere)*, Bloomington: Indiana University Press, 1961.

Robequain, Charles, *The Economic Development of French Indo-China*, London: Oxford University Press, 1944.

Rose, Saul, *Britain and South-east Asia*, Baltimore: The Johns Hopkins University Press, 1962.

Thio, Eunice, *British Policy in the Malay Peninsula, 1880-1910*, Kuala Lumpur: University of Malaya Press, 1967.

Thompson, Virginia, *French Indo-China*, New York: Octagon, 1968.

———, *Postmortem on Malaya*, New York: Macmillan, 1943.

Trager, Helen G., *Burma through Alien Eyes: Missionary Views of The Burmese in the Nineteenth Century*, New York: Praeger, 1966.

Tregonning, K. G., *A History of Modern Sabah, 1881-1963*, Singapore: University of Malaya Press, 1964.

Vlekke, B. H. M., *Nusantara: A History of Indonesia*, The Hague: van Hoeve, 1959.

Zinkin, Maurice, *Asia and the West*, London: Chatto and Windus, 1951.

9

Nationalist Evolution

There can be no doubt that our era has earned a permanent place in world history as the age of nationalism; and, unlike the names of previous periods that are associated with specific patterns, such as, religious ferment, exploration, or industrialization, the label for the present has global applicability. Never before has the entire world been caught up in a single process and, for that reason, the nationalist years are uniquely tumultuous. So much that seemed normal and changeless a generation or two ago has been swept away or recast in unfamiliar form that many once unquestioned, historical assumptions have been discarded. Class interests are not, as Marxists profess to believe, the ultimate determinants of collective behavior. China is no longer a giant in perpetual sleep. It now seems incredible that the West once assumed that its imperial role had been divinely ordained and, even more astonishing, that colonized Asians and Africans could do little but acquiesce. Nationalism has changed all that and much more.

Countless explanations for the rise of nationalism have been offered. All emphasize the necessity of exploiting certain minimal resources if a people is to become a nation. A common language, shared cultural and religious traditions, and a territorial homeland are ordinarily cited as all but indispensable. The turning point in the move to nationalism comes when a sufficient number of people somehow come to the conclusion that their individual interests can best be served when their segment of mankind prospers as a whole. Family, clan, tribe, caste, church, class, once the only foci of loyalty, may be relegated to the periphery of men's passions. The emotional change is most forcefully generated when an entire people is struck down by a common affliction. Colonial subservience is a prime example of such adversity, but because the victim has succumbed to unfamiliar forces, there is a substantial lapse of time before a positive response is possible.

Literature on the subject establishes that the effective nationalist mobilization of a colonized people typically is achieved only after a period of learning from the conqueror.[1] The organizational skills of popular leadership, the mechanics of mass propaganda, and the diplomatic art of winning outside support are all demanded in some measure. Moreover, nationalist movements in colonial or semi-colonial countries, such as China or Egypt, normally begin as expressions of frustration among the nascent middle classes. Products of the economic changes and educational innovations that have come under foreign rule, those on the middle rung of the social ladder are impeded by neither the isolation and inarticulateness of the peasantry nor the fading pretensions of the old aristocracy. However, the indigenous bourgeoisie, as a beneficiary of colonialism, does not initially agitate for national liberation. On the contrary, the earliest clamor is for equality with the overlords, especially in schooling and career advancement. Hence, incipient national movements are very likely to be conservative in purpose and timid in practice.

In due course, when the middle class realizes that its ambitions can be fully served only with the expulsion of an alien authority compelled by the logic of colonialism to preserve dominance, the movement becomes revolutionary. The leadership of the cause must then recruit manpower from the ranks of the urban poor and harness the power of endemic peasant discontent. Economic dislocations caused by faltering world trade, war, or lean harvests accelerate the enlistment process, and, once a nationalist upsurge becomes a destructive military struggle for independence, the flow of disaffected recruits to revolution is certain to increase.

[1] See Rupert Emerson, *From Empire to Nation* (Cambridge: Harvard University Press, 1960), for the clearest presentation of the subject available.

National liberation is naturally served by symbols, beliefs, traditions, and primordial loyalties from the pre-conquest era, but the fight, if it is to be victorious, cannot be negatively xenophobic, for it is precisely through its promise of material progress through modernization that nationalism exerts its most powerful appeal. Partly for that reason, traditional elites are rarely able to serve in campaigns that are revolutionary and reject so much of the old. Selective use of the past is symbolically necessary, but promises of material betterment and some form of popular sovereignty in the independent future are equally indispensable.

It is evident that nationalism takes hold first and most powerfully in countries that have undergone extensive change under colonialism. Developments that produce a middle class and put the peasants and urban workers at the mercy of international economic forces and administrative patterns that dispossess traditional elites are instrumental in the nationalist awakening. Therefore, colonies that have not moved very far toward modernity can be expected to remain politically dormant longer than relatively progressive lands. In Southeast Asia, the rule was more or less operative, though Malaya, despite phenomenal economic transformation, lagged behind in nationalism, due to both the comfortable and respected situation of the indigenous upper crust and the alien origins of the bourgeoisie. Elsewhere, the pace of nationalist advance was primarily determined by the extent and nature of the changes wrought by the Western impact. The Filipinos were the first to stir; the peoples of Laos still seek to become a nation.

THE OVERSEAS CHINESE

About the time Aguinaldo rose to command over the Philippine insurrectionists, the overseas Chinese began to form the second of Southeast Asia's nationalist movements. Though of alien origin, the Chinese of the region played a major role in the political awakening that in two generations would destroy colonialism. For one thing, their omnipresence ensured that Chinese successes in mobilization would be seen and studied by the indigenous peoples among whom they lived. Second, in the first years after the turn of the century, the Chinese convincingly demonstrated that political and economic concessions could be won from colonial regimes.

It was apparent that the strength of the Chinese lay in communal solidarity and organizational sophistication. Across Southeast Asia, Chinese chambers of commerce came into being to serve as bodies representative of unified communities. The power of the chambers was in their ability to press the authorities for reforms to remove legal disabilities that had come to seem humiliating or arbitrary, to secure educational advantages for young Chinese, and to ensure equity in taxation and business operations. Other pan-Chinese associations, particularly those responsible for the operation of community schools, were similarly influential. All of these bodies were served by the growth of Chinese newspapers, which sprang up where only the Western-language press had previously existed. To put it briefly, the Chinese demonstrated the means and utility of political modernization to increasingly receptive local audiences. Paradoxically, Southeast Asian nationalist campaigns that were initially so indebted to the overseas Chinese for technical guidance eventually turned against their mentors, for anti-Sinicism became a conspicuous feature of them all.

INDONESIA

The roots of the movement that ultimately drove the Dutch out of the Indies reach back to first years of this century. Characteristically, the initial expression of discontent with the colonial status quo was cautiously reformist, but, more significantly, it also represented a positive approach to the problem of coping with alien rule. Boedi Oetomo—or, according to recent orthography, Budi Utomo—was founded in 1908 for the purpose of fostering material and spiritual progress. The name of the association, customarily translated to mean "noble endeavor," was appropriately derived from Javanese, for membership was recruited all but exclusively within the ranks of the upper classes of central Java. The endeavor to be nobly supported was by no means a struggle for independence, as Boedi Oetomo's expressions of loyalty to the Dutch were reminiscent of those of the martyred José Rizal to the Spanish crown. The nationalist protypes of 1908 sought simply to win equality with the Dutch in education and official employment. The modest aims of Boedi Oetomo were very much like those of the Indian National Congress at the time of its founding (significantly, by an Englishman) a generation before; but whereas the Indian association eventually grew into a popular anti-colonial force, its Indonesian parallel never matured beyond an elitist infancy and was soon overshadowed by Sarekat Islam, the first pan-Indonesian mass movement.

Sarekat Islam came into being in 1912 as an expression of the anxieties of Muslim merchants in central Java threatened with collapse in the face of mounting Chinese competition; but the strength of the organization was quickly expanded beyond the shores of one island and the boundaries of a single social class. Some of the early leaders of the movement were no less aristocratic and Javanese than those of Boedi Oetomo and were similarly oriented toward goals of Western inspiration, but the newer group intelligently did not restrict itself to catering to elitist aspirations and provincial attachments. They also enjoyed the advantage of exploiting the general resentment against the Sino-Dutch partnership that had come to exercise monopoly control over most of the business life of the archipelago. Sarekat Islam thus harnessed both the passions of those who feared the Chinese and the dreams of those who championed progress along Western lines. The combination was potent.

Sarekat Islam presumably would have remained an alliance of restless men from the aristocracy and the bourgeoisie had it not been for an ability to reach the masses through its religious appeal. The choice of a name that translates as Muslim League was judicious, for it facilitated winning access to the faithful of the villages and small towns. Moreover, the variety of the levels of orthodoxy among Indonesian Muslims left individuals notably free to interpret their faith and to evaluate the claims of those seeking roles as spokesmen. Thus, Sarekat Islam could attract followers among those who consciously claimed to be orthodox as well as among those who enjoyed the comforts of relatively syncretic beliefs. In other words, the organization was able to address itself to some 90 percent of the people of the archipelago and, in fact, enlisted over 350,000 members in its first four years.

The speed with which Sarekat Islam grew was costly, for there was neither time nor machinery to ensure discipline within the rank and file of the movement. Each chapter was inclined to follow its own course; even the collection of dues was sporadic. Though the organization was massive, it was anything but monolithic, and that circumstance invited infiltration by men who hoped to exploit the numerical strength of

Sarekat Islam for their own political purposes. The move was made by the far left.

The inauguration of a social-democratic movement that in time produced through spin-off the first of Southeast Asia's Communist parties had come early, even before the initial nationalist stirrings. This phenomenon of radical politicization antedating national awareness is not as hard to explain as might be expected, for the pioneer Social-Democrats of the Indies were not Indonesians, but Dutch Eurasians who felt threatened by the expanding numbers of European Hollanders drawn to the colony by the economic advances of the period. Starting early in the twentieth century as an effort to mobilize Eurasian— or, to use the odd designation favored in the Indies, Indo-European— strength to influence municipal elections, political radicalism by 1912 had formed a party that was about 20 percent Indonesian and 80 percent Eurasian in membership. Too extreme to be tolerated by the government at Batavia, the party was soon ordered dissolved. Most of its Eurasian followers then drifted into milder communal organizations, while the banner of Marxism was transferred to new hands.

In 1913 Hendricus Sneevliet, a Dutch veteran of the Social-Democratic struggles in the Netherlands, appeared on the Indies stage and quickly set about revitalizing a leftist movement that had almost expired. Sneevliet was an experienced activist and organizer whose life was dedicated to a cause that in the 1920's was to take him to China as an agent of the Kremlin under a *nom de guerre*, Maring, and eventually would be ended by a Nazi executioner in his occupied homeland during the Second World War.

Sneevliet directed his considerable energies toward winning a voice for himself in the tiny labor movement of Java and into establishing in 1914 a small Social-Democratic nucleus largely composed of disaffected Hollanders who had brought their Marxism from home. Had the movement remained the preserve of disgruntled expatriates, nothing would have come of it; but the support of dissident Indonesians was actively invited. Soon the left was transformed from a discussion group into a political force through the recruitment of local followers, including a gifted Javanese youth, Semaun, who swiftly rose to revolutionary leadership. By 1917, aided by the economic discontent caused by wartime interruptions of export sales, he and a growing number of Marxist compatriots had insinuated themselves into Sarekat Islam and gained enough power in that mass organization to dominate the drafting of the league's manifesto for that year. In addition to routine calls for progressive reforms, the great Muslim movement came out against capitalism that was "sinful"—that is, foreign. The first real challenge to Dutch authority had been offered.

The Bolshevik victory at Petrograd in 1917 briefly impeded the growth of Indonesian Marxism, for Sneevliet and those who had by then joined him as Leninists were distracted by their childlike faith in the imminence of revolution in the West. To them, it was axiomatic that the course of history would be determined by the European proletariat; nationalists in the colonies were seen as part of a mere sideshow. The governor general at Batavia in 1918 inadvertently revitalized the left by expelling Sneevliet from the Indies, thereby ensuring that the mantle of Marxist leadership would pass to Indonesian radicals eager to resume the penetration of the nationalist movement.

Lenin, striving to consolidate his power over a country with substantial Muslim enclaves, was obliged to denounce pan-Islamic movements, for he could ill-afford to endanger the security of the one country that had lived up to revolutionary expectations. His stand naturally tarnished the attractiveness of the left within Sarekat Islam and in 1920 drove Indonesian Marxist-Leninists to found Southeast Asia's first Communist party, the PKI. Though continuing to work from within for the domination of Muslim nationalism, Semaun and his more famous successor, Tan Malaka, also sponsored a rival Islamic association in a quite forlorn attempt to lure members away from Sarekat Islam.

The next few years were characterized by PKI efforts to gain ascendancy in and over Sarekat Islam and the labor unions, while the non-Communist leaders of the Muslim body sought to contain the Marxist-Leninists. The shock waves of the predictable fight would grievously injure both parties to the contest. Sarekat Islam, already debilitated by its inability to digest the leftists, soon came under criticism from religious conservatives who were repelled by the wordliness of modernist Islam. Membership rolls began to shrink as many either turned to organizations that were specifically religious in purpose or simply reverted to apolitical hibernation.

The PKI, driven by fears of declining influence in the labor movement and by police efficiency that had already decimated its leadership, decided to rise in revolution before all hope of success evaporated. The

fateful year was 1926. Oblivious to the total inadequacy of their preparations for a campaign of violence and naïvely trusting that aid from
the Comintern would somehow prevent disaster, the Communists engineered a series of strikes and riots. The scale of the operations was tiny;
the coordination of the attack was chaotic. A single spark can indeed
ignite a prairie, but only when the climate is right. The authorities had
no trouble at all in stamping out the smouldering fire and scattering the
embers by forcing some Communists into flight abroad and sending
some 1300 others to a concentration camp in western New Guinea.
The PKI had launched the first of its three disastrous attempts at revolution. In 1948 and in 1965, the party would try again with the devastation growing on each occasion.

Just as these events were unfolding, Sukarno came onto the scene.
The young product of the Dutch engineering college at Bandung was
ideally suited to rise to nationalist leadership. He was at once deeply
rooted in Javanese mysticism and culture and firmly grounded in
Western technology. A man with a foot in each of two worlds, he was
a living case study of the synthesis that is colonial nationalism. Moreover, he was a captivating orator who could both electrify audiences
and refresh himself with his speeches. Sukarno was one of the few
leaders of his time who deserved to be described by the overworked
word "charismatic." Even after his political disgrace and downfall in
1965-66, the men who had toppled him felt obliged to treat him re-
spectfully and, when he died in 1970, they ordered a full-scale state
funeral in his honor. Charisma that endures in defeat and death is un-
questionably genuine.

Sukarno's genius essentially lay in the vagueness of his politics. Nominally Muslim, loosely Socialist, fervently patriotic, he could reach an
almost boundless cross-section of his countrymen. In 1927, expanding
from the nucleus of a political discussion group, the PNI or Indonesian
Nationalist Party was founded with Sukarno as its head. The platform
was uncluttered by ideological trappings; freedom from colonial rule
was the sole and specific goal. So successful was the leader in mustering
a following pledged to noncooperation with the authorities that within
a couple of years the Dutch took preventive measures by arresting him.
That action merely endowed Sukarno with increased notoriety. Upon
release from his first detention, he returned to agitation, was rather
promptly rearrested and sent into fairly comfortable banishment in the

eastern part of the archipelago, to derive benefit, as did so many colonial nationalists, from sabbatic leave from revolution. When he was ultimately released by the Japanese in 1942, he was fully ready to grasp the opportunity that history had brought him and his country.

Dutch policy was to stifle nationalist murmurs with kindness, through the Ethical Program, with controlled and cautious liberalization, as with the establishment of the Volksraad, and with police repression. The tactics of the government, reinforced by the organizational inadequacies of the Indonesian opposition, were remarkably effective. During the last few years before the Second World War swept into the Indies, the islands were quite tranquil. There were of course those in the local intelligentsia who wrote and talked about politics, but there was no mass movement. It seemed that potent nationalism had come and gone in two lively decades, from the founding of Sarekat Islam to Sukarno's exile from Java.

VIETNAM

The French conquest never smothered or even seriously challenged the cultural identity of the Vietnamese. Historic memories of the struggles to win and maintain freedom from China were a living part of their national heritage. In their days of glory, the emperors of Vietnam, modeling themselves after Chinese sovereigns, had required tributary expressions of inferiority from lesser rulers who sought to maintain harmonious diplomatic relations with Vietnam. The Chinese tribute system, in which of course Vietnam was herself a participant, was re-created in miniature to provide for exchange between the Vietnamese court and the monarchs of neighboring, generally weaker lands. Proud memories of all those achievements and more endured.

In further emulation of their Chinese cultural tutors, the Vietnamese considered themselves pre-eminently civilized. Alone among Southeast Asians, they contemptuously regarded those peoples who had not undergone Sinic cultivation as barbarous. The clash of values with the French, ethnocentric legends in their own right, became a lasting feature of the colonial era. Though a minority surrendered to Gallicization, most Vietnamese remained fundamentally convinced of the superiority of their Sinicized heritage.

The imperial institution and the mandarinate were preserved by the French in order to dress their rule with respected symbols of authority and legitimacy. However, insofar as the imperial puppets and their officials were taken seriously by colonized Vietnamese, the brilliance of the old traditions was recalled. The fact of nine centuries of sovereignty and high civilization before the French came was inevitably underscored. Furthermore, since their roots reached all the way back to the mythical and classical ages of China, the Vietnamese could boast of cultural ancestors who were polished and refined when the primitive Gauls were rude savages yet to be tamed by Rome.

The Vietnamese sense of cultural integrity and their feelings of ancient superiority were therefore strained but never erased by the French. For that reason, the Vietnamese were not plunged into confusion and despair to the same extent as the colonial peoples in, say, Burma or Indonesia. Accordingly, when modern nationalism began to materialize, a rich body of tradition awaited enlistment in the cause. This is not to say, of course, that the national movement was directed at turning back the clock of history. Like all such drives, it employed the symbolic legacy of the past to strengthen demands for independent progress in the future.

Japan, not China, fired the imagination in new and compelling ways as the twentieth century began. The triumph in 1905 over Russia, the Western giant, won by a small Asian country so recently lifted out of feudal isolation, reverberated around the colonial world. The European mystique was permanently dispelled. No longer would whiteness of skin be taken, albeit reluctantly or subconsciously, as evidence of invincibility. In Vietnam, as in many subject lands, the Japanese victory brought a loud and clear message: the attainment of modernization and national strength by a non-Western people did not require the sacrifice of self-respect and the abandonment of traditional values. Pan-Asianism centered on Japan became a rallying point for many colonial nationalists and was to provide an ideological basis for later Japanese expansionism under the slogan, "Asia for the Asiatics."

Adaptations from the Chinese model and inspiration from Japan were by no means the only elements in the story of the Vietnamese national awakening. Resistance to the French was carried on for many years after Vietnam was pacified on paper, and the spirit of those who fought kept national hope alive. Doubtless some of the enemies of the colonial regime were simply brigands who would have been lawless under any flag; but there were others, men of the scholar class who could have enjoyed material security as ornaments in the ceremonial mandarinate, who opposed the foreign masters for clear reasons of patriotism. Ho Chi Minh's father was such a man. In 1916, even the puppet emperor was implicated in intrigue preparatory to an armed rising. When the scheme came to light, the plotters were arrested and potentially mutinous colonial troops were disarmed. For his alleged part in the affair, the emperor was exiled to an island in the Indian Ocean. It can be noted that these events occurred when France was highly vulnerable, with so much of her manpower in the trenches.

The First World War had a far more lasting impact on Vietnam than that caused by the abortive rebellion of 1916, for to a degree unknown by the other peoples of Southeast Asia the Vietnamese were drawn into the global conflict. Close to 100,000 Vietnamese laborers or colonial soldiers were sent abroad to serve in the metropole or wherever French orders took them. Evidence strongly suggests that many of the men were coerced into service rather than recruited. Even more significant than the nature of their departure for France was the consequence of their return home. Exposure to trade unionism, to democratic institutions, and, perhaps most importantly, to the fact that not all Frenchmen were superior beings in white suits and pith helmets naturally made deep and disturbing impressions. It is surely not coincidental that the upsurge of nationalism as a popular wave soon followed the repatriation of the tens of thousands who had seen the outside world.

Historical continuity was served by the establishment of one of the first modern political organizations in Vietnam, the Nationalist Party, usually referred to as the VNQDD, for its structure and philosophy were imported straight from China. The 1926-28 reunification of China by the Nationalist Party, the Kuomintang, invited admiration to the South. A small band of Vietnamese, drawn largely from the urban intelligentsia, responded by forming a nuclear party modeled after the Chinese body and adopting its name in Vietnamese translation. It is doubtless a point of significance that the VNQDD was the only foreign protégé of the Kuomintang. There were of course overseas branches of the Chinese Nationalist Party, but they served compatriots abroad, not non-Chinese. Presumably only a land of Sinic civilization, like Vietnam, could accommodate a transplanted Chinese institution.

In emulation of the parent party in its long years of political weakness, the VNQDD functioned in the manner of a secret society. It was a brotherhood of some 1500 members, not a mass movement. Clandestine meetings, illicit publications, and terrorist acts were the party's stock in trade. The vigilance of the French police of course precluded the early mounting of an open offensive, but the VNQDD might have been wise to concentrate on the slow construction of a popular base rather than on the thrills of intrigue and the promise of violence. Like the early Kuomintang, the VNQDD was an elitist conspiracy remote from the people. The putsch was regarded as the best means to stimulate nationalist mobilization. The theory that the people would rise and throw off their foreign chains once an enlightened vanguard showed the way was soon tested with shattering consequences.

In 1930, the third year of the VNQDD's short life, panic combined with overconfidence to drive the party to premature, uncoordinated action. In anticipation of a mutiny by a colonial garrison and out of fear that the authorities were closing in, an uprising was ordered. Some soldiers in fact mutinied and there were isolated explosions of local violence, but the ease with which the French put down the pitifully mismanaged coup demonstrated the organizational inadequacies of the VNQDD and the ineptitude of its leadership. The party was effectively crushed, never again to play a meaningful part in the independence struggles that were to bring Vietnam decades of anguish.

The prime force in the expulsion of foreign control was of course generated by the Communists and their allies. Unfashionable though it is to examine history through the biography of a single figure, there is no way to study twentieth-century Vietnam without giving primary attention to Ho Chi Minh. Though many of his middle years remain partly hidden in the obscurity sought by a hunted revolutionary, the general outline of Ho's life is clear enough. Before going on to a brief biographical sketch, however, this is a logical place to offer a note of explanation on Vietnamese names.

Borrowing from the Chinese, the Vietnamese typically have names composed of three syllables. The first stands for the family name; the second and third in combination are the person's given name. But, whereas a Chinese, say, Mao Tse-tung is politely referred to as Chairman Mao; a Vietnamese named Vo Nguyen Giap is known as General Giap. The origins of the Vietnamese style are obscure. To compound the confusion, Ho Chi Minh observed Chinese usage and is now always known as President Ho. Presumably his years in China and his long association with Chinese account for this unique exception to the etiquette of Vietnamese names.

Ho Chi Minh was born in 1890, the son of a traditional literatus who was implacably hostile to French rule. A born member of the scholarly class, Ho was put through an educational program that sought to bridge the gap between Asia and the West by drawing upon the heritages of both. Qualifications earned in school, however, did not open many doors to careers for Vietnamese in the colonial environment. Thus, in 1911, Ho was compelled to take a menial job aboard a French liner that took him abroad to begin nearly thirty-five years of wandering and rarely interrupted exile. In the first part of that period, Ho spent several years as an apprentice pastry cook under the great Escoffier. Later, he earned his living retouching photographs in Paris, and it was there that his first memorable political acts took place.

Innocently assuming that the Wilsonian advocacy of national self-determination would sway the statesmen who assembled in 1919 to work out treaty settlements for the postwar world, Ho campaigned at the Versailles conference in a bleak effort to win freedom for his homeland. His predictable failure was not total, for the force of his personality and the skill of his pen won him a position writing for a French Socialist newspaper. Soon, he was enrolled in the Socialist Party and, when that organization was fractured in 1920 by the withdrawal of its left-wing to form the French Communist Party, Ho became a founding member of the new revolutionary force. From that time on, as a loyal Communist, he was to spend many years as an international agent of the Kremlin. At no point, however, is there any hint that the cause of Vietnamese independence was ever far from his mind.

Collaboration between the Chinese Communists and the Kuomintang during the mid-1920's enabled Ho to base himself at Canton. The site was attractive because of its proximity to the Tonkinese frontier and because it had become a haven for a handful of Vietnamese who had been linked to nationalist stirrings and forced into flight by the colonial regime. Working among his compatriots in the southern China city, Ho assembled a following that in 1925 banded together as the Association of Vietnamese Revolutionary Youth, a body that was directly ancestral to the Vietnam Communist Party born five years later. It is worth noting that Ho's first political organization bore a name designed to appeal to the widest possible audience, for the technique of suggesting nationalist coalition through the use of labels that avoided direct mention of communism was to be repeated.

The climate of discontent in Vietnam in 1930 prompted the Communists, as it had the VNQDD earlier in the year, to turn to violence, with peasant rage harnessed to the Marxist-Leninist cause. Rebellious outbreaks in the countryside and urban work stoppages profoundly alarmed the authorities but never menaced their ability to react. Military assaults on rural pockets of upheaval caused heavy loss of life; police sweeps netted thousands. Just as those events were transpiring, Ho Chi Minh was arrested in Hong Kong and by the narrowest of margins escaped extradition to Vietnam, where the guillotine stood poised. Freed on appeal to the Empire's highest court, the Privy Council, he promptly left the British colony to resume his often mysterious travels. The Communists, along with the VNQDD, were thus in tactical retreat by 1932.

The movements of right and the left already discussed were not the sole nationalist manifestations of the period. While the VNQDD and the Communists primarily worked for revolution in the north, other efforts were taking shape to the south, in Cochin China. Two movements that appear bizarre 'to foreigners but which were markedly attractive to villagers merit attention. Religious revivalism, rather than nationalism, was their basis, but, as challenges to the established order, both had clear political overtones and were manifestations of popular restlessness.

A variant Buddhist sect, known as Hoa Hao, was rapidly and enthusiastically embraced by peasant thousands after its founder, Huynh Phu So, underwent miraculous enlightenment in 1939. Purportedly guided by the spirit of a legendary holy man, the leader of Hoa Hao instructed the swelling ranks of the faithful in a simple doctrine unembellished by theological embroidery. More compelling, he claimed to possess magical powers of prescience. Sadly, it was this gift of clairvoyance that proved his undoing, for he predicted, among innumerable other things, that the French would be dislodged. The authorities concluded that the man was mad and had him confined to a hospital, where he promptly converted his psychiatrist. That missionary triumph left the French no alternative to banishing the Hoa Hao leader to a remote spot and ultimate obscurity.

The Cao Dai sect began a decade and a half earlier than Hoa Hao and is the more fascinating of the two. Seldom, probably never, has a religious movement displayed greater doctrinal eclecticism and ritual synthesis. Monotheistic though it was, the sect extended hospitable accommodation to a remarkable assembly of saintly beings, including Confucius, Joan of Arc, and Victor Hugo. Its theological basis was Buddhist, but Taoist, Christian, and animist elements were present in profusion. The elaborate and hierarchical structure of the movement's officialdom was borrowed from Roman Catholicism, as was a portion of the ceremonials. The architecture of Cao Dai houses of worship was an arresting mélange of neo-Gothic and Mahayana Buddhist approaches to the art of building. Down to the Second World War, the hundreds of thousands of Cao Dai faithful were regarded with patronizing amusement by the French, but the organizational strength and political potential of the movement eventually caused official uneasiness. That was quite understandable, for the sect was not without an anti-colonial flavor and followers were inclined to group themselves in self-contained village communities that could become enclaves of resistance.

Like the Dutch in the Indies on the eve of the Japanese move southward, the French could feel that their upper hand might be bruised but never knocked aside. Tragedy far from Indochina would soon prove them wrong, for the spring of 1940 brought German armor crashing through France. The French surrender in the forest near Compiègne, held with vengeful symbolism in the railway car where Imperial German commanders had capitulated a generation before, was accompanied by the establishment of a puppet regime at Vichy that could not defend Indochina against Japanese pressure. In a matter of weeks, French prestige in Vietnam would be dealt the first of a series of fatal blows.

BURMA

The British had found the pacification of Burma a trying process. In the sense that rural banditry, *dacoity*, remained endemic, the Burmese were never brought under rigid control. The spirit of resistance was reduced but not extinguished. The partial breakdown of patterns of village authority and the process of land alienation, discussed in an earlier chapter, could only contribute to lawlessness. The reservoir of peasant discontent was ready to be tapped, once coordinated leadership appeared. As throughout Southeast Asia and the rest of the colonial world, most of the nationalist leaders were to come from the urban middle class.

Religion provided the vehicle that initially carried sharpened national awareness to the countryside. Buddhism was the most substantial link between urban sophisticates and the peasantry and bound all Burmans together. Though not initiated for political purposes, the Young Men's Buddhist Association, founded in 1906, was soon drawn into nationalist activities. That was thoroughly appropriate, for the YMBA, consciously patterned after its Christian counterpart, represented the blend of tradition and innovation that is nationalism.

The first united campaign of the YMBA was mounted during the First World War to compel all visitors to pagodas, including otherwise unassailable Britons, to follow established custom by removing their shoes. It seems little short of incredible that the British resisted granting such a small, polite concession to local sensibilities and thereby magnified the issue. When the government at Rangoon eventually gave in to popular pressure, the Burmese had won a victory of symbolic significance. The might of mass action had been demonstrated and would soon be put to fresh use.

Hatred of the connection with India did not preclude learning from the Indian experience in nationalist agitation. When political devolution brought dyarchy to India in 1919, like benefits were demanded for Burma. The country was soon swept by broadly popular protest centering on secondary school and university students who had called a boycott of regular classes. That the students played such a catalytic role is far from surprising, for the youth of a colony are likely to embody the synthesis of old attachments and new aspirations.

The student strikes that began in 1920 would have been mere annoyances had not support come from the headquarters of the YMBA—now renamed the General Council of Burma Associations in order to expand its attractiveness to men—and women as well—who might be neither young nor Buddhist. The resultant broadening of the nationalist campaign brought in thousands of Buddhist monks who broadcast the message of rebellion throughout the countryside. So ominous did the situation grow that in 1921 the Parliament at Westminster reversed an earlier decision that had denied limited self-rule to the Burmese. Opposition to the British slowly began to subside but by no means evaporated.

Burmese leaders in the years after dyarchy was finally introduced into their country in 1923 were in something of a quandary. Such political reforms as had come had originally been devised for India; therefore, being under the viceregal authority of New Delhi was beneficial. Yet the driving force of much of the Burmese nationalist movement was generated by deep yearning for an end to the colonialist *mariage de convenance* that bound Burma to her large neighbor. Put most simply, a choice had to be made between divorce from the subcontinent and struggling alone, on the one hand, and, on the other, maintaining the union in the hope that the coming of independence might be accelerated by developments in India, where Gandhian techniques were proving highly productive. The debate inevitably dissipated the strength of the nationalist forces, though events in the early 1930's would make the issue somewhat academic.

The economic distress into which the world was plunged in the second of the interwar decades inflamed Burmese passions and made the course of political moderation virtually unthinkable. Tumbling prices for export commodities quickly worsened the lot of rice farmers already groaning under debt, while the Chettyars were blamed for the growing misery. Meanwhile, in urban areas, indigenous workers were forced out of their jobs by cheaper immigrant labor. Anti-Indian feelings, never far below the surface, and hostility to the relatively small Chinese minority reached unprecedented proportions and were translated into bloody riots in 1930 and 1931 that brought death to uncounted numbers of aliens and terrified the survivors.

The communal explosions in the cities in the early years of the depression were not directed against British rule per se, but against the clients of colonialism in Burma, the visible and vulnerable Indians and Chinese. In an especially impoverished rural district in Lower Burma, however, the turn of the white overlords had already come with the outbreak of a peasant rebellion, called the Saya San movement after its leader, a man who had grown weary of the debate over political gradualism. His uprising promised full freedom and the restoration of the

Burmese monarchy with Saya San on the throne. The appeal to tradition and the use of religious mysticism and magic brought the message to simple villagers. A rustic army was raised and attacks began with the murder of a British forestry expert in 1930. That act signaled the spread of outbursts of lethal fury to various parts of the country over the next two years.

The government responded to the risings by introducing modest steps to ameliorate the economic hardship that afflicted the most troubled districts. More important, the police, assisted by militia units raised among the Karens, a people always ready to fight Burmans, struck with swift efficiency. The rebels' primitive weapons could not match superior arms in the hands of disciplined forces. The talismans and tattoos which the trusting believed assured immunity against official bullets were even more worthless. Saya San was captured in 1931, and in 1937, after extended proceedings that brought national recognition to his attorney, Ba Maw, who will shortly reappear in this narrative, the royal pretender was hanged.

After the rebellion had been contained, most established Burmese political figures channeled their energies into speeding progress toward self-rule. The lure of official posts within the dyarchic government led many to seek political fortune through cooperation with the British. Accordingly, the nationalist banner was gradually shifted to more youthful hands, specifically to the followers of the Thakin movement, which came into full bloom in 1936.

The word "thakin," generally translated as "master," was the humble style of address politely used by many Burmese in speaking to Britons. At the University of Rangoon, large numbers of students began calling each other "Thakin" to dramatize their conviction that the Burmese were the equals of the British and therefore ought to govern their own country. Ideological influences on the Thakins came from a variety of sources, but a rudimentary Marxism-Leninism was the dominant force. Accordingly, the young revolutionaries with but limited success turned to efforts to organize and lead what there was of a Burmese urban proletariat.

In 1936 the Thakins found their cause. They rallied when two of their chiefs, Thakin Nu (later U Nu) and Thakin Aung San, both to achieve subsequent great fame, were expelled from the University as punishment for their nationalist labors. Student strikes were immediately called to protest against the colonial nature of education. The timing of the mass demonstration could not have been better chosen, for the examination season was about to open. There will never be any way to distinguish between those students who paralyzed the university out of patriotism and those who acted out of youthful *joie de vivre* reinforced by fear of examination failure. In any event, the strike was triumphant, as it spread to sister and secondary institutions, and ultimately obliged the government to accept many of the Thakin demands for organizational reform of the University. Far more significant, Thakin activities had thrilled many ordinary citizens and pushed into prominence men who would soon guide the destiny of the country.

In 1938 renewed rioting against Indians took place, with Thakin rhetoric helping to arouse the mobs. The outbursts were initially touched off by the appearance of a book that was of Muslim Indian authorship and seemed scornful of Buddhism. As on earlier, unhappy occasions, the casualty rolls were long. The restoration of order through rather heavy-handed action by the police left a residue of bitterness, particularly as the force was largely Indian in manpower.

The start of the Second World War in Europe was seen by many nationalists, notably the Thakins, as providing new opportunities to break the colonialist hold on Burma. Some hoped for Japanese support in the fight for independence; others simply expected that the over-extension of the British would result in imperial weakness and a willingness to grant concessions for the sake of political tranquility. Following the example of the Indian National Congress, the more militant Burmese leaders publicly urged the denial of support for the British war effort. Notable figures thus ran afoul of wartime laws against sedition and were quickly sent to prisons to savor political martyrdom.

It is reasonable to believe that Burma would have moved to full dominion status in less than a generation had war not speeded the pace of events. By 1941, the decline of imperial authority had been in progress for over two decades and could not have been reversed or even much retarded. The only question was whether change was to be under the command of the moderates who had comfortably fitted into dyarchy or the revolutionaries who had taken to the streets. The answer was not long in coming.

THE OTHER COLONIES

The Philippines, Malaya, Cambodia and Laos can be lumped together in a few paragraphs on nationalism before the Second World War. The experiences of those countries were certainly not the same, but in none was nationalist agitation the paramount or even conspicuous political theme.

Among Southeast Asians, Filipinos took deserved pride in the seniority of their national awakening. That the first phase of the struggle for independence had been ended by the American intrusion did not diminish the glory of Rizal and other patriots. All prominent political figures remained verbally bound to the cause of Philippine freedom, but they were outflanked by the American pledge that the period of United States rule would be brief and that administrative and legislative power would be transferred to Filipinos with deliberate speed. Consequently, the leaders of the campaign for independence were quite snugly accommodated within the establishment, where they made impassioned speeches on the blessings of liberty. As there was no mass movement capable of threatening either American tenure or the right of succession to power held by the Filipino landed and professional classes, nationalism was contained. The elite had neither the need nor the wish to generate revolutionary stirrings.

From the perspective of colonial administrators, Malaya was particularly blessed, for the country's ethnic composition discouraged the development of local nationalism. Insofar as they were politically articulate, the Chinese and the Indians, who together outnumbered the Malays, looked abroad to their ancestral homelands. Some Malays were beginning to think in terms of their nation, but there was no organized movement of opposition to foreign control. The Malay elite was inclined to relish the benefits that colonialism had brought to the sultans and to those who had entered civil service careers. The expulsion of the British was practically unthinkable.

Economic underdevelopment and systems of indirect rule behind façades of indigenous royal legitimacy minimized the French impact on Cambodia and Laos. The peasants of both countries were not shaken out of village traditionalism by material progress. The top strata of the two societies were reasonably satisfied with their lot; some lived in palaces, while others were won over by educational and career opportunities reserved for selected aristocrats.

THAILAND

Escape from colonialism by no means excluded Thailand from participation in the process of national regeneration that touched most of her neighbors. The same forces that produced national reactions among others had been felt by the Thais. Imperialism had been held at bay only at considerable cost in territory and sovereignty. Economic advance had reshaped demographic patterns through increased urbanization. Though the country remained essentially agricultural, centers of trade and light manufacturing grew where only administrative towns had stood earlier. The cleavage between urban and rural districts and peoples steadily widened, especially as a major proportion of those who prospered in the transformed cities and towns were alien in origin. A handful of Westerners held a few powerful positions in shipping, banking, timbering, and the import-export trade; vastly greater numbers of Chinese or Sino-Thais ran almost everything else.

Clearly the emergence of a new middle class was the single most important result of Thailand's entry into modernization. Some members of the class were in the professions; many others had risen in the civil and military services. Particularly successful were those who had acquired modern educations at home or abroad. All were consciously in pursuit of upward mobility; all were committed to some form of faith in national progress. To put it most succinctly, the emerging middle class of Thailand was able to produce precisely the same kind of leadership that strove for liberation in colonies. The difference lay in the fact the Thai modern elite was obliged to combat absolute monarchy rather than alien rule.

The year 1932 brought the end of the Thai king's total authority. It is somewhat paradoxical that efforts begun by Mongkut in the mid-nineteenth century and continued by Chulalongkorn and his heirs to reform Thailand ultimately and directly led to the stripping away of the monarchy's unbridled power. In a process obviously parallel to the self-destructive creation of restless middle classes in the colonies, the sponsorship of modern education by reformist kings generated the ideas and ambitions that in due course touched off a coup d'état. The leaders of the attack were representatives of the youthful group of professional men whose training and goals made royal absolutism seem responsible for the country's inferior status internationally and backwardness domestically. They were, in short, nationalists.

The military display that obliged the king to assume a limited constitutional role is customarily referred to as a revolution. The title seems extravagant. There was neither gunfire nor popular involvement. A disciplined force commanded by elitist conspirators simply presented demands that were meekly accepted by their sovereign.

Like so many other published promises of democratic advance that soon prove to be empty, the constitution proclaimed in 1932 was a wordy document that provided for everything but its own implementation. The engineers of the king's demotion in effect distributed among themselves most of the sovereign rights that the Chakri rulers had held. The party—or, more accurately, the clique—that assumed power jealously guarded its authority. The masses were urged to embrace a nationalist cult but not to aspire to participation in the making of decisions. As might be anticipated, the power elite soon began to divide and quarrel internally. Thus, Thai political history during the initial twenty-five years of constitutional monarchy was one of coups, some abortive, some victorious, all staged by a familiar cast with the principal actors engaged in a dreary minuet of transferring premierships, while the public watched in apathy.

READINGS

Ba, U, *My Burma: The Autobiography of a President*, New York: Taplinger, 1958.

Buttinger, Joseph, *Vietnam: A Political History*, New York: Praeger, 1968.

Coast, John, *Some Aspects of Siamese Politics*, New York: Institute of Pacific Relations, 1953.

Collis, Maurice S., *Trials in Burma*, London: Faber and Faber, 1938.

Donnison, F. S. V., *Public Administration in Burma: A Study of Development during the British Connection*, London: Royal Institute of International Affairs, 1953.

Emerson, Rupert, *From Empire to Nation*, Cambridge: Harvard University Press, 1960.

Ingram, James C., *Economic Change in Thailand since 1850*, Stanford, Stanford University Press, 1955.

Kartini, Raden Adjeng, *Letters of a Javanese Princess*, New York: Norton, 1964.

McVey, Ruth T., *The Rise of Indonesian Communism*, Ithaca: Cornell University Press, 1965.

Moscotti, A. D., *British Policy and the Nationalist Movement in Burma, 1917-1937*, Honolulu: University of Hawaii Press, 1974.

Neill, W. T., *Twentieth Century Indonesia*, New York: Columbia University Press, 1973.

Noer, Deliar, *The Modernist Muslim Movement in Indonesia, 1900-1942*, London: Oxford University Press, 1973.

Roff, William R., *The Origins of Malay Nationalism*, New Haven: Yale University Press, 1967.

Sjahrir, Soetan, *Out of Exile*, New York: Greenwood, 1969.

Skinner, G. William, *Chinese Society in Thailand: An Analytical History*, Ithaca: Cornell University Press, 1957.

Trager, Frank N., *Burma—From Kingdom to Republic*, New York: Praeger, 1966.

Van Niel, Robert, *The Emergence of the Modern Indonesian Elite*, The Hague: van Hoeve, 1960.

Vella, Walter F., *The Impact of the West on Government in Thailand*, Berkeley: University of California Press, 1955.

Wertheim, W. F., *Indonesian Society in Transition: A Study of Social Changes*, 2nd ed., The Hague: van Hoeve, 1959.

Williams, Lea E., *Overseas Chinese Nationalism: The Genesis of the Pan-Chinese Movement in Indonesia, 1900-1916*, Glencoe, Ill.: Free Press, 1960.

10
Japanese Interregnum

In the immediate postwar period, it became an article of colonialist faith to blame the Japanese for having sired and nurtured revolutionary nationalism in Southeast Asia. It was routinely alleged that Japan had planted a time bomb set to explode in the faces of Western rulers when they returned in victory. That simplistic analysis was doubly appealing: it excluded the reality that nascent nationalism had been generated under prewar colonial circumstances; it suggested that patriots striving to liberate their homelands were collaborationist traitors or, more charitably, mere dupes.

The truth, comfortably available through historical retrospection, is found in familiar facts. National consciousness well antedated the arrival of the Japanese and doubtless would have grown to triumphant maturity without cataclysmic outside prompting. It is inconceivable that, in the absence of war, the colonies would have quietly vegetated. The social and economic changes that came with colonialism and that produced the initial nationalist awakening would surely have gained in momentum over time and thereby stimulated growing political ferment. By way of comparative illustration, it can be observed that India and much of the colonial and semi-colonial Middle East went through national revolutions without the direct assistance of military invaders.

There is no logical reason to suppose that Southeast Asia would have acted differently. In brief, the Japanese intrusion accelerated processes that had begun earlier and were not to be reversed. Wartime occupation may have compressed a generation of history into three and a half years, but it did not redirect the course of events.

CONQUEST

The Japanese decision to invade Southeast Asia was made late, only after international events permitted the action. Tokyo had long been rightly fearful of war on two fronts, one to the north against the Russians, one to the east and south against the Western colonial powers. The attack on China begun in 1937 increased Japan's anxieties, for a major part of her army was immobilized in the inconclusive contest on the mainland. However, when the British and the French documented their cowardice at Munich in 1938, their Asian colonies began to appear appealingly vulnerable. The defeat of France in the spring of 1940 and the siege of Britain that then began added to the attractiveness of a Japanese southward thrust. By late 1941, dread of the Soviet Union had faded with the signing of a Russo-Japanese neutrality pact in April of that year and, more compellingly, with the shattering advance of the Germans deep into the Soviet homeland that began in June. With Hitler's armies almost within sight of Moscow, the warm months of 1942 would surely see the final collapse of the Russians. Thus Japan felt free to move south to win easy prizes and access to the resources her islands had been denied by a niggardly nature.

Well before the final choice between fronts was made, the initial push into Southeast Asia had already come. In August and September 1940, the Vichy French were pressed to permit the Japanese to enter Tonkin to use port facilities and airfields and to maintain small garrisons. The purpose was twofold. First, China's access to the sea via the Kunming-Hanoi railway was closed, while Japanese troops were free to use Tonkin as a staging area for assaults on Chinese resistance forces. Second, the Japanese won a stepping stone on the southward route. In a matter of months, all Indochina came under the new invaders who had neither to occupy territory nor administer affairs, since the compliant and collaborationist French comfortably served as their deputies.

The presence of Japanese forces was euphemistically designated by the French a *stationnement;* and, until 1945, the tricolor continued to wave, though perhaps not as proudly as before.

Concurrent with the spread into Indochina was a diplomatic offensive designed to win Thailand to the Japanese side. The rightist head of the incumbent junta at Bangkok, Phibun Songgram, one of the leaders of the 1932 coup, may be presumed to have been personally inclined toward fascism and to have admired Japan's forceful strides. He also was a realist who saw that, at least over the short run, Tokyo would be dominant in the Far East and that accommodation ought to be sought. Finally, Japan bought Phibun's cooperation in early 1941 by compelling the French gubernatorial puppet at Saigon to cede to Thailand those extensive areas in western Cambodia and in Laos that had been lost by the Thais during the flood tide of late nineteenth-century imperialism. Accordingly, within a few months of the collapse of metropolitan France, Japan was free to control and exploit Indochina and could hope for Thai complicity as the march into Southeast Asia progressed. At that point, however, the United States intervened.

This is not the place to go into the intricacies of United States gravitation toward war. American sympathy for beleaguered China and attendant hostility toward Japan motivated diplomatic actions that brought Washington and Tokyo into ever more ominous confrontation. By 1941 Roosevelt had begun to use heavy economic pressure in an effort to oblige the Japanese to withdraw from Indochina and end their aggression in China. Particularly menacing was the American attempt to cut off the flow of oil that was vital to the running of Japan's war machine. In the fall of that year, the decision to strike in the south, where petroleum was to be had, was given final approval.

The Japanese had hoped that the Dutch in the Indies, whose homeland was by then under German occupation, would follow French example and timidly yield to demands that would put the islands at Japan's service. Partly from stubbornness and partly due to American encouragement, Batavia stood firm. Dutch collaboration would not be forthcoming.

The British and the Americans were expected to resist militarily, but the former already had enough on their hands and the latter were believed to be emotionally incapable of sustained warfare. A bolt of lightning at Pearl Harbor would reduce the Americans to impotence in the Pacific; defeat of the British would take some time but was deemed certain. Thus, the design of the initial campaign took shape and was soon to be brilliantly and dreadfully successful. Japan's only mistake was to count on winning her goals in a short war that would be concluded through negotiations with humbled, defeatist Anglo-Americans.

As Japanese carrier pilots began their mission against the home base of the United States Pacific Fleet, other warriors of the emperor struck in the Philippines and in Malaya. Landings on Luzon were easily accomplished, and the advance through the archipelago begun. Despite the fact that Filipinos were the only Southeast Asians to rally to the defense of the established order, in a short time the binational American-Filipino army was driven onto the Bataan Peninsula across from Manila to await relief that never came. In early April 1942, the peninsula fell; a month later, the island fortress of Corregidor at its tip was surrendered. Four centuries of Western colonialism in the islands had ended.

The pace of conquest was similarly swift elsewhere. The Japanese invasion fleet that took troops from Indochina to landing beaches in the extreme south of peninsular Thailand were obliged to cross only some two hundred miles of open sea. Thai token opposition to the arrival of Japanese troops on their territory was momentary. Coming ashore just north of the Malayan frontier, the invaders made a bloodless landing. The sinking of two capital ships of the Royal Navy, three days after hostilities opened, paralyzed the British in Eastern waters and allowed a steady flow of Japanese reinforcements and supplies to be moved across the South China Sea to the invasion beaches.

The entire Malayan campaign took a bit over two months. Japanese soldiers averaged around ten miles a day as they moved toward Singapore. The United Kingdom, Indian, and Australian defenders at all times enjoyed numerical superiority over the enemy, but that advantage was an empty one. Untrained in jungle warfare in a country that was three-fourths jungle, terrified of leaving the false security offered by Malaya's fine highways, the British repeatedly were outflanked as they manned successive roadblocks, each to the south of one just abandoned.

In mid-February 1942, Singapore surrendered. Plans for the defense of the island, of course, had been premised on the conviction that attack would be seaborne. Frantic eleventh-hour preparations for meeting an assault across the Johore Strait were quite pitiful. Even the demolition of the causeway linking the island to the Malay Peninsula was mismanaged; at low tide, men could still wade across on remnants and rubble.

Less than a month after the capitulation of Singapore the Dutch gave up on Java. Their air force and navy already destroyed, they never committed the bulk of the colonial army to battle. By then the invasion of Burma, mounted from Thai territory, was progressing ahead of schedule. Rangoon had been taken and the retreat of British, Chinese, and American defenders had become a rout. The whole of Southeast Asia came under a single authority for the first and only time in its history.

OCCUPATION

The conquerors faced great problems in the establishment and implementation of their rule, but the most pervasive resulted from the inadequate supply of competent Japanese administrators. Not many Japanese commanded the requisite resources for governing their exotic prizes. Few knew indigenous languages; rare indeed was the Southeast Asian who had mastered Japanese. In acknowledgment of these circumstances, in the former Anglo-American colonies and in Thailand, English was regularly pressed into service as the only available vehicle of communication. When one considers the abysmal quality of the English spoken by all but a handful of Japanese, the awkwardness of the arrangement is obvious. Fortunately, Malay-Indonesian of the bazaar variety could be mastered quite quickly and was used in its homelands. To compound their linguistic difficulties, the Japanese had only a shallow knowledge of local cultures and societies. Acknowledgment of that inadequacy was made early, when the occupation commands assigned research teams to investigate a remarkable variety of subjects that are normally reserved to academicians.

Interest in the human composition of the captured lands was understandably born of the hope that Southeast Asians could be enlisted in the service of Japan. Wherever inter-ethnic animosities awaited exploitation, as between the Chinese and host peoples, or between majorities and minorities, policies of rule through communal division were adopted. Where religion was seen as a vital force in society, as in Burma or Indonesia, the Japanese strove to present themselves as defenders of Buddhism or, somewhat less credibly, of Islam. Where members of the established ruling or reigning elites were ready to cooperate, as in Indochina, the Philippines, Thailand, and Malaya, they were used. Where national movements appeared to be malleable, as in Burma or Indonesia, they were cautiously encouraged. Over all, Japan shone as the "leader of Asia, the protector of Asia, the light of Asia."

Policing the occupied countries was generally not a bothersome task, for the populations were inclined to receive the Japanese dispassionately. Only in the Philippines and Malaya was there resistance of consequence. Filipinos, on the eve of full independence when war came, were uniquely recalcitrant. Partisan bands harassed the Japanese throughout the occupation, though even in the Philippines, there were many who were prepared to collaborate with the conquerors. The postwar fate of such men would briefly be a central issue in the country's politics.

In Malaya, opposition to the Japanese came all but exclusively from Chinese oriented to Communism. A small number of Chinese leftist revolutionaries were trained at the last minute by the British to operate as saboteurs and guerrillas behind the line of Japanese advance. When the entire peninsula was overrun, the Communist Chinese took to the jungle to carry on the fight. Never able to engage substantial Japanese units, the jungle fighters were more an annoyance than a threat. Their real usefulness would have come if the Allies had been able to counterattack by landing an invasion force. As it eventually turned out, the Chinese guerrillas fought their bitterest campaign after the war, when they launched a struggle against the perpetuation of British colonialism.

Even though most of occupied Southeast Asia was quite placid, the Japanese were extremely apprehensive. Their secret and military police, never idle, terrorized the entire region. Torture and death were meted out to untold thousands. The Chinese were treated with particular savagery, but no people was immune. Any one suspected of pro-Allied leanings or even of skepticism toward Japan's pan-Asian mission was liable to be a target of the justly dreaded Kempeitai, the terror arm of the occupation.

Appalling though Kempeitai excesses were, far more people suffered and perished under conditions of economic disintegration than from police cruelty. The widespread breakdown of internal transportation caused hunger and even starvation in food-deficient areas. Devastating food shortages existed in some places, while other places were glutted with grain. Productivity in mining, lumbering, and petroleum extraction was depressed or interrupted as the result of damage inflicted during the invasion. Burma had been hit especially hard due to British scorched-earth destruction of oilfields and transportation systems. People whose livelihoods had been derived from working in facilities that were destroyed by war were made jobless. Far greater numbers, however, were reduced to poverty by the virtual cessation of export trade. All productive and service operations that had been developed to supply the world with tin, rubber, rice, and less important goods were affected. Japan had hoped to redirect the flow of exports for the support of her own industry and for the general welfare of the "Greater East Asia Co-Prosperity Sphere," but shipping tonnages were inadequate for the task. It was not long before Allied severance of Far Eastern sea lanes all but isolated Japan from her new empire. The naval blockade, established primarily by American submarines and aircraft, had a direct and painful impact on the economies of Southeast Asia.

Subsistence agriculture, since it was not geared to market demands, suffered the least under wartime conditions. For that reason, many of those thrown into unemployment or poverty by economic deterioration turned to marginal farming. The return to the land was most significant in Malaya, where many tens of thousands of Chinese who had formerly been employed in mining or estate agriculture scratched bare livings from plots on the fringes of the jungle. Those people, to be known later as squatters, were to cause much official concern during the postwar Communist insurgency.

Many destitute men who were unable to find land to till or who lacked peasant skills sought security by joining labor gangs organized by the Japanese for the construction of transportation lines or military installations. Indonesians in particular were recruited for such work, but all the occupied countries contributed men to the labor battalions. The world is familiar with the brutal treatment of Allied prisoners of war; less well known is the story of the misery of the masses of Southeast Asian laborers who were marched off, quite often never to return.

THE SPONSORSHIP OF INDEPENDENCE

The ideological justification of Japanese expansion rested on the promise of emancipation for East Asia through the expulsion of Western control and exploitation; and, however much the Tokyo directors of the enterprise may have acted tongue in cheek, expediency dictated that local support and cooperation be enlisted whenever possible. Consequently, national independence was pledged to a number of countries and, under rigidly circumscribed conditions, selectively granted.

Thailand of course could not be handed the freedom she had always possessed, so Japan treated her as an ally. Until after the tide of war had turned against his patrons, Phibun Songgram seemed thoroughly satisfied with the new pattern of power in Southeast Asia. He was grateful for Japanese support that had secured the return of parts of Cambodia and Laos to Bangkok's sovereignty. Further territorial expectations were stirred and national pride was served by the Japanese decision to permit Thai forces to occupy those parts of northern Malaya that the British had once removed from the shadow of Thai suzerainty. Phibun's appreciation was expressed by a Thai declaration of war against Britain and the United States, though the latter country found it useful to render the ultimate diplomatic insult by ignoring the matter.

The American refusal to consider Thailand an enemy was not designed solely to offend Phibun. A pro-Allied faction of Thais was supported by many influential men, including Pridi, another veteran of the 1932 coup and Phibun's chief rival. The Free Thai, as the members of the anti-Japanese movement were known, were represented in Washington by the Thai ambassador, who in effect headed a government in exile abroad, while Pridi worked behind the scenes at home. The activities of the Free Thai facilitated the establishment in wartime Thailand of a flourishing American espionage apparatus. In recognition of these facts, when peace came, the United States, regarding Thailand as a liberated friend and a symbol of self-determination in a world that had begun to reject colonialism, persuaded the British to ease their retributive claims.

In 1943 both Burma and the Philippines were proclaimed independent by the Japanese. Naturally, conditions in the two countries were quite different, but they had traveled far closer to political freedom than their neighbors. As a few representatives of the Thakin movement had actively assisted the Japanese in the conquest of Burma, there seemed to be a nucleus of local figures around which a puppet regime could be formed. Aung San had actually gone to Japan a year before the outbreak of war in the Pacific, and had subsequently recruited some thirty Thakins as the cadre of an "army" that took part in defeating the British. Ba Maw, who earlier had achieved fame as the defense attorney for the leader of the Saya San movement and who had risen to the premiership of a prewar coalition government, was similarly ready to serve the new masters of his country. Accordingly, Ba Maw was designated chief of a Japanese-sponsored state, while Aung San was put in command of Burmese military forces. Neither man was to remain loyal to Japan when an alternative presented itself.

The Philippines had not produced an organized body of activists sympathetic to Japan, but there was no scarcity of collaborationists once the archipelago had been incorporated into the Greater East Asian Co-Prosperity Sphere. After all, generations of the Filipino elite had known privilege and limited power under two colonial orders; the patronage of the most recent conqueror was not to be spurned. Thus, when independence of a sort was proclaimed in 1943, many familiar names were listed in the ruling ranks. José P. Laurel, who had been a Supreme Court justice in happier times, was picked to be president. He and all other servants of the Japanese stoutly claimed later that their actions had been motivated solely by a patriotic desire to protect the people against the invader and the afflictions of war.

The Indochina states remained under French administration until a few months before the end of the war. The arrangement would no doubt have lasted longer had the Japanese not grown uncertain of the reliability of their European agents. By March 1945, when the Japanese struck, it was clear that few Frenchmen could be counted upon to support the Axis cause; their homeland had been cleared of Germans and Hitler was within weeks of his ignominious end. More compelling, the Americans appeared capable of crossing to Vietnam from the recently liberated Philippines. The Japanese understandably were disturbed by the prospect of trying to defend the beaches of Indochina against American landings with untrustworthy French troops in the rear. Accordingly, the Japanese launched a *coup de force* and, after crushing lively resistance, disarmed and interned all French soldiers except for a few who heroically fought their way to free Chinese territory.

With the Europeans toppled from power, it became necessary to create a new façade of political authority. To his surprise, Emperor Bao Dai, the reigning symbol of the Vietnamese dynasty, was elevated from glittering obscurity to assume imperial power under Japanese auspices and supervision. The emperor had neither the authority nor the administrative machinery to lend effectiveness to his short-lived regime. The country sank into chaos. The Japanese were preoccupied with clinging to their military defenses; the reborn imperial Vietnamese state existed only in name.

In Laos and Cambodia, events followed essentially the same course as in Vietnam. The French were used by the Japanese until their obedience was in doubt and then overthrown. The two kingdoms of course continued to be reigned over by their royal figureheads. The Cambodian king, Norodom Sihanouk, was regarded as commendably docile, for he had been placed on the throne through irregular action in 1941 due to French fears that the more legitimate claimant might prove intractable. From a later perspective, the French choice of puppets would come to seem not a little curious.

Indonesia was not declared independent until after the Japanese capitulated in mid-August 1945. Preparations for the nominal transfer of sovereignty had been in progress for some time, but the war ended before they could be implemented. Nevertheless, the years of occupation brought much change to the Indies. In comparison with other colonies, the Dutch possession had contained an exceptionally large population of Europeans and Eurasians, who were given preferred treatment in employment in government and modern economic enterprises. As few Indonesians were able to compete for such opportunities, only a handful had received advanced training or enjoyed sophisticated experience. The need for men to replace the interned Dutch, however, obliged the Japanese to promote substantial numbers of Indonesians to middle- and upper-level posts which earlier would have been far beyond reach. Perhaps the efficiency of the new managers and administrators was low, but the ability of the country to survive without the Dutch was established in a lesson not to be forgotten. The formation by the Japanese of a local military organization similarly demonstrated that the arts of war were not to be mastered only by Europeans and Christian Amboinese.

While no puppet government was created in wartime Indonesia, there was movement in that direction. In 1943 an advisory body of local notables was formed for the purpose of giving Indonesians a role in policy formulation and administration. The group was headed by Sukarno, with Hatta serving as second in command. The volume of advice produced and accepted was minimal, but Sukarno was most helpful in his work to enlist up to 300,000 destitute men for labor service, from which many failed to return.

COLLAPSE AND CHAOS

The suddenness of Japan's military disintegration took Southeast Asia by surprise and, welcome though it was, the initial effects were painful. As just slightly more than a week elapsed between the bombing of Hiroshima and the emperor's broadcast acknowledging that "the war situation [had] developed not necessarily to Japan's advantage," Allied plans for the post-surrender period had to be hastily thrown together. More than a fortnight passed before the formal ceremony of capitulation could be held; and, over an extended period after that event, Allied troops could move but slowly to disarm and replace the Japanese in most of the countries they had occupied. Thus, for a considerable time after the middle of August 1945, turmoil and uncertainty reigned widely as various nationalist and partisan bodies sought to settle old scores and win power during the twilight between Japanese rule and Western recovery.

Burma and the Philippines, the two most cruelly damaged countries of the region, in a sense were fortunate, for much of the wartime destruction inflicted upon them had come during the process of liberation from the Japanese. In April 1945, after months of secret parleys with the British, Aung San threw in his lot with the Allies and turned on his erstwhile patrons. His Burmese soldiers joined the Anglo-Chinese-American force that had already chased the enemy halfway to the sea and would take Rangoon in a matter of days. The Philippine islands had been reached by the American juggernaut in October 1944 and were effectively liberated within a few months. Both countries, therefore, were compensated for wartime losses by the comparatively smooth re-establishment of administrative control—though the fragmented ethno-political character of Burma would soon bring fresh insecurity.

In Indonesia and in Vietnam, as the Japanese crumbled, nationalists rushed to win power before Western domination could be reimposed. The Allied blueprint for a brief period of postwar transition provided that American forces would control the Philippines, while British units would be stationed in all other colonial parts of Southeast Asia—except in Vietnam north of the sixteenth parallel, where Nationalist Chinese soldiers were to be assigned. The task of local nationalists, then, was to act with speed before foreign military commanders could transfer power to internationally recognized legitimate authorities—that is, to reconstituted colonial governments.

In view of Sukarno's subsequent style of political operations and ora-torical flamboyance, it is difficult to understand the Indonesian leader's apparent timidity at the time of Japan's surrender. He did not instantly proclaim his country's freedom but had to be abducted by younger, more impatient patriots and argued into issuing a declaration of inde-pendence on August 17th, two days after Tokyo sued for peace. De-layed though it was, the announcement touched off a great wave of nationalist activity, most of it at first uncoordinated and therefore de-structive of public order, but all directed toward the prevention of a Dutch return.

In March 1944, a year and a half before the end of the war, Ho Chi Minh had organized a provisional government for Vietnam that was committed to the destruction of both Japanese military occupation and French colonialism. When surrender came, the Communists and their confederates in the revolutionary movement, generally known as the Vietminh, moved rapidly. On the same day that brought Indonesia's declaration of independence, Vietminh personnel initiated the smooth seizure of authority in Hanoi. Saigon for a time remained a scene of confused maneuvers among contending political and religious forces, since the Communists were relatively weak in the southern part of the country. However, organizational discipline and the fact that during the final months of the war Ho Chi Minh had won a measure of recognition and support from the Kuomintang Chinese and, more im-portantly, the Americans soon promoted the Vietminh to majority control over a newly improvised administration in Cochin China. Meanwhile, an improbable drama took place in Annam, where Bao Dai relinquished the imperial throne at Hué to be rewarded with an advisory position in the Vietminh.

The pace of events was so swift that, a little more than a fortnight after the end of Japanese control, Ho Chi Minh could proclaim the inauguration of the Democratic Republic of Vietnam. Ho headed the new government, and other Communists were placed in charge of the significant ministries, though the formula for uniting all patriots in a common stand against the French continued to be honored at least symbolically. The viability of the coalition would soon be severely tested, and in the south the nationalist alliance would be broken. September 1945 marked not the end of Vietnamese suffering, but rather the start of a more brutal phase of national agony.

The smouldering animosities that divided the peoples of Malaya fueled violence in the chaotic weeks after the Japanese collapse. Chinese guerrillas came out of the jungle determined to assume control. Their numbers did not permit the establishment of a centralized regime that might seek to deny entry to the British, but there were more than enough armed men for the purpose of inflicting punishment on those considered guilty of having aided the enemy. Though Chinese traitors were held to be the chief culprits, many Malays had carried on quite comfortably in wartime positions in the administration and the police, and members of their community were also singled out for vengeance. The predictable outcome of course was the ignition of widespread, grisly, intercommunal riots. The death toll will never be known, but a distressingly fixed pattern of latent fear and recurrent bloodshed was set.

Only tranquil Thailand escaped the consequences of Japan's overnight distintegration. No Western force was poised to strike against the country's freedom; no partisans made a bid for power. The higher-ranking politicians, who had been pro-Japanese, including Phibun, had been replaced by neutralists well before the end of the war. With the Allied victory, it was only necessary to elevate Pridi to power to ensure an unruffled transition. The nationalist struggles that engulfed their neighbors as they strove to prevent colonialist restoration did not touch the Thais.

READINGS

Abaya, Hernando J., *Betrayal in the Philippines*, New York: Wyn, 1946.

Agoncillo, Teodoro A., *The Fateful Years: Japan's Adventure in the Philippines, 1941-1945*, Manila: R. P. Garcia, 1965.

Anderson, Benedict, *Java in a Time of Revolution; Occupation and Resistance, 1944-1946*, Ithaca: Cornell University Press, 1972.

Aziz, M. A., *Japan's Colonialism and Indonesia*, The Hague: Martinus Nijhoff, 1955.

Barber, Noel, *A Sinister Twilight: The Fall of Singapore, 1942*, Boston: Houghton Mifflin, 1968.

Benda, Harry J., *The Crescent and the Rising Sun: Indonesian Islam under the Japanese Occupation, 1942-1945*, The Hague, van Hoeve, 1958.

———; James K. Irikura; Kishi Koichi, *Japanese Military Administration in Indonesia: Selected Documents*, New Haven: Yale University Press, 1965.

Chapman, E. Spencer, *The Jungle Is Neutral*, London: Chatto and Windus, 1954.

Collis, Maurice S., *Last and First in Burma*, London: Faber and Faber, 1956.

Elsbree, Willard H., *Japan's Role in Southeast Asian Nationalist Movements, 1940-45*, Cambridge: Harvard University Press, 1953.

Friend, Theodore, *Between Two Empires: The Ordeal of the Philippines, 1929-1946*, New Haven: Yale University Press, 1965.

Hartendorp, Abraham van Heyningen, *The Japanese Occupation of the Philippines*, Manila: Bookmark, 1967.

Jones, F. C., *Japan's New Order in East Asia, 1937-1945*, London: Oxford University Press, 1954.

Lebra, Joyce C., *Japan's Greater East Asia Co-Prosperity Sphere in World War II: Selected Readings and Documents*, New York: Oxford University Press, 1974.

Maung Maung, ed., *Aung San of Burma*, The Hague: Martinus Nijhoff, 1962.

Nu, Thakin, *Burma, under the Japanese*, New York: St. Martin's, 1954.

Percival, A. E., *The War in Malaya*, London: Eyre and Spottiswoode, 1949.

Steinberg, David J., *Philippine Collaboration in World War II*, Manila: Ann Arbor: University of Michigan Press, 1967.

Trager, Frank N., ed., *Burma: Japanese Military Administration, Selected Documents, 1941-1945*, Philadelphia: University of Pennsylvania Press, 1971.

Tsuji Masonobu, *Singapore, The Japanese Version*, Sydney: Ure Smith, 1960.

Willoughby, C. A., comp., *The Guerrilla Resistance Movement in the Philippines, 1941-1945*, New York: Vantage, 1972.

11
Nationalism Triumphant

The Western powers returned to Southeast Asia with confidence born of their collective ignorance of the transformations that had taken place during the years of war. It was widely assumed that popular restlessness could be contained once wartime dislocations were set right and economic recovery begun. No doubt, as in prewar days, a few nationalist firebrands would have to be brought under control; but surely the general passivity of the masses could not have been much altered. The Americans in the Philippines and the British in Burma anticipated continued evolution toward local sovereignty, but they also envisioned the retention of political influence and economic dominance. Elsewhere, the Dutch and the French simply could not accept the thought of substantive changes in their colonies and protectorates, while the British could not imagine Malaya without their experienced hand at the helm. Only the United States was justified in its assuredness; and even in the Philippines, there were men prepared to resist outside manipulation.

THE PHILIPPINES

The transitional decade between colonial status and liberty for the Philippines was drawing to a close as the war ended, and there was no wish among Americans or Filipinos to postpone the transfer of sovereignty. Hence, freedom for the Philippines came, as promised and scheduled, in 1946, on the fourth of July, a date chosen to reaffirm the institutional similarity and emotional compatibility of the former master and the new state. To underscore the symbolism of celebrating independence on the same day, other, more concrete bonds between the two countries were devised. It is not far from the mark to regard those tangible ties as neo-colonial, for they clearly infringed on Philippine freedom of action and served to keep the islands dependent upon the United States.

In both the military and economic realms, the celebration of Philippine independence meant next to nothing. The American Congress enacted legislation intended to bind the economy of the islands to the United States for at least a generation. The terms of the act of 1946 provided for free trade between the United States and the Philippines for a period of eight years, to be followed by two decades in which tariffs would be levied at rates to be increased by 5 per cent annually, until the final abolition of preferences by 1974. It was argued that the gradual liquidation of free trade would give Philippine exporters an opportunity to find markets outside the United States, the destination of two-thirds of their prewar shipments. Of course, not by accident, American goods entering the Philippines under favored terms would be sold at prices not to be matched by competitors.

A second American device to limit Philippine economic autonomy was monetary. By law, the peso was welded to the dollar at the artificial rate of two to one. The disadvantages to the Philippines would be substantial and costly. Island products were not competitive in the world market, for their prices in dollar terms were unreasonably high. Furthermore, an outflow of Philippine capital was stimulated by the availability of dollars at bargain rates. Indeed, the chief purpose of the fiscal arrangement appears to have been to provide smooth trans-Pacific passage for American funds previously invested in the Philippines that might eventually seek repatriation.

The section of the 1946 Congressional act that most outraged the Filipinos required that American individuals and corporations in the Philippines be treated on a basis of full legal equality with local citizens and enterprises. There was no reciprocal arrangement to protect Filipino interests in the United States, though the granting of such a concession would certainly not have been expensive. The insistence on parity for Americans in Philippine extractive industries and public utilities was received with dismay and hostility in Manila.

Responding with a total lack of delicacy, Washington made it clear that the provision of economic aid to support postwar recovery in the Philippines would be contingent upon the granting of the unique privilege of parity to Americans in business in the islands. An amendment to the constitution of the new state that would extend to Americans rights denied all other foreigners was bitterly opposed in legislative debate in Manila and passed by but one vote. Thereafter began the flow of millions of United States dollars to the Philippines to repair the devastation of war, to recompense Filipinos who had fought alongside the Americans, and to begin construction for economic development. The help was sorely needed, for at the time the transportation systems of the archipelago were a shambles, mines were flooded, machinery on agricultural estates was unusable, and much of Manila looked like the face of the moon.

The special position of the Americans in the economy was matched by parallel military arrangements. Philippine leaders feared that the withdrawal of United States forces would leave the islands vulnerable to outside attack and, more immediately, to internal rebellion. When independence came, Communist-led insurgents, initially organized to fight the Japanese and known as Huks, held extensive areas of northern Luzon and seemed capable of attacking the capital itself. In addition to the security to be afforded by a continued foreign military presence, a considerable amount of money was involved. Service personnel spent huge sums locally, and American installations gave direct or indirect employment to tens of thousands of Filipinos. Consequently, the Philippine government was more than ready to permit American retention of more than a score of bases and to grant extraterritorial legal rights to those who manned them. Moreover, the Philippine armed forces were kept under decisive American influence by an official pledge that virtually all equipment and supplies would be obtained from the United States.

It presumably goes without saying that the alien economic and military dominance maintained over the Philippines after independence ensured continued American political influence, particularly in foreign affairs. When the cold war spread to Asia, Manila would unswervingly follow the line laid down by Washington. In time, however, when Philippine national pride made humble subservience to the United States intolerable, the restrictions and concessions of 1946 came under mounting attack and were eventually modified through actions to be considered in the next chapter.

BURMA

There was no timetable for the freeing of Burma. Britain was prepared to negotiate, albeit with some reluctance, but it was initially believed that the transfer of sovereignty would be made slowly and hedged by safeguards to protect British interests. Time, however, did not permit gradualism. Burma was astir with nationalism; Britain, enfeebled by two world wars, no longer could do anything about the erosion of her imperial grandeur.

Before Anglo-Burmese consultations could begin, the issue of collaboration by nationalist leaders with the Japanese required resolution. When Aung San took his army over to the winning side in the climactic final weeks of the war, the question was expeditiously settled. The British issued a formal declaration to the effect that nobody who had acted out of sincerity was to be condemned, even if the actions had been anti-British. The rule was certainly more tasteful than the arrangement imposed on the Philippines, where Douglas MacArthur arbitrarily exonerated his friends and political allies, while other Filipinos stood indicted. The injustice of the American general so muddied the collaborationist issue that it soon lost meaning, especially after Manuel Roxas, a prominent wartime puppet, was restored to general's rank by MacArthur and subsequently elected to the presidency of his country in 1946.

Despite inept efforts by the first postwar British governor to foster a political alternative, Aung San was clearly in command of the main force of Burmese nationalism. He headed a coalition of anti-colonialists that had originated as an underground resistance movement during the Japanese occupation and proudly retained its wartime name, the Anti-Fascist People's Freedom League. When an extremist faction of Communists in its ranks was expelled after an abortive bid for power early in 1946, the AFPFL acquired enhanced respectability in British eyes. In August of that year a new governor, Sir Hubert Rance, took over from his rather inflexible predecessor and began to implement the extrication from empire sought by the postwar Labour government in Britain. The march to Burmese independence was accelerated and, despite grievous setbacks, would be completed in less than a year and a half.

Aung San led an AFPFL delegation to London in January 1947, in response to an invitation to participate in Anglo-Burmese talks on the political future of his country. The conversations went extremely well, possibly because it was clear to both sides that failure would have touched off a massive insurrection that neither moderate Burmese nor the British could have hoped to control. Strikes then immobilized much of the economic and administrative life of Burma; Communist dissidents seemed capable of swinging the nationalist struggle to the far and violent left. As always, the various minority peoples, especially the Karens, appeared ready to take up rebellious arms to avoid Burman hegemony.

The agreement signed at the conclusion of the London negotiations provided that Burma would immediately become self-governing under circumstances that gave the country de facto dominion status under a cabinet headed by Aung San. Accordingly, elections for a constituent assembly were scheduled for April 1947. The balloting would bring the public into the drafting of a constitution for post-colonial Burma; more important, an electoral triumph for Aung San and the AFPFL would represent popular endorsement of relative moderation and the rejection of the extremists who opposed peaceful advance to independence. The people more than lived up to expectations; the AFPFL routed the divided opposition, winning seats in a ratio of about seventeen to one over their political enemies.

At that point, fate struck most cruelly. A political rival of Aung San who had defected from the AFPFL, charging that the party's leader was insufficiently revolutionary, and who, for lack of a more productive plan, had boycotted the April elections, engineered a murderous plot. In mid-July two hired killers were sent to break into a cabinet meeting and gun down those present with automatic weapons. Aung San and six of his ministers died. U Saw, the perpetrator of the assassinations, had planned to blame the crime on the British, thereby plunging

Burma into a conflagration of revolutionary violence to be exploited by himself. Instead, his insane plan was exposed, and after a sensational trial, U Saw went to the gallows.

The murders seemed to leave Burma without top leadership. The nominal second-in-command of the AFPFL, U Nu, was immediately installed as head of the Rangoon government. He was known primarily as a rather dreamy man of profound religious dedication. Nevertheless, it was up to U Nu to lead the country through the transitional months before complete independence and to be its first prime minister after the transfer of power.

The Union of Burma officially came into being on January 4, 1948, at an uncomfortable and improbable predawn hour selected as auspicious by trusted astrologers. The troubled subsequent history of the new state suggests that their reading of the stars may have been imperfect. In any event, the British were out, though still pledged to extend economic and military aid to their former possession, and Burma could begin her experiment in constitutional democracy. Awesome problems would arise as ethnic and political minorities sought to challenge the central authority of Rangoon. Internationally, Burma sought to avoid all foreign entanglements, even to the extent of refusing membership in the British Commonwealth. The goal of total diplomatic independence, like that of secure internal unity, would not be fully attained.

INDONESIA

The Indonesian fight for independence was both costly and protracted. Sporadic warfare against the Dutch, interspersed with periods of political maneuvering, continued from the defeat of Japan till the end of 1949. The pain and the bitterness of the contest resulted from a number of factors. For one thing, the archipelago was by no means united in opposition to colonialism. The primary strength of the nationalists was found on Java; many of the peoples on other islands were either apolitical or fearful of Javanese domination. Even within the nationalist camp, there was fragmentation, for the Communists in the movement had their own revolutionary aspirations. The Dutch naturally sought to take advantage of Indonesian divisions.

Perhaps more influential than the hope that the centrifugal forces in

Indonesian politics could be exploited was the Dutch view of the islands. To great numbers of Hollanders, Indonesia was home; and, directly or indirectly, the country was the chief source of the livelihoods of a major proportion of the people in the Netherlands. The emotional and economic stakes were simply too high to permit the Dutch to bow out gracefully. Moreover, Indonesian nationalism had been seen as a minor phenomenon prior to the Japanese invasion and had been quite handily controlled. Certainly, the postwar turmoil was abnormal and could be ended through proper action once the Netherlands presence in the archipelago was effectively re-established.

During the war Queen Wilhelmina had promised, from exile in London, that peace would bring a re-evaluation of the political relations among her various territories; and in 1945 the Dutch were ready to talk about readjustments that would lead to progress toward home rule for the Indies. The Indonesian revolutionaries, for their part, held that independence was a *fait accompli*—that since August 17, 1945, there had been nothing to talk about other than the speedy liquidation of all vestiges of colonialism. The impasse made war unavoidable.

Unexpected though it might seem, the first skirmishes and battles fought by the Indonesians were not directed against the Dutch but against the Japanese, and the British forces caught in the middle. The surrender terms imposed on Japan required that her troops in occupied countries maintain order pending the arrival of Allied units. Thus, numerous clashes took place between Indonesian revolutionaries and the Japanese in the weeks after Sukarno's declaration of independence. When British forces disarmed and replaced the Japanese, the task of holding the Indies fell to them; and the largest military engagement of the transitional period, the battle of Surabaya in early November 1945, resulted in the expulsion of Indonesian power from the east Java city by Anglo-Indian troops. The occasion was the last on which Indian soldiers served under alien command in major combat. There had, in fact, been some apprehension among the British over the possibility that the Indians might refuse to fire on fellow Asians who, like their countrymen at home, were valiantly trying to break colonialist chains. Indian soldiers, however, had been sufficiently provoked by Indonesian attacks and excesses to remain obedient to their commanders.

While the British tried to keep the peace, an effort that was essentially confined to the cities, the Dutch returned to claim the prize they had held for three and a half centuries. The campaign for colonial re-conquest was ultimately to involve some 150,000 Dutch troops, a huge force in proportion to the Netherlands population base and in terms of the impoverished resources of a country that had suffered cruelly under German occupation. Some of the Dutchmen had somehow managed to get to the United States or Australia to receive military training during the war; others were veterans of the prewar colonial army; many had been newly inducted at home.

The size of the Indonesian nationalist army cannot be confidently gauged, for units might exist solely on paper or be understrength. Furthermore, a great number of men were irregulars whose discipline and accountability were less than reliable. A large proportion of the officers had been trained within an auxiliary army created by the Japanese; a far smaller number had begun military careers in the old Indies colonial army. The most exuberant and hence the least predictable Indonesian fighters came from the ranks of the restless young. The *pemuda*, as the youthful militants were known, were inclined to independent and violent action that considerably embarrassed Sukarno in his efforts to negotiate with the enemy. Dutch intransigence, of course, was an equally formidable obstacle to the peaceful determination of the country's political future.

Nevertheless, Dutch-Indonesian negotiations went on, largely under the pressure of outsiders, most conspicuously, the Americans. The consequent internationalization of the issue of Indonesian freedom can be regarded as having originated in the first attempt of the United States to dominate the Southeast Asian scene as the old colonial powers departed with a measure of grace or were expelled by force of arms.

American intervention came only as the Indonesian situation deteriorated. Initially, Britain played the more influential role, specifically by bringing the Dutch and the revolutionaries to the conference table late in 1946. A sense of urgency prevailed, since the Anglo-Indian occupation force was about to begin its departure and sought to leave stability in its wake. The Dutch did not then feel strong enough to open a campaign to smother the revolution; the Indonesian leadership, beset by internal challenges, was also prepared to talk. The result was the conclusion of an agreement at Linggadjati, initialed in November 1946 and signed the following March.

The agreement was a realistic compromise, but it was subject to conflicting interpretation and was dependent solely upon the good faith of signatories who deeply mistrusted each other. Its terms, distilled to essentials, called for the early establishment of a new sovereign state, the United States of Indonesia, consisting of three parts, each internally self-governing. The largest of the three would be Java and Sumatra joined together under Sukarno's republican government. The other two components would be a new Bornean state and a unit comprised of all the lesser islands that make up the eastern half of the archipelago. The federal pattern clearly was designed to quarantine revolution inside its home and protect the peoples of Borneo and the eastern islands against infection. The preservation of a measure of Dutch political power in Indonesia would thereby be ensured.

The Linggadjati accord also provided for the founding of a Netherlands-Indonesian union, envisaged as a partnership of equals under a shared symbol, the Dutch crown. In the preparatory period leading to the emergence of the United States of Indonesia, Dutch sovereignty, de jure, was to continue over the archipelago; Dutch property rights were to be protected; and the preservation of peace in Java and Sumatra was gradually to be made the responsibility of Sukarno's forces. The storm arising from quarrels over the last point soon caused the détente to founder.

By late July 1947 the fragile peace was broken. Feeling justified by the inability of the Indonesians to control lawlessness in republican territory or to let Netherlands forces do the job, the Dutch sent motorized troops to capture almost all the urban areas of eastern and western Java plus the richer sections of Sumatra and to maintain an uneasy hold on them. The offensive was swift and quickly attained its objectives, but was nevertheless a failure. Indonesian units continued to roam most of the countryside and never ceased partisan warfare. More decisive, foreign opinion was profoundly shocked. Batavia could call the operation a "police action," but in much of the world it was condemned as colonialist aggression.

The debates at the United Nations generated by events in Indonesia produced a resolution calling for a cease-fire and later brought about the creation of a tripartite commission charged with sponsoring fresh Indonesian-Dutch negotiations. The commission was composed of diplomats from Australia, Belgium, and the United States, with the representative of the third inevitably thrust into dominance.

After much backing and filling, in mid-January 1948, the warring sides signed an agreement named after the American naval destroyer *Renville*, aboard which talks had been convened. The document was basically a repetition of that drawn up at Linggadjati in 1946, except that the revolutionaries, much reduced in territory by Dutch attack, were obliged to agree to the scheduling of plebiscites to allow the peoples of Java and Sumatra to determine their relations with the Sukarno republicans within the projected United States of Indonesia. Needless to say, the Renville agreement was no more viable than its predecessor; in a very few months, the war was resumed on a grander scale.

Most of 1948 was a busy time for the contenders in Indonesia. The Dutch worked fast to plant cooperative regimes in territories under their control and to starve the republic into docility through the imposition of a blockade; the republicans were obliged by their enfeebled military circumstances to look to sympathetic foreign governments for salvation. Each side of course complained that the other sought to destroy the Renville agreement. Whatever truth there may have been in the accusations, the question was soon made academic, for the resumption of hostilities came in December.

Before the final round of Dutch-Indonesian fighting, however, Sukarno was able to win a signal victory over enemies within the nationalist movement and to gain new international stature. Misguided by the conviction that their time to strike had come, the Indonesian Communists attempted to seize command of the revolution. Hungry victims of the Dutch blockade, patriots disillusioned by the failure of the West —particularly the United States—to restrain the Dutch, and demobilized, irregular soldiers were recruited for the Communist enterprise. The coalition of extreme leftists and various disgruntled elements was loose and undisciplined. When a coup against Sukarno came in mid-September in the region of the central Javanese city of Madiun, the jerry-built structure was speedily demolished. No general rising of the masses was touched off; most of those military men who had seemed to waver between loyalty to Sukarno and Communist sympathies continued to waver or stood with the republicans. In a matter of days, the republic's best troops chased the putschists of Madiun into the mountains where, after some weeks punctuated by shifting skirmishes, the rebels were captured or destroyed.

Communist greed and ineptitude, viewed retrospectively, were manifested at a most auspicious moment for Sukarno. Before September 1948 foreign observers, notably within the American officialdom, feared that the Indonesian struggle for independence seemed to be coming under the domination of Stalinists. The Dutch naturally encouraged the view that hostilities in Indonesia were the product of cold-war rivalry, that the choice was between democracy and Communism. The rebellion at Madiun cleansed Sukarno of the red taint; his crushing of the Communists promoted him, in Western eyes, to unquestioned legitimacy as a moderate nationalist. Had the Communists not obligingly introduced their unintended *deus ex machina*, the Indonesian war might well have been internationalized in the pattern that was soon to take shape in Indochina.

The Madiun rebellion hurt the Dutch as much as it helped Sukarno. Consequently, the colonialists decided on a dangerous and desperate course. An ultimatum was issued demanding that the republic accommodate itself to inclusion within a federal structure subject to Dutch manipulation. Though Sukarno's government ruled about 40 percent of the people of Indonesia, it was to be treated as a mere constituent part of a federation that would also admit to full membership fifteen small puppet states created by the Dutch in areas under their military occupation. Apparently fearful that the hard-pressed republicans might feel obliged to accept the odious terms of the ultimatum, the Dutch insisted that a reply had to come within eighteen hours—a period too short to permit a response of any sort, for none was wanted. A military operation against the republican capital of Jogjakarta had already begun to roll.

On December 19, 1948, at the traditional dawn hour, the Dutch blow came. Bombing and a paratrooper landing at the Jogjakarta airfield quickly gave the attackers a base from which to mount a swift advance. By late afternoon the city was in Dutch hands, and Sukarno and most of the revolutionary leadership were prisoners. During the balance of the week before Christmas, Dutch forces gained control over the main roads and towns of republican territory. They were then faced with the problem of holding and exploiting their gains.

Guerrilla resistance plagued the victorious Hollanders and soon had them on the defensive; the public was powerfully inclined toward noncooperation with the conquerors; the captive republican leaders refused to call on their forces to quit the fight; most decisive, a tide of international denunciation engulfed the Dutch. The young United Nations went through the motions of asking for a cessation of hostilities and the release of Sukarno; subsequently, other well-intended demands were issued and ignored. Far more influential were rumblings from the United States Congress, where powerful legislators threatened to block the flow of American postwar aid to the Netherlands unless the Dutch agreed to negotiate in good faith with the Indonesian republicans. It was clearly a form of diplomatic blackmail; and, helped by anti-colonial political elements in Holland, the tactic succeeded. By June 1949 Sukarno and his lieutenants had been freed from detention and were back in Jogjakarta, once again the republican capital. The next month brought a Dutch-republican cease-fire and the opening of discussions at The Hague that resulted in Indonesian independence by the end of the year.

Incorporated in the Dutch-Indonesian agreement that ended nearly three and a half centuries of Netherlands rule in the Indies were some concessions to Dutch pride and to Indonesian regionalism. The federal structure so favored by the Dutch was preserved. A Dutch-Indonesian Union, under the symbol of the Netherlands crown, was established to facilitate binational consultation and cooperation. The western half of New Guinea was to remain under Dutch sovereignty pending eventual disposition. Only a few months passed before independent Indonesia abandoned federalism to become a unitary state. The Dutch-Indonesian Union never became a reality. The New Guinea question was to remain uneasily dormant until reactivated in a time of renewed Dutch-Indonesian quarreling a decade later. The former Dutch half of the huge island was finally handed to Indonesia by the United Nations in 1963.

INDOCHINA

The republican triumph in Indonesia demonstrated that Western material and technical superiority no longer could be counted upon to smother a determined people, galvanized by nationalism and capable of turning the political and diplomatic artifice learned from the colonialists against their oppressors. The message ought to have been loud and clear, especially to the French, who by 1949 were in the third year of war in Vietnam. But, of course, France did not equate herself with Holland. She was a great power; her greatness, as de Gaulle said at the time, largely derived from the possession of colonies girdling the earth. Moreover, as the Vietnamese nationalist revolutionaries were led by Communists, the French imagined their colonial war to be a sacred undertaking, a noble sacrifice to halt Stalinist expansion. Not incidentally, the United States was inclined to accept the crusading pretensions of France and, by 1953, would pay 80 percent of the financial costs of the colonial war. (Many Dutchmen must have envied the French for their ability to exploit American anxieties.)

The confusion of the weeks following Japan's surrender had permitted the French to re-establish their authority in Cochin China. The British general in command of the Anglo-Indian force sent to disarm and repatriate Japanese soldiers south of the sixteenth parallel was either unimaginative or implacably colonialist, for he actively aided the French in their seizure of Saigon in late September 1945. At that time, newly arrived French paratroopers, supported by units of the colonial army that had just been freed from six months of Japanese internment and rearmed by the British, took control of the city and disbanded the factionalized Vietnamese coalition regime that had sought to govern Cochin China. The French celebrated their victory by mounting a campaign of cruelty against Vietnamese thought to lean toward nationalism. The counterproductivity of such vengefulness in a land aflame with nationalism can be readily imagined. Determined guerrilla resistance denied most of the hinterland of the south to the French, even though they were militarily supported in their offensive by both British and Japanese forces.

In the north, Chinese Nationalist occupation troops did not interfere with the consolidation of administrative control by the Vietminh. For one thing, the Chinese were frankly hostile toward the French, from whom they had suffered much during the century of China's semi-colonial humiliation. For another, the soldiers of Chiang Kai-shek may simply have been too busy looting to take a serious interest in politics, for the months of the Chinese presence in Tonkin and northern Annam were spent in boisterous pilferage of historic proportions.

Evacuation of the Chinese force in the north was the prime objective of the French, who expected that colonial stability could then be restored. China charged a stiff diplomatic price for her cooperation. The Franco-Chinese agreement achieved in late February 1946 cost France all her special treaty rights in China and won new security for Chinese nationals resident in Indochina; in exchange, the Chinese occupation army was ordered home almost immediately.

Rid of the Chinese encumbrance, France still had to deal with the Vietminh in order to return to the north. Ho Chi Minh—no longer hopeful that American professions of anti-colonialism might be translated into political support; denied encouragement by Stalin, who was then preoccupied with the European theater of cold-war operations; and admittedly fearful of Chinese designs on Tonkin—concluded an agreement with the French early in March 1946. The terms of the accord included French recognition of the Vietminh state in the north as an autonomous member of an Indochinese federation and of the French Union, *née* empire. In return, Ho approved the movement of French troops into Tonkin primarily for the purpose of protecting French civilians in the Hanoi area. In a few months, the French force in the north would open a full-scale offensive against the Vietminh, and thus begin a war that would go on for eight years and be followed by an even longer and more terrible conflict.

Both the French and the Vietminh spent most of 1946 playing for the time needed to prepare for the next round of their contest. France sought to build up her armed strength in the north, while securing the south as a pacified base area; Ho Chi Minh knew well that the deficiencies in arms and training of his troops could not be speedily corrected. Accordingly, negotiations and intrigue occupied both sides as Vietnam moved toward war. At one point, Ho even led a delegation to France in a futile effort to win concessions. Though neither side could reasonably expect a political solution to save Vietnam, France was the more eager to resolve the issue by force of arms, and from her came the first blow.

Confident that their superiority in arms would quickly break the Vietminh, the French in late November 1946 moved to take Haiphong and its environs. The battle continued for several days and killed between six and twenty thousand civilians, depending on whose figures are believed. The high death toll was primarily the result of a naval bombardment of Vietnamese residential areas that was militarily pointless, though the destructive role of the French ships seemed to please Admiral d'Argenlieu, the high commissioner at Saigon, an unabashed imperialist who, rather curiously, had spent the years between the two world wars in a monastery.

Even after the loss of Haiphong, Ho Chi Minh tried to avoid full-scale war. For a month, while military preparations went forward, the Vietminh continued to negotiate with the French. It was a futile exercise, for the French, certain of their invincibility, demanded the surrender of Hanoi. Ho's rejection of the French ultimatum was signaled by the outbreak of hostilities in the Vietminh capital on December 20, the date the First Indochina War officially began.

The war followed a now familiar course. Cities were held by Western troops; most of the countryside was essentially in the hands of nationalist revolutionary forces. French convoys moving along the roads linking strongpoints were regularly ambushed by the Vietminh. It was combat between an army made sluggish by a wealth of arms and equipment and an elusive enemy whose greatest assets were determination and popular support. Successive French commanders arrived in Indochina bearing new plans for breaking the stalemate, for achieving final victory. Finally, in early 1954, the Vietminh soldiers were drawn into the open, lured into combat for a fixed position, where French armed superiority would surely decide the contest. An obscure town near the Laotian border was the site of the battle expected to be in the European style for which the French generals had yearned. The small town was, of course, Dienbienphu.

The decision to make Dienbienphu a fortress was not solely based on the hope that the Vietminh would be tricked into attacking an impregnable position. The place also guarded the chief route into northern Laos, and therefore had to be held to prevent major Vietminh incursions into the landlocked kingdom. The French reasonably felt that their difficulties in Vietnam would be disastrously compounded if Laos were also set aflame.

The battle of Dienbienphu, one of the pivotal engagements of history, opened in mid-March 1954. By that time the French had grown impatient for a chance to make telling use of their assumed material mastery. The delayed start of the Vietminh attack actually resulted from the care invested in preparations by General Vo Nguyen Giap, an academician by training, who had proved to be an inspired military tactician. Giap had used the months prior to the assault to ring Dienbienphu with men and, more tellingly, artillery, all concealed in the forested hillsides that surrounded the French position. Formidable supply problems were overcome through the use of bicycles to move food, ammunition, and disassembled heavy weapons and equipment. Thousands of men pushed laden bicycles along jungle paths to deliver cargoes and, then, returned to Vietminh base areas for new loads. Logistics really decided the issue. The Vietminh, greatly strengthened by guns sent from the People's Republic of China, simply smothered the French, who at the beginning were totally dependent upon deliveries by aircraft and soon had to rely on uncertain parachute drops.

Giap's army developed the art of tunneling to new levels of refinement. Night after night, assault troops burrowed closer to the French lines. Guns, as well as men, were moved up unseen. Howitzers and, contrary to orthodox expectations, anti-aircraft weapons were dragged through the tunnels to fire point-blank at the defenses and the airfield of Dienbienphu. The surprise and gloom caused by the Vietminh cannonade were dramatized by the French artillery commander who committed suicide on the second day of the battle in a gesture that doubtless did little to inspire confidence among comrades left behind.

Through April and the first week of May, the French perimeter was relentlessly reduced. A series of assaults by the Vietminh caused grisly losses among the besieged garrison of metropolitan Frenchmen, colonial Africans, men of the Foreign Legion (largely German), and Vietnamese under French command. The Vietminh lost even more killed and wounded before the fortress and its surviving defenders were captured on May 7, 1954. Though only a small percentage of the total French force in Vietnam was destroyed at Dienbienphu, the political impact of the defeat broke what little remained of the will of the government and the electorate in France. Settlement at virtually any price seemed inescapable, particularly as direct American intervention—periodically advocated by Secretary of State Dulles and Vice President Nixon, among other cold warriors—had been ruled out by Eisenhower in what may well have been his most perceptive presidential moment. As a matter of fact, the international conference that would end French colonialism in Indochina had begun its deliberations even before the final days of the great battle.

The cease-fire agreement devised at Geneva and concluded in late July 1954 militarily divided Vietnam at the seventeenth parallel of latitude. Vietminh troops were to move north of the line; French forces were to be sent south and repatriated. For three hundred days, civilians were allowed to migrate from one zone to the other. Some 900,000 people consequently left the north to become refugees in the strange and generally inhospitable south. About two-thirds of the northerners taking flight were Roman Catholics; the rest were people in fear of Vietminh reprisals or were overseas Chinese who sensed that it was unlikely that free enterprise would prosper under Communism.

According to the Geneva agreement, the ultimate destiny of Vietnam was to be determined in July 1956, when a nationwide election would enable the populace to choose between reunification under Ho Chi Minh's government at Hanoi or under the non-Communist administration at Saigon. But, of course, the plebiscite was never conducted, and the country remained split. The only positive political consequence of the Geneva agreement was the final liquidation of French colonialism in Vietnam, no small achievement in itself, though only a first step toward lifting the country out of the misery that had engulfed it.

As the Vietnamese rid themselves of French rule, their neighbors in Laos and Cambodia followed suit. Indeed, the two protectorates had been granted independence somewhat earlier than Vietnam. In the autumn of 1953, as the war against the Vietminh approached its finale, the French formally surrendered their authority over Laos in order to lessen the burdens of empire. At about the same time, Norodom Sihanouk, no longer the pliant adolescent the French had installed in 1941, won freedom for his country. In the theatrical manner that became so characteristic, the young monarch went into exile swearing not to return to his court until France quit Cambodia. The French could not endure the embarrassment of the situation, especially as Cambodia without its king seemed likely to become a new war zone. In a few months, Sihanouk achieved his goal and returned to Phnom Penh as the triumphant liberator of a fully sovereign kingdom.

MALAYA

The progress of the Malay States toward independence understandably followed a unique course. The prewar absence of a forceful, indigenous nationalist movement, and the pattern of ethnic fragmentation that confined Malays, Chinese, and Indians to self-contained, mutually suspicious communities, simplified and smoothed the reimposition of British authority in 1945. So easy was the process of colonialist restoration, in fact, that the British tended to be oblivious to the reality that changes had occurred under Japanese occupation and that Malaya was no longer politically somnolent. The first assault on British confidence came, quite surprisingly, from the Malays; a second and far more threatening one was launched by Chinese Communists.

In partial recognition of the inequity of continuing to have non-Malays in the country treated as aliens without rights and in part to punish the sultans and the nobility for having accommodated themselves so effortlessly to Japanese rule, Britain imposed new constitutional arrangements on the peninsular states in April 1946. Postwar treaties had by then been forced on the sultans, who otherwise might have been vulnerable to accusations of wartime treachery. The treaties ended British protection and transferred sovereignty from the Malay rulers to George VI in order to establish direct colonial authority. The sultans, so long denied the power to rule, were thereby stripped of the right to reign; all they had left was nominal authority in matters of Malay custom and the Muslim religion.

With the sultans apparently put out to pasture, the British created a new colonial polity, the Malayan Union. Centralized under the government at Kuala Lumpur, the Union comprised the nine peninsular sultanates plus Malacca and Penang, while Singapore remained a separate crown colony. Union citizenship was made readily available to all, so that the Indians and the Chinese, who together formed a majority of the population, might enjoy rights equal to those of the Malays. The plan appeared both rational and progressive, but it was thoroughly unworkable and operated for less than two years. Chinese and Indian apathy joined with Malay hostility to kill the scheme.

In an act of symbolic defiance, the sultans declined invitations to attend inaugural ceremonies in celebration of the birth of the Union. That demonstration of pique by rulers expected to be humbly grateful for British guidance was disturbing; but far more unnerving to the colonial masters was the rapid growth of a mass movement of protest, largely led by Malay aristocrats and named the United Malays National Organisation, or UMNO. The first substantial expression of indigenous nationalism, UMNO spoke for all those who opposed the Malayan Union formula. Thus, it joined together men of royal and aristocratic

lineage resentful over the downgrading of the sultanates and common-
ers fearful of the consequences of extending citizenship rights to non-
Malays. The combination was potent. Britain was soon compelled to
dismantle the Union for the sake of maintaining harmonious relations
with a people long cooperative and friendly. UMNO, still under largely
elitist leadership, has remained the dominant power in Malay politics
ever since.

At the beginning of February 1948, the wreckage of the Union was
pushed aside with the establishment of the Federation of Malaya. The
change restored sovereignty to the sultanates, under British protection
and direction, and reaffirmed the special privileges of the Malays. However, the principle of administrative centralization under Kuala Lumpur was retained; and, as a concession to the notion that non-Malays
ought to be made loyal to the country, access to federal citizenship was
granted to a minority of the Chinese and Indians.

The Federation enjoyed but a few months of relative tranquility
before its very survival was challenged by Chinese Communist insurgents. The war—or, as British understatement put it, the Emergency—
began in June 1948 and continued by official reckoning until 1960,
though the last flames of the conflagration have yet to be finally extinguished. The struggle was much more than a contest between colonialism and revolutionary nationalism. In addition to its ideological
dimensions, the Emergency for a time seemed to take on the coloration
of an intercommunal civil war, pitting the Malays against the Chinese.
Had the fight, in fact, become one between the country's two chief
ethnic groups, the Emergency could never have been contained. Indeed, Malaya would not have survived in recognizable form. Fortunately, British skill supported by Malay stability and, far more decisive,
the refusal of the general Chinese community to join in revolution
prevented disaster.

The blueprint for revolution was simple, First, the economy and political stability of the country were to be destroyed through terrorism.
Second, the Communists hoped to establish secure base areas of "liberated territory." Finally, the insurgents expected to invest and subsequently capture cities and towns amid general popular acclaim. At that
point, a new Malayan state would come into being under Communist
direction. Only the initial campaign of terrorism was mounted, though
even that was but partially successful. Rubber trees were slashed; min-

ing equipment was sabotaged; transportation lines were broken. Attacks on isolated police stations, manned largely by Malays, threatened village security. The murders of the European managers of remote rubber estates and tin mines were designed to cause economic paralysis. Although a tenth of the targets of that effort were killed, the production of Malaya's principal exports was not significantly affected. More telling was the dreadful work of Communist assassination squads sent to exterminate Chinese held to be pro-government or condemned for refusals to give support to the revolutionary cause. In consequence, the first years of the Emergency were a time of deep fear for thousands of ordinary Malayans.

The Communist plan for victory may have been sound in terms of ideological orthodoxy, but it was doomed to fail within the socio-political environment of Malaya. Despite the claim that the fight was between the agents of colonialism and the forces of the exploited masses, regardless of ethnic heritage, and despite a contrived effort to legitimize the claim by giving prominence to token Indian and Malay participants in the insurgency, the Communist movement was almost totally Chinese in manpower and leadership. The task of the government, then, was to ensure that the rebels in the jungle, never numbering more than five to seven thousand, were denied support by the 40 percent of the country's population that was Chinese. Once given the opportunity, the Chinese populace proved to be cooperative with the authorities, or at least eager to avoid involvement in the struggle.

The terrorists began their attack with two advantages. First, the nucleus of the jungle force was composed of veterans of the wartime anti-Japanese resistance movement who had retained both their guerrilla skills and a cache of arms. Second, the earlier flight of great numbers of impoverished Chinese victims of the economic dislocations born of depression and war had created belts of settlement, typically on abandoned rubber estates, between the jungle sanctuaries of the Communists and the strongholds of the British. The subsistence farmers, referred to as squatters by the authorities, were required by the Communists to supply them with food, shelter, and intelligence. Caught unprepared to combat the terrorists, the British could do little but hold on for the first two and a half years of the Emergency. Gradually, however, the police and millitary forces of the government gained skill and grew in size as multinational reinforcements were recruited. A home guard was formed among the Malays to protect their villages. Scots highlanders, English riflemen, Malays, scouts from Sarawak, Gurkha warriors from Nepal—the most fearless of all—and many others gained expertise at "jungle bashing," as the pursuit of elusive terrorists came to be called.

Most instrumental in putting the terrorists on the defensive was the implementation in 1951 of a vast resettlement plan to insulate the squatter population against Communist manipulation. Close to half a million Chinese were removed from the borders of the jungle and re-established in "new villages," numbering more than five hundred, where they were provided with land, housing, schools, public health care, and, not incidentally, security against terrorist pressure. The government's substantial investment in the construction of the resettlement communities paid great dividends. As anticipated, logistical problems soon obliged the terrorists to retreat deeper into the jungle in search of small clearings where food might be grown. Perhaps less expected, though crucial, was the fact that the resettlement program went forward without meeting noteworthy opposition. Had half a million people refused to be transported to "new villages," which after all were ringed with barbed wire and therefore resembled detention camps, the authorities would have been thwarted. Even passive resistance would have defeated the government. Neither Chinese popular opinion in Malaya nor the sensitivities of the British public at home could have tolerated the spectacle of squatter families being clubbed and kicked into cooperation. Resettlement succeeded primarily because the squatter masses, far from having been won over by the Communists, preferred stability to revolution. In a parallel expression of choice, the Chinese of the cities remained peaceful throughout the Emergency. As has been said elsewhere, the British won the battles; the Chinese population won the war.

As the Emergency became manageable, the political evolution of Malaya was resumed. UMNO was transformed into an independence movement; a new Chinese party was formed to promote the interests of a community that was still largely alien in nationality and therefore particularly defenseless in the midst of the upheavals rocking the country. The Malayan Chinese Association, or MCA, represented the first major political effort of the resident Chinese that focused on local concerns rather than on developments in distant China. Thus, the creation of MCA expressed recognition of the fact that Malaya, not China, was home. The party's first moves were directed at improving the lot of re-settled squatters and, of more enduring significance, at pressing for broadened openings to Malayan citizenship for non-Malays.

In 1952, UMNO and MCA joined forces in a victorious electoral campaign for control of the Kuala Lumpur municipality. The success of the Sino-Malay political coalition soon attracted participation by the Malayan Indian Congress, or MIC, in the country's first viable, multi-communal party, the Alliance. Individuals still joined their own ethnic parties; there was no direct membership in the Alliance, which functioned as the coordinating center of its three constituent parts.

As the Alliance took shape, the British came to the conclusion that progress toward Malayan independence would counter the Communist assertion that the Emergency was a colonialist war. Consequently, Malaya's first general elections were held in 1955 to select the members of a national parliament that would be the legislative heart of a transitional government. The Alliance won fifty-one out of fifty-two parliamentary seats—a triumph that remains virtually unique in the history of democratic elections. The formula for Alliance success, perhaps over-simplified, was straightforward. The Malay elite, in return for the right to dominate both the party and the government, offered non-Malays expanded access to Malayan citizenship and promised that their communal and economic interests would be safeguarded. Put more basically, the Malays would run the country; the Chinese would continue to control the economy; the less numerous Indians could feel secure in their jobs.

The head of the Alliance was Tengku (or Prince) Abdul Rahman, a son of the sultan of Kedah, who had spent his youth and early middle age as a thoroughly amiable *bon vivant,* much of the time in England, where distractions interrupted his legal studies and delayed his being called to the bar for some twenty years. Though never losing his appreciation of the good life, the Tengku, as he is universally known, became a forceful political leader. Upon becoming Malaya's chief minister after the elections of 1955, he conducted a campaign to win full national independence from Britain, arguing that the most effective method of destroying the Communists lay in the speedy ending of colonialism. The British, who were inclined toward a similar view, were

soon persuaded. The Federation of Malaya, under the Tengku's premiership, became a sovereign state at the end of August 1957.

With Malaya independent, the future of Singapore, Sarawak, Brunei,
and British North Borneo became subject to re-examination. Britain
was in the process of withdrawing to west of Suez and no vital interest,
political, economic, or military, was to be served through the continuation of colonial rule over the eastern detritus of empire. On the contrary, freedom for those territories would help combat the pernicious
fiscal anemia that has endangered British solvency since the First World
War. The obstacles to ending colonialism in Singapore and Borneo
were not created by the British; they were of local origin.

The peninsular Malays fear, above all, drowning in a sea of Chinese.
Though willing to accept the economic paramountcy of the Malayan
Chinese, at least temporarily, UMNO was pledged to maintain the
political supremacy of the Malays. The incorporation of Singapore
within the Malayan state was anathema, for the island's population was
about three-fourths Chinese in origin. To bring Singaporeans into the
Malayan electoral process would tip the political balance away from the
Malays.

In Singapore itself, a vigorous anti-colonial movement led by Lee
Kuan Yew, clearly the most intellectual and dynamic leader in Southeast Asia, had by 1959 assumed internal administrative authority. The
British retained nominal sovereignty during a transitional period, but
Singapore's colonial era was virtually over. In 1961 the Tengku aston-
ished the public by reversing his previous stand and declaring that Singapore and Malaya ought to be joined together in a federal arrangement.
His reasoning was that the creation of an independent Singapore, with
a socialist government and a militant, leftist electorate, would pose a
greater danger to Malaya than the incorporation of the island within an
expanded Malayan state. Happily, Lee Kuan Yew also believed that
Singapore's future would best be served through marriage with Malaya. In 1963, after extended negotiations and following a plebiscite in
Singapore, the island was brought into a political union with the peninsula under a formula that protected both Malay parliamentary strength
and the special economic and communal interests of Singaporeans. It
was an intelligent arrangement, but the scheme proved itself to be unworkable in less than two years.

A sign in the Botanic Gardens, Singapore, suggests that communications are awkward in a multilingual society. (Lea E. Williams)

The Borneo territories presented different kinds of problems. Most conspicuously, a long history of conflict between Muslim Malays based on coastal enclaves and many of the indigenous Borneans of the interior had left a residue of bad feeling and suspicion. Moreover, the Borneans had barely begun to develop the' political resources that might be needed in the defense of their interests should their homelands be joined to Malaya. The fear of coming under the overlordship of the Malays appeared to be widespread among non-Muslims, including some in the substantial Chinese communities. Yet, the Borneo territories were not equipped to go it alone; federation with Malaya seemed inescapable.

Preliminary conversations between Bornean and Malayan spokesmen were followed in 1962 by a study tour of Sarawak and North Borneo conducted under the chairmanship of an English peer. At the end of two months of investigation, to the surprise of no one, the study commission announced that opposition to uniting the two Bornean territories with Malaya was little more than marginal. That conclusion was of course precisely what the British, the Malays, and those Bornean politicians who had been won over wanted to hear. Elections were then scheduled to be held in Sarawak and North Borneo, soon to be renamed Sabah, to secure popular endorsement of the proposed federation. Guaranteed special safeguards for their own local interests, the Bornean public proved cooperative. The creation of Malaysia, comprised of the peninsular states, Singapore, Sarawak and Sabah was set to take place in August 1963.

Brunei stood aside as these events unfolded, the sultan of that tiny British protectorate ultimately opting for continuation of the status quo. An abortive revolutionary coup directed against the sultanate in late 1962 had understandably frightened the monarch and made him more dependent upon British support. There was also the question of his precedence within the ranks of Malaysia's remarkably numerous royalty. If Brunei were to join the proposed federation, its sultan might be relegated to the end of the queue of peninsular rulers waiting to succeed, one every five years, to the rotating kingship of the whole country. Finally, Brunei sits on a rich, though diminishing, foundation of petroleum reserves. In all Southeast Asia no other state boasts a higher net national income on a per capita basis, though inevitably only a small proportion of the wealth ever goes directly to the ordinary subject of the sultan. In short, Brunei could live peacefully and in unique prosperity outside Malaysia, and that is precisely what she has done.

As the formation of Malaysia neared completion, denunciation of the plan grew in volume in neighboring Indonesia and the Philippines. Sukarno attacked the idea as "neo-colonial"; in Manila, old and dubious claims of Philippine sovereignty over Sabah were resurrected. The motivations and consequences of these attacks will be considered later; at the moment it is necessary merely to record that, after a brief postponement to permit the United Nations to certify the legitimacy of the enterprise and thereby seek to calm Indonesia and the Philippines, Malaysia was established in mid-September 1963. Except in Brunei and the forgotten fragments of Timor that then remained under Portuguese rule, colonialism was gone; thus, attention must now be directed to the triumphs and the troubles of the era of post-colonial independence.

READINGS

Ba Maw, U, *Breakthrough in Burma: Memoirs of a Revolution, 1939-1946*, New Haven: Yale University Press, 1968.

Barber, Noel, *The War of the Running Dogs: The Malayan Emergency, 1948-1960*, New York: Weybright and Talley, 1971.

Bone, Robert C., *Contemporary Southeast Asia*, New York: Random House, 1962.

Brimmell, J. H., *Communism in South-East Asia*, London: Oxford University Press, 1959.

———, *A Short History of the Malayan Communist Party*, Singapore: Donald Moore, 1956.

Buttinger, Joseph A., *A Dragon Embattled: A History of Colonial and Post-colonial Vietnam*, New York: Praeger, 1967.

Chen, King, *Vietnam and China, 1938-1954*, Princeton: Princeton University Press, 1969.

Clutterbuck, R. L., *The Long, Long War*, New York: Praeger, 1966.

———, *Riot and Revolution in Singapore and Malaya, 1945-1963*, London: Faber and Faber, 1973.

Fall, Bernard B., *Street without Joy*, 4th ed., Harrisburg, Pa.: Stackpole, 1964.

Furnivall, John S., *The Governance of Modern Burma*, New York: Institute of Pacific Relations, 1958.

Gullick, J. M., *Malaya*, New York: Praeger, 1963.

Hammer, Ellen J., *The Struggle for Indochina*, Stanford: Stanford University Press, 1954.

Hanrahan, Gene Z., *The Communist Struggle in Malaya*, New York: Institute of Pacific Relations, 1954.

Holland, W. L., *Asian Nationalism and the West*, New York: Macmillan, 1953.

Jacoby, Erich H., *Agrarian Unrest in Southeast Asia*, New York: Columbia University Press, 1949.

Kahin, George McT., *Nationalism and Revolution in Indonesia*, Ithaca: Cornell University Press, 1962.

Kennedy, J. A., *A History of Malaya*, London: Macmillan, 1962.

Kim Sung Youg, *United States-Philippine Relations, 1946-1956*, Washington: Public Affairs Press, 1968.

Lacouture, Jean, *Ho Chi Minh: A Political Biography*, New York: Random House, 1968.

Lancaster, Donald, *The Emancipation of French Indo-China*, London: Oxford University Press, 1961.

Leifer, Michael, ed., *Nationalism, Revolution and Evolution in Southeast Asia*, Hull: Centre for South East Asian Studies, 1970.

McAlister, John T., Jr., *Vietnam: The Origin of Revolution*, New York: Knopf, 1969.

McKie, R. C. H., *The Emergence of Malaysia*, Westport, Conn.: Greenwood, 1973.

Miller, Harry, *Jungle War in Malaya: The Campaign against Communism, 1948-60*, London: Barker, 1972.

————, *Prince and Premier*, London: Harrap, 1959.

Nasution, Abdul Haris, *Fundamentals of Guerrilla Warfare*, New York: Praeger, 1965.

O'Ballance, Edgar, *The Indo-China War, 1945-54: A Study in Guerrilla Warfare*, London: Faber and Faber, 1964.

————, *Malaya: The Communist Insurgent War, 1948-1960*, London: Faber and Faber, 1966.

Palmier, Leslie H., *Indonesia and the Dutch*, London: Oxford University Press, 1962.

Pluvier, Jan, *South-East Asia from Colonialism to Independence*, New York: Oxford University Press, 1974.

Purcell, Victor, *Malaya: Communist or Free?*, London: Gollancz, 1954.

————, *The Revolution in Southeast Asia*, London: Thames and Hudson, 1962.

Pye, Lucien W., *Guerrilla Communism in Malaya: Its Social and Political Meaning*, Princeton: Princeton University Press, 1956.

Roy, Jules, *The Battle of Dienbienphu*, New York: Harper and Row, 1965.

Shaplen, Robert, *The Lost Revolution*, New York: Harper and Row, 1965.

Smail, John R. W., *Bandung in the Early Revolution, 1945-1946: A Study in the Social History of the Indonesian Revolution*, Ithaca: Cornell University Press, 1964.

Steinberg, David J., et al., eds., *Cambodia: Its People, Its Society, Its Culture*, New Haven: Human Relations Area Files, 1957.

Tanham, George K., *Communist Revolutionary Warfare: The Vietminh in Indochina*, New York: Praeger, 1961.

Thayer, P. W.; Philips, W. T., *Nationalism and Progress in Free Asia*, Baltimore: The Johns Hopkins University Press, 1956.

Thompson, Virginia, and Richard Adloff, *The Left Wing in Southeast Asia*, New York: Sloane, 1950.

Trager, Frank N., ed., *Marxism in Southeast Asia*, Stanford: Stanford University Press, 1960.

Tregonning, K. G., *A History of Modern Malaya*, London: University of London Press, 1964.

Vo Nguyen Giap, *People's War, People's Army. The Viet-cong Insurrection Manual for Underdeveloped Countries*, New York: Praeger, 1962.

Von der Mehden, Fred R., *Religion and Nationalism in Southeast Asia*, New York: The Free Press, 1963.

————, *Southeast Asia, 1930-1970*, New York: Norton, 1974.

Wehl, David, *The Birth of Indonesia*, London: Allen and Unwin, 1948.

Wolf, Charles, Jr., *The Indonesian Story: The Birth, Growth and Structure of the Indonesian Republic*, Westport, Conn.: Greenwood, 1973.

12
Independent Paths

The struggle for freedom from colonialism left much of Southeast Asia in a poor state to meet challenges common to developing countries around the world. The euphoric belief that the departure of alien rulers would signal the opening of a nationalist millennium was soon broken. More debilitating than the physical damage suffered where military operations had taken place were the human costs of the campaigns for independence. Many who had earlier been bravely hopeful grew frustrated and embittered as the problems of the post-colonial period multiplied and remained unsolved. Some disillusioned patriots sank into apathy or corrupt opportunism; others, feeling compelled to renew the fight for national uplift, enlisted in revolutionary causes that threatened the survival of the new states.

During the years of political ferment that preceded independence, ethnic animosities endemic across the region had become more virulent and were destined to worsen further. Nationalist definitions of alien rule were selfishly narrow, referring only to Western colonialism. Once sovereignty had been transferred, national unity, not self-determination, became the watchword from Rangoon to Manila. Minority peoples who aspired to a meaningful measure of local autonomy were condemned as state enemies. Small or vulnerable ethnic communities had to bow to the nation-building will of their new masters; powerful, bold, or desperate minorities often turned to violence. Hence, not a single country has been spared misery born of the union of ancient rivalries and nationalist ambitions.

Peaceful efforts to safeguard minority interests, as well as militant separatist movements, were denounced as subversive. Both were attacked as products of the divisive administrative policies of the discredited past. Minorities that had not actively supported the campaigns for independence were open to charges of pro-colonial treachery. Hill peoples, geographically isolated from revolutionary struggle, and the overseas Chinese, living in urban areas garrisoned by Western forces, had unavoidably been obliged to seek security through political detachment, which the nationalists interpreted as hostility. Other groups, notably the Indians of Burma, had been so heavily dependent upon Western patronage that they could not be accommodated within the post-colonial scheme of things. Of course, a record of colonial military service against nationalist forces was unpardonable, which became known to the thousands of East Indonesians who sought asylum in the Netherlands.

Contrary to the expectations of many, freedom from colonialism did not bring relief to the economically distressed. Subsistence agriculture in the countryside and urban poverty endured; in fact, conditions generally worsened. Southeast Asia inevitably suffers along with most of the rest of the world from the modern plague of runaway population growth. As the pressure of people on rural resources increased, peasant life became harder year by year. Millions migrated to cities and towns that offered little other than misery in settings more bustling than those abandoned. The rapid advance of unplanned urbanization brought into painfully sharpened relief the barrier that divides the comfortable classes from the destitute. No longer were the impoverished masses invisible in their villages. Hideous, squalid slums spread into and around most of the cities of the region. No place was totally immune to the blight, though Singapore was best able to defend itself. Elsewhere, the ravages of interminable war drove people into Saigon and the lesser centers of South Vietnam; the population of Jakarta was doubled and redoubled by an endless flow of refugees from hunger; the juxtaposition of wealthy neighborhoods and pitiful shanty towns earned Manila the sad distinction of being a place of unparalleled extremes.

The proliferation of people directly impeded or stalled economic growth. As little, if any, production escaped immediate consumption in most countries, investable capital was scarce. Rising living standards could be achieved only where the production and processing of exports for the world market flourished. Malaysia and Singapore were conspicuously blessed in that respect; at the other end of the economic spectrum stood Burma and Laos.

Regional deficiencies in capital formation were not effectively offset by infusions of foreign funds. Government aid from abroad was largely directed toward maintaining consumption levels, as in devastated Vietnam, or into the construction of unproductive showplaces like the huge sports stadium in Jakarta. Similarly, private investment was no more than marginally helpful. Corporate funds from overseas naturally did not flow to countries that were deemed unstable; and, where investment capital was made available, it financed extractive industries or other undertakings operated primarily for the benefit of the outside investor, not the local economy.

The political styles of some leaders added to the problems of capital accumulation for rational economic development. The image of a new state was often judged to be more important than its substance. To make matters worse, corruption raised the costs of striving for prestige and the acquisition of the symbols of power. Thus money went into building monuments, enriching the elite, military expansion, and the operation of such ventures as international airlines that were neither economically viable nor remotely useful to the village millions.

THAILAND

The comparative tranquility of early postwar Thailand clearly may be credited in part to the fact that no alien regime had to be dispossessed. The passions and expectations generated during a time of nationalist revolution did not rise among the Thais. Administrative continuity was preserved; basic political stability was not shaken. The coup d'état, preferably bloodless, continued to be the acceptable instrument for changing leadership at the top, while life went placidly on at lower levels.

It is not to be supposed, however, that Thailand has been either inert or unruffled under circumstances that are general across Southeast Asia. Unrest and violence were ignited by tensions between the Thai majority and numerous minorities—Malays in the far south, Lao and hill peoples in the north and northeast. Cold-war politics eroded Thai sovereignty. Authoritarian, self-serving men ran the country as their private preserve.

Nevertheless, the kingdom has fared far better than most of her neighbors. World War II left no damage, physical or human. Though technically allied to Japan, Thailand had enjoyed de facto neutrality, while the rest of the region experienced invasion and occupation. In 1944, once Japanese defeat was certain, Phibun was shunted aside to prepare for the restoration of amity with the West. It was a wise move. As soon as Thailand withdrew from the Indochinese and Malayan territories with which Japan had bought Phibun's cooperation, the embarrassing past was erased. Thai rice and timber production gained in volume to meet demands in the world marketplace. Moreover, as postwar developments cut exports from Vietnam and Burma, Thailand faced decreasing competition.

The political history of Thailand in the quarter-century after the Second World War was quite predictable. Factions of the elite carried on in the pattern that had been established after the liquidation of the absolute monarchy in 1932, transferring the premiership within a tiny circle. Pridi was dominant as regent and through the medium of a handpicked premier for a brief time after the war, when it seemed diplomatically expedient for the kingdom to be governed by liberals untainted by records of happy cooperation with the Japanese; but power was not to be his for long. Early in 1946, he was compelled by the shifting allegiances of the elite to give up the security of his role as an *éminence grise* and accept the vulnerability of a premiership. Within three months tragedy came to Thailand; the youthful king was fatally shot in his bed by a person yet to be identified. Whether the royal death was by accident or design, whether the act was suicide or regicide remain unanswered questions. Though not an iota of evidence linked Pridi to the calamity, suggestions that the prime minister must bear ultimate responsibility were circulated by his political enemies and by the gossips of Bangkok. Charges of corruption and partisan favoritism

Buddhist temple architecture and sculpture at Bangkok. (Lea E. Williams)

were coupled with innuendo to force him to step down in favor of a new premier, a non-controversial centrist whom Pridi hoped to manipulate from the wings. Early disappointment lay ahead.

The rightist faction, largely made up of military men, had already begun to regroup for a fresh round in the contest for power. By late 1947 it was time to move. For one thing, condemnation of Pridi and other liberals persisted; for another, as Soviet-American confrontation had become the dominant fact of international political life, crypto-fascists were no longer ostracized by the West, provided they were noisily anti-Communist. The confidence of the military clique was justified, for the moderate premier was handily driven from office, and Pridi himself was obliged to flee the country. A compliant civilian figurehead was then installed as prime minister for the sake of appearances, only to be removed in early 1948, when Field Marshal Phibun regained the premiership he had lost four years earlier in the whirlwind of Japanese collapse. Moves to establish military dictatorship were immediately initiated, and Thailand was to be ruled by a succession of soldiers until 1973.

The restored premier was of course not unchallenged; the habits of political infighting die hard in Thailand. In particular, the officers of the navy and, to a lesser degree, the air force chafed under army domination. Moreover, for a time, constitutional advances gave a powerful voice to an elected lower chamber of the legislature and obliged Phibun to curb his authoritarian impulses. In late 1951, after three years of endangered existence, the popularly chosen lower house was disbanded; the practice of appointing half of the people's representatives was resumed. It is not remarkable that most of the appointees were military men beholden to Phibun.

In 1955, presumably to strengthen his hand against top deputies who increasingly demonstrated recalcitrance, Phibun reversed himself and initiated steps to rebuild parliamentary democracy. Turmoil ensued. Relatively free political discussion generated rising waves of criticism aimed at military rule that frightened Phibun's lieutenants and left the leader himself riding a tiger from which he could not safely dismount. Elections held early in 1957 were denounced by Phibun's enemies as fraudulent and served merely to create a climate of confusion in which ambitious men might plot.

Within a month after the elections, the government was overthrown by Field Marshal Sarit, a junta chieftain whose loyalty to Phibun had crumbled as his hunger for power increased. A second set of elections was quickly staged to endow the new regime with symbolic legitimacy. By then, Pridi had long been settled in asylum in the People's Republic of China. (He had originally sought refuge in the United States, only to be rebuffed by the State Department, which feared offending the Thai military.) Phibun had also been forced into exile, and vocal critics of authoritarianism had been silenced. Thus secure, Sarit installed his second-in-command, General Thanom, in the premiership and went abroad seeking medical treatment for a multiplicity of complaints brought on by a life of debauchery that had made the field marshal a legend in his own time.

In less than a year, his assortment of terminal diseases briefly arrested, Sarit flew home, pushed Thanom aside, and made himself the absolute ruler of a country in which all effective opposition had been obliterated. As the wits of Bangkok put it, Sarit had made the game of coup d'état a form of solitaire. His tenure was ended in 1963, when death finally overtook him. The dictatorship then passed to Thanom, who had been selected to succeed. The peacefulness of the transition suggested that Thailand had at last found authoritarian stability. A decade later, however, Thanom, too, was to fall in a coup—one of unprecedented violence, led by newcomers to the main arena of Thai politics.

There is no ready explanation for the jumble of events that overthrew military dictatorship in Thailand. The simple truth is that, as 1973 unfolded, public frustrations, resentments, and fears approached and ultimately reached flash point. Official corruption, injury inflicted on the middle classes by inflation, dismay over the fact that the kingdom's relations with the outside world were controlled by the United States politically and dominated by Japan economically, and hurt done national pride by the presence of huge American bases with their complements of alien soldiers, all combined to fuel unrest. Urban intellectuals grew increasingly disenchanted, being both middle class in origin and particularly aware of their country's conditions. Moreover, they saw themselves as uniquely endowed to save Thailand from further decline and humiliation. It is not surprising that the overthrow of the junta became the dream of thousands in the universities. When the militarists blundered into bloody confrontation with articulate students and their sympathizers, twenty-five years of rule by men on horseback ended.

Youthful idealism and courage powered a movement of protest first organized at one university in June 1973 to voice complaints against the authoritarian head of the institution. In a matter of days, repression in general and that of the military regime in particular became the targets of street demonstrations. Support for the protests came from swelling numbers of students and professors and from a few public figures of liberal persuasion. The clamor for constitutional democracy grew as the sweltering months passed; in October, battle was joined.

Predictably, Thanom and his deputy, Field Marshal Prapas—who in fact had become the most powerful man in the country—ordered the arrest of a few leaders of the campaign for constitutionalism and accused them of serving as the agents or dupes of a Maoist conspiracy. Student demands for the release of those detained reached a level of menace that eventually obliged the regime to back down; even the demand for early promulgation of a constitution was accepted at the last minute, though the time for negotiations had passed. The demonstrators suspected that the conciliatory gestures of the government were insincere and deceitful; the militarists mistakenly assumed that armed might would clear the streets of some 150,000 activists, who were supported by a flood of public donations of food, money, and good will.

The ensuing violent scenario that left hundreds dead was one that has become tragically familiar in many countries, but it was outside Thai experience and, therefore, doubly shocking. Paramilitary police units, soon reinforced by army tanks and helicopters mounting machine guns, attempted to scatter the demonstrators with firepower. A gentle people to whom bloodshed in political contests was abhorrent, ordinary Thais were horrified. The massed students and their supporters were enraged; fighting back with improvised weapons, they laid siege to government buildings, burning a number, and eventually drove the police into retreat and hiding. The collapse of the government came swiftly. Sanya Dharmasakti, an elderly scholar from Thammasat University, the nerve center of the rising, was named prime minister by the king, to serve in the transitional period prior to the promulgation of a new constitution and the holding of a general election. Thanom escaped to the United States; Prapas and his family found congenial refuge in Taiwan.

The place of the monarchy in these events deserves special mention. The king emerged as a symbol of hope and moderation to all those in opposition to the junta. A sensitive man of the twentieth century, he became a campus hero, meeting with student leaders, even providing palace refuge to youths fleeing military gunfire. Marching demonstrators, about to be shot down as terrorists, carried national flags and portraits of their king.

Democracy is a fragile thing in any environment and, in a land but recently freed of despotism, it must necessarily be especially delicate. Yet Thailand can prove to be a fertile field for the growth of parliamentary institutions. Clearly, the educated classes are emotionally committed to liberal ideals. Moreover, the urban population in general rallied to the cause when the overthrow of dictatorship became attainable. That the revolution of 1973 was a victory of moderation over extremism is the most encouraging consideration of all. Under the royal symbol of national unity, Thailand may well progress toward secure democracy faster than any of her neighbors—provided the counter-revolutionary impulses of the military are held in check and festering insurgency in districts populated by minority peoples is contained.

BURMA

By the logic of contemporary history, the troubles that have beset the Union of Burma since its establishment in 1948 ought to have destroyed the country. Militant separatist movements of minority peoples, notably the Karens and the Shans, have challenged the central government repeatedly. At times, guerrilla warfare has been waged by two bodies of Communist revolutionaries, one at first vaguely Titoist and later crudely Maoist, the other more orthodox and oriented toward Moscow. The intrusion of Chinese military and civilian refugees from Communism after 1949 created a new minority problem in northern frontier areas. Insurgency became so general in the early years of independence that little of the country beyond the city of Rangoon was under effective government control. The expulsion of shiploads of Indians denied Burma the services of a corps of experienced commercial, managerial, technical, and clerical manpower. Stumbling moves to establish socialism in a poor, agrarian land ruled by soldiers have caused stagnation and dislocations that put Burma in a tie with Laos for last place in the race for economic development in the region.

Yet the multiplicity of threats and weaknesses never came close to killing the Union, at least as an ideal and as a fact of international law. Rangoon remained, in a formal diplomatic sense, the capital of a sovereign state. The government was never compelled to acquiesce in the partition of the country. No separatists and no Communist revolutionaries, whether inspired by Moscow or by Peking, neared victory. The explanation for Burma's improbable ability to escape total catastrophe seems to be quite simple. Due in part to the government's efforts to avoid crippling foreign entanglements and, perhaps in equal measure, due to sheer good fortune, the country has not become the victim of great power rivalries. In short, Burma's internal weaknesses were never successfully exploited by outsiders seeking yet another cold-war battleground. It is only necessary to consider the horror inflicted on Indochina to recognize the costs of the internationalization of domestic conflict.

By fits and starts, the Burmese government has moved toward the pacification of the minority peoples and the quelling of insurrections. Periodic offers of amnesty have persuaded the more faint-hearted or exhausted rebels to surrender. Other dissidents have been won over or at least placated by central government steps to transfer local administrative responsibility to state authorities in minority areas. The more sinister of the two Communist movements obligingly killed off most of its own leadership in an intramural bloodbath caused by doctrinal and personal quarrels; the other has virtually disintegrated, its leader turning himself in to the government. Where rebels have refused to lay down their arms or engage in self-destruction, the armed forces of the Union have fought an endless chain of skirmishes and slowly gained the upper hand. Though insurgency continues to embarrass the government, there no longer appears to be any likelihood that Burma will soon crumble.

The presence of thousands of Chinese Nationalist soldiers in the remote borderlands of the north after 1950 was much more than an annoyance. Rangoon grew fearful, perhaps with justification, that the army of the People's Republic of China might be ordered to pursue the Nationalists across the frontier between Yünnan and the Shan State. In 1953, in response to Burmese pleas, the United Nations urged that alien forces leave Burma. Thus encouraged, the American government pressed Chiang Kai-shek to abandon the hope that Mao might be overthrown by a Nationalist invasion from the south. Between five and six thousand Chinese Nationalist veterans were then evacuated from Burma, using transshipment facilities in Thailand and aircraft from the United States. Though uncounted numbers of Chiang's old soldiers still remained in Burma to settle into placid lives of banditry and narcotics smuggling, the danger of immediate Chinese Communist intervention in the Shan State had been removed.

The survival of the Union may also be credited in part to the fact that the country has had only two chief executives during most of the years since the end of colonialism. Admittedly, the first, U Nu, allowed events to overtake and engulf him, while the second, Ne Win, has been the victim of his own political and economic dreams; but stability of sorts has been promoted by the relative absence of coups and erratic power shifts.

The assassinations that pushed U Nu into the leadership of the AFPFL in 1947 soon put Burma under the premiership of a decent, devoutly Buddhist figure, who was unable to maintain discipline within his own party. In due course, the fissures in AFPFL solidarity could no longer be patched over. Official malfeasance and the clash of ambitions among the top men of the party finally drove U Nu into semi-retirement in 1956-57. He was quite naïve in his hope that contending party lieutenants and corrupt officials would somehow be made to see the error of their ways by the shock of his withdrawal into a life of religious study. Political deterioration continued and, early in 1958, obliged U Nu to seek to exercise power by forming an improbable alliance of AFPFL stalwarts personally faithful to him and leaders drawn from the opposition and minority people's parties. The coalition was built on shifting sand and soon collapsed. At that point, General Ne Win was asked to assume command over a provisional government committed to the political regeneration of Burma. Remarkable as it might seem, early in 1960 the general concluded that the success of his housecleaning efforts enabled him to step aside and permit U Nu to regain the premiership of a new, popularly elected government. The second trial for parliamentary democracy was short-lived. Only two years passed before Ne Win, uninvited this time, led the army in seizing full power. U Nu and other civilian politicians were arrested; since 1962 the military regime has run Burma.

Burma is hardly unique in having a military dictatorship, but the ideological content of Ne Win's regime does endow it with a special flavor. Like military officers in political command around the world, those of Burma present themselves as disciplined and efficient patriots equipped with moral qualities that the dispossessed civilian politicians are supposed to have lacked. Beyond such commonplace assertions, however, the Rangoon junta upon taking power claimed particular wisdom in the socio-economic sphere and promised to lead the country along "the Burmese way to socialism."

The consequences of Ne Win's socialist innovations have been devastating. In 1973, for the first time in its modern history, Burma had to suspend the export of rice. The country's ability to earn foreign exchange to finance economic growth was thus ended. The scarcity of rice must be directly blamed on the weariness of peasants disgusted with a state marketing system that pays artificially low prices for harvests in order to subsidize socialism in the non-agrarian sectors of the economy. Unable or unwilling to collectivize or otherwise regiment agriculture, Ne Win has been injured by rural apathy and disillusionment translated into enfeebled production.

Urban Burmese have not fared notably better than their village compatriots. Consumer shortages, even in such basic necessities as cloth, are general and work cruel hardships on people of modest means. The shelves of the state retail outlets are permanently bare, while the wares of the black marketeers command ever higher prices. Bureaucratic corruption, a prime target of Ne Win's coup, is now said to be uninhibited. Army officers and the remaining civil officials charged with both administering a government and managing commerce, transportation, industry, and banking are understandably overextended and undereducated for their tasks.

Meanwhile, looking to the future with the same vision that has made a shambles of the present, Ne Win prohibits any form of population control, lest thirty million Burmese be submerged by the one and one-third billion people of India and China. Outnumbered by forty-five to one, Ne Win's subjects have been given a formidable assignment.

Impoverished countries, however, manifest a curious strength of their own. Subsistence, not progress, is the traditional goal of their rural millions. The misguided and inept actions of the central government and the grandiose schemes of visionary rulers can have but little meaning to villagers preoccupied with simple survival. City people in their concentrations are less inclined to passivity, but military regimes normally have the police resources to maintain urban order. Present-day Burma appears to fit into this pattern, as was shown when university students in late 1974 were defeated in their riotous attempt to pay posthumous honor to an old foe of Ne Win, the late Secretary General of the United Nations, U Thant.

THE PHILIPPINES

Without pushing the argument to the point of absurdity, it is possible to suggest that the Philippines have followed a course parallel to Burma's in the post-independence years. The two countries were particularly injured during the Second World War, for they alone experienced the expulsion of the Japanese by force of Allied arms. Both have been plagued by Communist insurgency and the unrest of minority peoples. In neither have the institutions of parliamentary democracy survived, though in the Philippines the democratic experiment went on longer. Perhaps Filipinos were given a decade more of constitutionalism after the Anglo-American model because their homeland remained so securely tied to the United States. In Burma, the work of decolonization was begun much earlier and performed far more energetically.

As the years of independence passed, it became routine among observers of the Philippines to predict the death of democracy in the islands. The formal political system seemed so alien and artificial. What might be appropriate for the United States patently did not fit Philippine realities. Most conspicuously, electoral contests could have little meaning in a country dominated by a remarkably cohesive elite in control of both chief parties. The ordinary voter was simply permitted to express a preference for one party over an all but indistinguishable adversary. The frequency and impunity with which politicians shifted their announced loyalties revealed the near identity of the contending organizations. Politics was very much a matter of personalities and personal obligations; doctrinal differences were of no meaningful significance.

The electorate gravitated between the parties and was normally inclined to cast negative votes against incumbents who failed to grapple with the lengthening list of economic injustices. Only one presidential candidate in the dismal parade seemed to offer hope that government might be made to serve the general public and not merely cater to the favored few who owned land, held concessions for the exploitation of natural resources, or were in command of major enterprises. In 1953 Ramon Magsaysay won some two-thirds of a popular vote of unprecedented size in one of the few honest and comparatively peaceful elections in Philippine history. He had earlier risen from modest origins to hold the defense portfolio in the cabinet of his presidential predecessor. In that capacity Magsaysay was primarily responsible for the direction of a military offensive against the Huk movement, as previously noted, a Communist-led guerrilla effort that had been born in the years of resistance to the Japanese occupation and kept alive by the bitterness of the landless peasants of Luzon. Recognizing that the destruction of the Communists would be an empty victory unless the government abandoned its traditional lack of concern for peasant welfare, Magsaysay directed his phenomenal energies into seeking to understand the needs and grievances of rural Filipinos. That alone made him unique and won him the presidency.

A man of the people, endowed with boundless drive and unblemished integrity, Magsaysay was emotionally and ideologically committed to reform. Unfortunately, good intentions were not enough. Keeping the door to the presidential office open to citizens with something to say did not alter the fact that Congress remained under the sway of wealthy and privileged power brokers. Touring the countryside to listen to the voice of the downtrodden did not bring restructuring and progressive leadership to the Nacionalista Party that Magsaysay had led to victory but could never transform. The example of the President's personal honesty had but passing influence on the corrupt and self-serving Philippine bureaucracy.

It was tragically in character for Magsaysay to meet his death early in 1957 in an airplane crash possibly caused by the weight of extra passengers who had been hospitably invited to go along on a presidential

flight in the provinces. The loss to the nation was keenly felt by griev-
ing millions. Like the American President, who was to fall to an assas-
sin's bullets early in the next decade, Magsaysay was mourned not for
his achievements, which were modest, but for the hope his symbol had
inspired among the inarticulate and the defenseless. And, as was to hap-
pen in the United States, a loss of faith in the future poisoned the political atmosphere.

Magsaysay was followed in office by a dreary procession of men. His
immediate successor is remembered primarily for the splendor of the
presidential yacht he had built for himself. The second in line was an
improvement, for he managed to break some of the neo-colonial bonds
that linked the economy of his country to the United States, most significantly by winning freedom for the peso from its tie to the dollar,
thus permitting Philippine exports to be priced competitively in world
markets. The third President after Magsaysay will be immortalized in
history as the man who replaced constitutionalism, however inadequate
it may have been, with personal dictatorship.

It is not to be assumed that the declaration of martial law by President Ferdinand Marcos in 1972 was unrelated to the fact that the man's
second term in office was due to expire at the end of the following year.
He had been a spectacularly successful politician; a handsome war hero
with a strikingly beautiful wife, Marcos in 1969 had won the distinction
of becoming the first Philippine president since independence to gain
re-election. He soon concluded, however, that personal popularity was
not enough to enable him to use the instruments of democracy to combat inflation, mass poverty, insurgency, an epidemic of crime, and outbursts of political violence. The country was obviously in distress, but
there were those who argued that Marcos contrived evidence to frighten
the public with reports of Maoist plots and terrorist bombings. Whether
or not the president set his own Reichstag fire to justify the action will
long be debated; in any event, in September 1972 he declared martial
law and assumed dictatorial command.

Developments in the post-democratic period have followed a de-
pressingly familiar course. Critics of the regime, liberals, and old opponents have been rounded up in the usual pre-dawn sweeps. The press,
once flamboyantly free, is now chained and muzzled. The citizenry has
lost the rights of assembly and public expression. No longer are the accused protected by due legal process in the courts. A carefully orches-

trated referendum was staged to legitimize dictatorship as the will of the people.

Perhaps surprisingly, in view of their history of political volatility, Filipinos have been generally docile under the new order. The beginnings of land reform have doubtless given a measure of hope to the peasantry. Bureaucratic housecleaning to curb corruption has been beneficial to all, except those malfeasant functionaries swept out. The business community reportedly welcomed with anticipated enthusiasm the imposition of rigorous controls over lawlessness and official dishonesty. Few Filipinos must regret the dissolution of the private armies of thugs that once served the great landowners and other provincial notables. Repealing the right of individuals to bear arms could only have been a blessing in a land where there were more guns and more shootings per capita than in any other. On that matter, incidentally, it is instructive to consider that it had formerly been necessary to require senators and congressmen to surrender their weapons to an attendant before going onto the floors of their parliamentary chambers to walk in the footsteps of Webster and Calhoun.

Once the positive moves of the dictatorship, such as they are, have been considered, there still remain broad areas of uncertainty. Philippine living costs continue to soar, while wages remain depressed. Hunger and degradation have not been driven from urban slums; exploitation of the peasants is not a thing of the past. Communist insurrection is certainly not ruled out for the future; in the southern part of the country, warfare between Muslim villagers and Marcos's Christian soldiers drags on. In short, the coup of September 1972 seems to have solved nothing fundamental. The enduring ills of the Philippines endure and may well destroy the dictator just as they contributed to striking down democracy.

MALAYSIA AND SINGAPORE

There is nothing in the post-independence development of the former British holdings in maritime Southeast Asia that is not ultimately related to the fears and hatreds generated by communal divisions. In colonial times, administrative plans and actions were based on the premise that only a sure alien hand in control could keep the peace. Since the transfers of sovereignty in 1957 and 1963, Sino-Malay balance has remained the preoccupation of the men in power, though the fact that the rulers are now men of local origin has changed the style and purpose of politics. Today, the emphasis is on building the nation by bringing the various communities—or, to use the local term, races—together within a common identity. The declared goal in Malaysia is material advance for the Malays and "Malayanization" for others. The theory is that democratic viability can be assured only when the Malays have caught up economically with the more affluent Chinese, and when non-Malays have demonstrated loyalty to the country by shedding expatriate attachments, most conspicuously by mastering and using the "Malaysian" language—that is, Malay. Put another way, the Malay elite promises to share power once the Chinese and Indians have abandoned their cultural separatism and lost their dominance in the modern sectors of the economy. In Singapore, there is similar insistence that there must be general acceptance of the unsentimental values of the English-educated Chinese who run the place. It is argued that only with the creation of a multiracial Singaporean identity can the state be secure. Meanwhile, external loyalties must be crushed.

The allegiances of the Malay aristocrats in control at Kuala Lumpur and those of the pragmatic materialists ruling Singapore were destined to clash throughout the two years that the essentially Chinese island was incorporated within Malaysia. Singapore was neither politically digestible nor capable of shaping the newly formed Malaysian state in its own image. Inevitably, the conflict became centered on the personalities and commitments of the Tengku and Lee Kuan Yew.

It is likely that the first Malaysian experiment would have foundered even earlier than it did had it not been for Sukarno's campaign of confrontation against it. The Indonesian leader, by declaring pseudo-war against the Malaysian-Singaporean union at the time of its birth in September 1963, was of course driven by his own domestic and international ambitions; but "konfrontasi," as the campaign was called, also served to hold the component states of Malaysia together in the face of an outside threat directed at them all. Once it was obvious that the Indonesian attack would be limited to rather inept raids and isolated terrorist bombings, communalism resumed command over Malaysian politics. In short order therefore, Singapore was ejected from the federation.

By the middle of 1965, tensions between Kuala Lumpur and Singapore made the divorce of the two unavoidable. Lee Kuan Yew had stepped on sensitive Malay toes by calling for a "Malaysian Malaysia"—that is, a state serving the interests of all communities without favoritism to one. The slogan became the theme of an offensive carried on by Lee and his followers in the political arena of the peninsular states, despite a tacit understanding that the moderate socialism of Singapore was not to be exported from its home island. Moreover, Lee began to make unflattering, injudicious remarks on the quality of the Malay leadership of the country his state had joined. Provocative though the Singapore prime minister's actions may have been, however, the final decision to expel the Chinese city-state was primarily prompted by the Tengku's fear that the more extreme Malay communalists in his own party might bolt UMNO to shatter the Alliance and bring about the collapse of the government. The danger lay in the fact that a rightist political alternative, the Pan-Malayan Islamic Party, stood ready to exploit the anxieties and the Sinophobia of Malays who might conclude that multiracial Malaysia would eventually come under the authority of the Chinese, especially those of Singapore. Consequently, the Tengku decided that considerations of his own political survival and the security of his people dictated setting Singapore adrift after less than two years of stormy marriage.

Since the separation, Malaysia and Singapore have moved farther and farther apart. The gap between the two has widened most perceptibly in the economic realm. Limitations on the issuance of work permits to the nationals of one country wishing to seek employment in the other; customs barriers to cut the flow of goods from Singapore into Malaysia; the efforts of Kuala Lumpur to encourage shippers to use peninsular ports rather than Singapore; and, most significantly, the end in 1973 of free convertibility for their respective currencies have pulled the two neighbors apart. Even so, established commercial patterns, continuing mutual interdependence, and geographic proximity dictate that economic ties endure. Moreover, in terms of international politics, the two governments find themselves allied through coordination in diplomacy and military defense.

Thus, though the years of separation have been punctuated and enlivened by outbursts of acrimony, there is no reason to suppose that the present pattern of coexistence will not go on indefinitely, provided economic prosperity is maintained. Should a depression strike, however, the situation would deteriorate most dangerously. Malaysian well-being is especially vulnerable to world price fluctuations; Singapore can support itself only as an entrepôt and regional industrial center. If tin and rubber exports and earnings were sharply cut, Malaysian affluence would evaporate. If customers were to stop paying for Singapore's goods and services, the city-state would explode. In either circumstance, violence born of economic deprivation would spill from one country to the other and engulf both.

In both Malaysia and Singapore, the chances for democracy have been made slim by the pressures of communalism. The former country erupted in deadly rioting after parliamentary elections in 1969, when modest gains by anti-Alliance parties seemed to threaten Malay hegemony. The precise death count will remain uncertain; but there can be no denying that, when Malay uneasiness was translated into mob action, scenes of horror followed. Kuala Lumpur, in particular, was stained with blood, most of it Chinese; lesser disturbances broke out elsewhere up and down the peninsula. Fearful that civil war would soon follow, if the Chinese struck in full retaliation against Malay attacks, the government ordered rigid curfews and put the country under a state of siege. For a time, rule by decree replaced parliamentary government.

Slowly and cautiously, the late Tun Abdul Razak, who succeeded to the premiership in the aftermath of the riots, directed a partial return to democracy. Though no one was permitted in speech or in print to incite intercommunal hostility, parliament was reconvened some months after the riots and national electoral contests were resumed in 1974. A new political front, led by the prime minister, swept the field that year, capturing 135 of 154 parliamentary seats. The front was no doubt helped by the fact that opposition candidates had little access to the mass media and by the exclusion from debate of the one subject that encompasses and overshadows all others, relations among the different ethnic communities.

The two Bornean states have followed courses of their own since they were joined to Malaysia in 1963. As a direct result of Sukarno's confrontation of the new federal experiment at the time of its inception, Sarawak was disturbed by terrorist raids carried out by bands of local Chinese Communists who had been trained and armed in Indonesia. The

Typical Singapore street. The stress on new construction, cleanliness, greenery, and public transportation is apparent. (Courtesy Government of Singapore)

end of confrontation in 1965-66 left the Sarawakian Maoists without an Indonesian base, but they have continued a sputtering campaign in the jungles, doubtless sustained emotionally by a parallel effort on the Malay Peninsula, where Communist diehards seek to perpetuate the struggle of the Emergency, especially along the Malayo-Thai border.

Sabah has been the more peaceful of the Bornean territories, though it has been anything but unmoved by post-colonial developments. Most conspicuously, the chief executive of the state, a singularly ardent Muslim, has been assiduous in his efforts to serve Islam by attracting newcomers to the faith through the power of the government to offer bureaucratic appointments, political rewards, and economic incentives to the converted and the devout. It is conceivable that dangerous inter-communal friction may be generated by the pressures for Islamicization in a state where substantial Chinese, Christian, and animist minorities live, but thus far the general prosperity of Sabah, a booming frontier-land, has contributed to public order.

Finally, after over a decade of independence, the sovereign republic of Singapore has become something of a political curiosity—a one-party democracy, where opposition to the administration of Lee Kuan Yew is inevitably denounced as anti-national, though the forms of parliamentary government are preserved. Jury trials, press freedom, and uninhibited speech have disappeared; but elections are still held, and the government works hard and constructively to win popular loyalty. Special vigilance is maintained to curb communal chauvinism, particularly of the Maoist variety, but the stability of the city-state is based far more on the economic benefits enjoyed by the populace than on police repression. With per capita incomes second in Asia only to those of the Japanese and with public housing and government services that would be unimaginable in 90 percent of the world, Singaporeans collectively are not likely to risk political adventures while times are good. However, the end of prosperity for some two million people, on an island measuring roughly ten miles by twenty, would quickly reactivate the militant left that once commanded the communal and ideological loyalties of at least one-third of the population.

INDONESIA

The Indonesians, half the human beings of Southeast Asia, have lived through a turbulent quarter-century since becoming independent. Like the archipelago and the people themselves, the recent history of the country has been rich in variety and promise. It has also been full of uncertainty and anguish. Ethnolinguistic heterogeneity, religious divisions, and economic imbalances have played major roles in the drama. Deadly overpopulation on Java, the only place in the region to know endemic malnutrition, has contrasted with the enormous potential for development of the outer islands and generated centrifugal forces that have threatened to tear the country apart. The largest Communist movement outside those states of the world ruled by ideological descendants of Marx and Lenin for a time seemed destined to defeat all opponents and win mastery over the country. All these elements and pressures have shaped independent Indonesia; and interacting with them during the most tumultuous years of the period was Sukarno, whose presidential authority rested on personal charisma and a talent for maneuvering contentious people and factions into dependence upon him. Until the final cataclysm, when the experiment blew up in his face, Sukarno was a master alchemist.

Constitutional democracy was foredoomed in a fragmented land that had known only alien rule and protracted revolution. The transitory life of effective cabinet government spanned only four years and was terminated in 1953 with the collapse of the last in a series of ruling coalitions. Based on centrist and right-of-center support, the coalitions had been committed to finding pragmatic solutions for the innumerable difficulties of a country debilitated by over a decade of economic retrogression. From 1953 on, though successive cabinets continued to be named, Indonesia moved rapidly into presidential dictatorship, as parties and the public as a whole were drawn toward opposing ends of a political spectrum that ran from the Communist left to the nationalist-religious right. Sukarno found the polarization of politics much to his liking, for he was able to juggle the contenders, all of whom trusted the master performer to keep them airborne and in circulation.

Recurring cabinet crises had forced the postponement of national elections during the four years of constitutional vigor, and when the people finally were given a chance to express themselves in the latter part of 1955, the time for popular consensus had passed. Indeed, the parliamentary elections served merely to underscore the fact that Indonesia was as split politically as it was geographically, with the fractures running along the same lines. Four big parties won some three-fourths of the parliamentary seats, while several lesser ones divided the balance. The electoral strength of the PKI ranked somewhat beneath that of any one of the other three major parties, but the Communists had demonstrated organizational vitality and discipline not to be matched. Potentially more ominous, the left, both Communist and nationalist, had gained most of its support in eastern and central Java, while the religious and moderate parties were favored elsewhere. With the boundaries of territorial loyalty geographically conterminous with those of political faith, there arose the specter of civil war between the Communists of Java and their enemies on the other islands. Sukarno henceforth presented himself as the keeper of the peace, the one figure who could prevent disaster. His strategy, most simply put, was to play the Communists off against the military and their civilian allies and to keep both sides reliant upon him. The first presidential move was to call for the early inauguration of "guided democracy"—a contradiction in terms if ever there was one.

Economic degeneration, bureaucratic ineptitude, and corruption had long worried many; and when Sukarno revealed his dictatorial ambitions, concern was transformed into rebellion by military officers—in Sumatra in late 1956 and in eastern Indonesia a few months later. The regional separatists, including some distinguished civilian figures, were motivated by their fears of Javanese-Communist domination under the plan for "guided democracy." They were materially sustained by an ability to finance rebellion through the export of the products of the rich outer islands. The rebels also received some backing, including limited air support, from the Chinese Nationalists on Taiwan and from American intelligence operatives. The intrusion of foreign anti-Communists was doubtless counterproductive, however, for the development enabled Sukarno to appeal to the national loyalties of those military officers on Java and elsewhere who were not yet mutinous, but who might have been reluctant to fight friends and colleagues.

The affair dragged on for nearly two years, during which Sukarno escaped an assassination attempt staged by religious extremists and decreed the expropriation of all remaining Dutch holdings. Both moves strengthened his hand, the first by discrediting the far right, and the second by pleasing the revolutionary left. In 1958, when Jakarta's armies took the field against the regional rebels, organized resistance evaporated in Sumatra and was rather quickly overcome in Celebes, the two territorial bases of the insurgents. The country reunited, the president justifiably felt himself to be stronger than at any time since the revolution. The establishment of "guided democracy" was finally and promptly proclaimed.

While Sukarno had indeed won additional prestige and authority, he by no means held a monopoly of power; both the army and the Communists had emerged from the two years of separatist strife with greatly expanded political resources. The state seizure of Dutch property had put military officers in control of a major segment of the economy. Profits from estate agriculture and other undertakings could be made to serve army purposes; jobs for those worthy of army patronage could be awarded. The Communists, for their part, basked in a climate of political radicalization and were delighted to see their old electoral opponents in disarray—pushed aside by the leftist tide or popularly discredited by earlier association with regional rebellion. Thus, more than ever, Sukarno was obliged to be artful in tacking between Scylla and Charybdis.

Under "guided democracy," as it developed, the representative parliament was replaced by bodies composed of the spokesmen of "functional groups" or particular economic, religious, or ethnolinguistic interests. The new assemblies·were not empowered to legislate, but they were expected to serve as conduits for the exchange of information between the rulers and the ruled. Government policy was nominally set by Sukarno, though his hand was restrained by the realities of the accelerating power struggle between the Communists and the military. Such limited civil liberties as had been enjoyed earlier were destroyed. The economy of the country fell to pieces due to official mismanagement, the squandering of resources on adventurism abroad, and political showmanship at home, for the president's style of operations, both personal and official, was expansive and expensive.

State visits to foreign capitals, reciprocal hospitality for those statesmen who paid return calls, the staging of spectacular events described as international conferences, the holding of an Afro-Asian olympiad, and the confrontation of Malaysia were some of the costly divertissements designed to impress outsiders and Indonesians alike. The endless speaking tours undertaken by the president served both to refresh him and to offer inspiration to the populace, even when the best advice presented was the 1963 call for the nation "to live dangerously"—or, as Sukarno oddly put it, *vivere pericoloso*. The man's plurality of wives and the legend of his extramarital displays of machismo transformed him into a modern *devaraja* in the admiring eyes of many countrymen. Except for the hungry, the people who knew or feared political arrest, and the outraged members of the youthful intelligentsia, Indonesians lived in a giddy circus atmosphere until, as was unavoidable, the bubble burst in 1965. As with so many past events, the development was shaped by Sukarno's charisma; or more precisely, the debacle came when the leader's departure from the office of president for life seemed imminent.

Rumors that Sukarno's considerable inventory of diseases would soon combine in deadly attack had circulated for years, but they gained fresh currency and credibility as 1965 wore on. The president's face in photographs was puffy and aging; worse, on one occasion Sukarno faltered in the middle of a public address and had to be helped from the platform before the eyes of shocked thousands. Though the man was in fact destined to survive five more years, evidence of his declining health clearly contributed to the growth of political anxiety that culminated in violent upheaval.

Even a decade after the event, it is impossible to understand precisely what precipitated the coup of September 30-October 1, 1965, known to history by an acronym, "Gestapu," formed by the initial parts of the Indonesian words for "the September 30th movement." Concern over Sukarno's physical decline clearly had caused both the Communists and the military to anticipate an early resolution of their contest for supremacy. The generals may or may not have engaged in planning a pre-emptive strike to shatter the PKI, but they were understandably alarmed by Communist efforts to establish a popular militia force under PKI command to complement moves to infiltrate the lower ranks of the army. The PKI, for its part, obviously concluded that a bid for power had to be made while Sukarno was still on the scene to serve as a symbol of national continuity.

In the first hours of October 1, armed squads killed or captured for immediate and barbaric execution six generals, including the commander of the army. The defense minister, General Nasution, fled assassination in a burst of gunfire that took the life of his infant daughter. When dawn came, Jakarta radio announced that a coup to prevent military treachery had succeeded and that a revolutionary council would soon assume control over the country. Sukarno, significantly enough, had spent the bloody predawn hours at a nearby air force base, where he chatted with reported affability with the men who had engineered the coup and had the mutilated bodies of the six murdered generals flung down a well.

Nasution was not the only top military figure to escape death. General Suharto, a Javanese of village birth who had climbed to command over the army's strategic reserve, had the good fortune or, as some maintain, the prescience to be away from his house when the killers assigned to him arrived. Together with Nasution and other officers, Suharto swiftly initiated a counterattack against Gestapu forces. Loyal army units were quickly mustered to march against the rebels at the air force base and in the center of Jakarta. Within twenty-four hours, except for limited guerrilla activity, Gestapu was broken, though months of turmoil lay ahead.

The collapse of Gestapu touched off a vendetta of unmatched proportions and savagery, as nationalists, active Muslims, and the army lashed out at the PKI. Estimates of the numbers killed range from as high as a million down to less than a hundred thousand. Communists, including Aidit, leader of the PKI, members of revolutionary front organizations, and countless innocents somehow caught in the tide of vengeance fell before army gunfire or mob attack. Idyllic Bali was soaked in blood; rivers in central and eastern Java were said to have been dammed by bloated corpses. The Communists of Indonesia had suffered their third and most terrible defeat.

During the months of bloodletting, Sukarno sought to save himself. The president's reputation had been more than a little sullied by his questionable behavior during Gestapu. Moreover, his old stratagem of balancing the Communists against the military had made him appear pro-PKI to many. Apparently blinded by desperation, Sukarno brought about his final downfall by seeking to restore equilibrium between left and right. The cabinet he named after the coup gave ministerial powers to men widely thought to be Communist sympathizers. To make his point clear to all, Sukarno took the defense portfolio from Nasution in a supremely injudicious move. Students filled the streets of Jakarta in massive protest. Their hopeful idealism had been frustrated once too often; for too long their youthful sense of propriety, typically prudish, had been assaulted by Sukarno's lechery and extravagance. Watched with indulgence by the military, the young people paralyzed the city. In early March 1966, Sukarno was driven to retire under army protection, while General Suharto became acting president and de facto ruler of the land.

The post-Sukarno era has been one of selective reconstruction. Though carefully directed national elections were eventually held to give Suharto presidential legitimacy, the country in reality remains under firm military dictatorship. No meaningful progress toward the restoration of democracy has been attempted. Organized dissent is impossible; thousands of political prisoners have been under detention ever since 1965. Such forward steps as have been taken have been in the direction of economic development. The national currency has been stabilized; exports have risen; state enterprises, notably the petroleum industry, though corrupt, claimed high levels of efficiency and productivity. Foreign loans and investments have flowed to a country that not long ago was a notorious international credit risk. Japanese, American, and—once again—Dutch capital and enterprises, among others, are welcomed. Investors are confident. Revolutionary unrest seems a thing of the past, as was perhaps best symbolized by the Jakarta crowds of 1972 who cheered the state visit of a lady they affectionally called *Oma* (the Dutch word for "grandmother"), Queen Juliana of the House of Orange.

Outside the better neighborhoods of the capital and a few other places, however, signs of economic advance are rare, and reassurance that Indonesia has attained lasting political stability is hard to find. The villagers of central and east Java, whose population is greater than that of either France or the United Kingdom, remain precariously on the thin line between subsistence and catastrophe. The urban poor continue to multiply in numbers and sink deeper into misery, their quest for steady and secure employment frustrated, their hopelessness unrelieved. The intellectual proletariat—students and jobless graduates—though presently obliged to be circumspect, still voice disgust with the government, complaining of corruption, favoritism, and insensitivity. From time to time, eruptions of protest occur, though they leave the invulnerable junta untouched, lashing out instead against defenseless Chinese shopkeepers, the traditional targets of violence in Southeast Asia.

All in all, it seems reasonable to conclude that, while Indonesia has partially recovered from the chaos of the Sukarno period, the present leaders of the country have yet to initiate moves to overcome the great and unresolved problems. It is no doubt beneficial to provide hospitality and security for foreign investments in the modern sectors of the economy, but most Indonesians are pre-industrial villagers unrewarded by growth financed in New York, Amsterdam, or Tokyo. The rigidity of the regime is normally conducive to the maintenance of public order, but the absence of any means of popular expression other than the riot invites disaster. In short, the basic difficulties of Indonesia have not been attacked and could generate renewed upheaval at almost any moment.

The states of Indochina have not been considered in this chapter on post-colonial developments because their recent collective history has been primarily shaped by external forces rather than by domestic events. This is not to deny the significance of changes that have been internally generated, particularly in Cambodia under Sihanouk and in North Vietnam; but the organizational approach of this study makes it both appropriate and convenient to consider the Indochinese states within an examination of the place of independent Southeast Asia in international politics, the next and final subject for discussion.

READINGS

Basche, James, *Thailand: Land of the Free*, New York: Taplinger, 1970.

Bellah, Robert N., ed., *Religion and Progress in Modern Asia*, New York: Free Press, 1965.

Bloodworth, Dennis, *An Eye for the Dragon: Southeast Asia Observed, 1954-1970*, London: Secker and Warburg, 1970.

Butwell, Richard A., *U Nu of Burma*, Stanford University Press, 1969.

Cady, John F., *Post-war Southeast Asia: Independence Problems*, Athens, Ohio: Ohio University Press, 1974.

Corpuz, Onofore D., *The Philippines*, Englewood Cliffs, N.J.: Prentice-Hall, 1965.

Dahm, Bernhard, *The History of Indonesia in the Twentieth Century*, New York: Praeger, 1970.

De Young, John, *Village Life in Modern Thailand*, Berkeley: University of California Press, 1955.

Donnison, Frank S. V., *Burma*, New York: Praeger, 1970.

Du Bois, Cora, *Social Forces in Southeast Asia*, Cambridge: Harvard University Press, 1962.

Feith, Herbert, *The Decline of Constiutional Democracy in Indonesia*, Ithaca: Cornell University Press, 1962.

Geertz, Clifford, *Peddlers and Princes: Social Change and Economic Modernization in Two Indonesian Towns*, Chicago: University of Chicago Press, 1963.

——, ed., *Old Societies and New States: The Quest for Modernity in Asia and Africa*, New York: Free Press, 1963.

——, *The Religion of Java*, New York: Free Press, 1959.

George, T. J. S., *Lee Kuan Yew's Singapore*, London: Deutsch, 1973.

Ginsburg, Norton, and Chester F. Roberts, *Malaya*, Seattle: University of Washington Press, 1958.

Golay, Frank H., *The Philippines: Public Policy and Economic Development*, Ithaca: Cornell University Press, 1961.

Grossholtz, Jean, *Politics in the Philippines*, Boston: Little, Brown, 1964.

Gullick, John Michael, *Malaysia*, London: Benn, 1969.

Halpern, Joel M., *Government, Politics and Social Structure in Laos: A Study of Tradition and Innovation*, New Haven: Yale University Press (Southeast Asian Studies Monograph, Series 4), 1964.

Hanna, Willard A., *Bung Karno's Indonesia*, New York: American Universities Field Staff, 1960.

——, *Eight Nation Makers: Southeast Asia's Charismatic Statesmen*, New York: St. Martin's, 1964.

Hindley, Donald, *The Communist Party of Indonesia, 1951-63*, Berkeley: University of California Press, 1964.

Holt, Claire, ed., *Culture and Politics in Indonesia*, Ithaca: Cornell University Press, 1972.

Hughes, John, *Indonesian Upheaval*, New York: David McKay, 1967.

Insor, D., *Thailand: A Political Social and Economic Analysis*, New York: Praeger, 1963.

Jay, Robert R., *Javanese Villagers: Social Relations in Rural Modjokuto*, Cambridge: Massachusetts Institute of Technology Press, 1969.

Josey, Alex, *Lee Kuan Yew*, rev. ed., Singapore: Donald Moore, 1971.

Kahin, George McT., ed., *Governments and Politics of Southeast Asia*, 2nd ed., Ithaca: Cornell University Press, 1964.

Keith, Agnes, *Barefeet in the Palace*, Boston: Little, Brown, 1955.

Lachica, Eduardo, *The Huks: Philippine Agrarian Society in Revolt*, New York: Praeger, 1971.

Lebar, Frank M., et al., *Laos: Its People, Its Society, Its Culture*, New York: Taplinger, 1960.

Legge, John D., *Sukarno: A Political Biography*, New York: Praeger, 1972.

Leifer, Michael, *Dilemmas of Statehood in Southeast Asia*, Vancouver: University of British Columbia Press, 1972.

Liddle, R. William, *Ethnicity, Party and National Integration: An Indonesian Case Study*, New Haven: Yale University Press, 1970.

Marcos, Ferdinand E., *The Democratic Revolution in the Philippines*, Englewood Cliffs, N.J.: Prentice-Hall, 1974.

Maung Maung, U. *Burma and General Ne Win*, New York: Asia Publishing House, 1969.

McAlister, John T., Jr., ed., *Southeast Asia: The Politics of National Integration*, New York: Random House, 1973.

McVey, Ruth T., ed., *Indonesia*, New Haven: Human Relations Area Files, 1963.

Means, Gordon Paul, *Malaysian Politics*, New York: New York University Press, 1970.

Mills, Lennox A., *Southeast Asia: Illusion and Reality in Politics and Economics*, Minneapolis: University of Minnesota Press, 1964.

Milne, Robert Stephen, *Government and Politics in Malaysia*, Boston: Houghton Mifflin, 1967.

——, and K. J. Ratnam, *Malaysia: New States in a New Nation; The Po-*

litical Development of Sarawak and Sabah in Malaysia, London, Cass, 1973.

Mintz, Jeanne S., *Mohammed, Marx and Marhaen: The Roots of Indonesian Socialism*, London: Pall Mall, 1965.

Mortimer, Rex, *Indonesian Communism under Sukarno: Ideology and Politics, 1959-1965*, Ithaca: Cornell University Press, 1974.

Mossman, James, *Rebels in Paradise: Indonesia's Civil War*, London: Jonathan Cape, 1961.

Nash, Manning, *The Golden Road to Modernity: Village Life in Contemporary Burma*, New York: Wiley, 1965.

Osborne, Milton E., *Region of Revolt: Focus on Southeast Asia*, Harmondsworth, England: Penguin, 1971.

Palmier, Leslie H., *Communists in Indonesia: Power Pursued in Vain*, Garden City, N.Y.: Doubleday, 1973.

————, *Social Status and Power in Java*, New York: Humanities Press, 1969.

Pye, Lucian W., *Politics, Personality and Nation Building: Burma's Search for Identity*, New Haven: Yale University Press, 1962.

Quirino, Carlos, *Magsaysay of the Philippines*, Quezon City: Phoenix, 1958.

Rabushka, Alvin, *Race and Politics in Urban Malaysia*, Stanford: Hoover Institute, 1973.

Ratnam, K. J., *Communalism and the Political Process in Malaya*, London: Oxford University Press, 1965.

Riggs, Fred W., *Thailand: The Modernization of a Bureaucratic Polity*, Honolulu: East-West Center, 1966.

Romulo, Carlos P., and Marvin M. Gray, *The Magsaysay Story*, New York: John Day, 1956.

Scott, James Campbell, *Political Ideology in Malaysia: Reality and Beliefs of an Elite*, New Haven, Yale University Press, 1968.

Shaplen, Robert, *Time out of Hand: Revolution and Reaction in Southeast Asia*, New York: Harper and Row, 1969.

Sharp, Lauriston, et al., *Siamese Rice Village: A Preliminary Study of Bang Chan, 1948-49*, Ithaca: Cornell University Press, 1953.

Smith, Donald E., *Religion and Politics in Burma*, Princeton: Princeton University Press, 1965.

Smith, Robert A., *Philippine Freedom, 1946-1958*, New York: Columbia University Press, 1958.

Smith, Roger M., *Southeast Asia: Documents of Political Development and Change*, Ithaca: Cornell University Press, 1974.

Somers, Mary F., *Peranakan Chinese Politics in Indonesia*, Ithaca: Cornell University Press, 1964.

Starner, Frances L., *Magsaysay and the Philippine Peasantry: The Agrarian Impact on Philippine Politics, 1953-1956*, Berkeley: University of California Press, 1961.

Sutter, John O., *Indonesienisasi: Politics in a Changing Economy, 1940-1955*, Ithaca: Cornell University Press, 1959.

Taruc, Luis, *Born of the People: An Autobiography*, New York: International Universities Press, 1953.

Taylor, George E., *The Philippines and the United States*, New York: Praeger, 1964.

Thompson, Virginia, *Labor Problems in Southeast Asia*, New Haven: Yale University Press, 1947.

———, and Richard Adloff, *Minority Problems in Southeast Asia*, Stanford: Stanford University Press, 1955.

Tilman, Robert O., *Man, State and Society in Contemporary Southeast Asia*, New York: Praeger, 1969.

Tinker, Hugh, *The Union of Burma; A Study of the First Years of Independence*, 4th ed., London: Oxford University Press, 1967.

Trager, Frank N., *Building a Welfare State in Burma, 1948-1956*, New York: Institute of Pacific Relations, 1958.

Vandenbosch, Amry, and Richard Butwell, *The Changing Face of Southeast Asia*, Lexington, Ky.: University of Kentucky Press, 1966.

Van der Kroef, Justus M., *The Communist Party of Indonesia: Its History, Program and Tactics*, Vancouver: University of British Columbia Press, 1965.

Vitachi, Tarzie, *The Fall of Sukarno*, New York: Praeger, 1967.

Wallace, Ben J., *Village Life in Insular Southeast Asia*, Boston: Little, Brown, 1971.

Wang, Gungwu, ed., *Malaysia: A Survey*, New York: Praeger, 1964.

Williams, Lea E., *The Future of the Overseas Chinese in Southeast Asia*, New York: McGraw-Hill, 1966.

Willmott, Donald E., *The Chinese of Semarang: A Changing Minority Community in Indochina*, Ithaca: Cornell University Press, 1960.

Willmott, William E., *The Political Structure of the Chinese of Cambodia*, London: Athlone, 1970.

Wilson, David A., *Politics in Thailand*, Ithaca: Cornell University Press, 1962.

Wilson, Richard G., *The Future Role of Singapore*, London: Oxford University Press, 1972.

13
Southeast Asia in Global Politics

Southeast Asia has been twice discovered by the outside world. Starting in the sixteenth century, the West was drawn to the region by the lure of trading profits; and Japan during the Second World War sought to build a new Pacific empire based in substantial measure on the natural wealth of the lands to her south. Both discoveries generated rivalry and fostered greed. The colonialist penetration that followed the first has been discussed earlier; it is now time to consider the consequences of the second, to recognize that the Japanese invasion and occupation established a precedent for others seeking general domination of the region. Before 1945, nobody spoke of tropical East Asia as a vacuum; since that cataclysmic year, many have talked, thought, and acted as if the region were a void, particularly as independence came to one country after another.

Prompted by the conviction that the end of colonial control had created instability and vulnerability that would be exploited as a matter of course by one or more of the great powers, elaborate arguments were devised to justify foreign intervention. It goes without saying that a populous region, rich in natural bounty and strategically situated, invites the attention of giants engaged in multifaceted competition and confrontation; but it is useful to realize that a power vacuum, like beauty, exists in the eye of the beholder. Small states become the objects of foreign concern only when some interest of an outsider appears to be at stake.

AMERICAN IMPERIAL SUCCESSION

No country has surpassed the United States in preoccupation with the notion that the lands of Southeast Asia need and ought to welcome intervention. The titan of international politics at the end of the Second World War, America felt called upon to pick up the pieces as old empires were dissolved. Diplomacy, economic aid, military support, and meddlesome plotting drew the United States deeper and deeper into the vacuum it had defined. Involvement ranged from political support for Indonesians fighting the Dutch to the maintenance of a neo-colonial grasp on the Philippines; from assistance for economic reconstruction in Burma to covert backing for rebels in Sukarno's Indonesia and in Laos; from Peace Corps efforts to the formation of an international absurdity, the Southeast Asia Treaty Organization. The domino theory was simply an expression of the belief that some physical law dictates domination of the small by the mighty. The horror of the Second Indochina War was the logical result of the American obsession.

It must be objectively recognized that the United States was not unique in seeing the world in terms of solids and vacuums. The American record has simply been the most fully documented, publicized, and criticized. Moreover, it should be acknowledged that Americans, in the years after the Second World War, felt with considerable justification that their prewar isolationism had been a cause of much of the misery that subsequently afflicted mankind. The determination to prevent a repetition of history may have been commendable in theory; it certainly was expensive in practice.

American moves toward the assumption of imperial burdens in Southeast Asia can be interpreted as the unforeseen result of the wartime China policy of the United States. Franklin Roosevelt had rested his plans for the Far East on the reasonable belief that with the restoration of peace, the Japanese would be confined to their home islands and Western colonialism would be in retreat. Under those circumstances, according to the reasoning of the day, China would come to play a vital part in the re-establishment of Asian stability by redressing the disturbed international balance. Thus, Washington strove to elevate the Chinese state to great power status, as was formally symbolized by initiating her into membership in the "big five" of the Security Council of the United Nations.

The end of the war brought swift disillusionment. China dissolved into civil war, and in 1949 came under Communist rule. Many in the United States, in a curious expression of national conceit, blamed their own country for "the loss of China"—as if the homeland of a fifth of mankind had ever been America's to lose. While the fatuous debate on the internal history of China gathered momentum, Washington moved uncertainly toward the development of a new policy of partial disengagement in the Far East, a course made necessary by the turn of events in China and by the intensification of the contest with the Soviet Union for paramountcy in Europe. Only a few months passed, however, before the outbreak of hostilities in Korea in June 1950 made Asia the main theater of cold-war operations. With that shift, China was again given a central position in American calculations. The consequences for Southeast Asia were immediate and enduring.

Already four years old, the substantial war then in progress in Vietnam had attracted growing American concern as Chinese Communist forces pushed to the Sino-Tonkinese frontier. With the eruption in Korea, Vietnam came to be regarded as the second front of a larger struggle to check Communist expansion. The stand of the French against the Vietminh was seen as supportive of American resistance in Korea. With the appearance in Korea of troops of the Chinese People's Liberation Army, Washington was persuaded to channel great quantities of military equipment and supplies to the French in Indochina. As noted earlier, such aid was eventually to cover 80 percent of the costs of the First Indochina War; and the United States came within a shade of ordering its air force to lend a hand in the defense of besieged Dienbienphu.

The French debacle of 1954 prompted the United States to attempt the construction of a new defense perimeter to block any further advance by the Communists. The exercise in international engineering consisted of two interrelated moves: the establishment of the Southeast Asia Treaty Organization, and efforts to build a militarily viable state in South Vietnam.

SEATO was doomed to impotence from the start. Even its name was ridiculous, since membership was accepted by only two Southeast Asian countries, Thailand and the Philippines—both then malleable clients of Washington. The other member states were Britain, New Zealand, Australia, France, Pakistan and, of course, the United States. The commitment of SEATO was as inappropriate as the body's name. The collective responsibility of participants in the organization was essentially restricted to blocking the open invasion of the region by any power that might be prompted, presumably by nostalgia, to fight in the traditional manner rather than wage irregular warfare. Generals are inclined to be prepared for the last, rather than the next war; and SEATO was proof that diplomats, as exemplified by John Foster Dulles, can be equally hypnotized by history. Since no invader obligingly marched in with banners and bugles, SEATO remained inert in one of the world's most disturbed areas. Admittedly, the headquarters of the organization in Bangkok provided sinecures for career soldiers and civil servants.

The American attempt to pump vitality into South Vietnam was, in a restricted sense, a more successful venture than SEATO. Without United States support, the South Vietnamese state could never have survived for more than twenty years, though it would be difficult to justify that survival in human terms.

In 1950, in a forlorn attempt to win Vietnamese popular support for their colonial war, the French had brought Bao Dai back from Hong Kong, where the fallen emperor had been obliged to live in temporary exile. The purpose of the French maneuver was not to rejuvenate the Nguyen dynasty but to use Bao Dai as *chef d'état* of a new Vietnamese state that was alleged to exercise sovereignty "in association" with France. Although the former monarch's monumental lack of charisma and the transparency of the French scheme combined to defeat the enterprise, the puppet government at Saigon lived on to inherit authority when colonialism was finally killed at Dienbienphu. At that point, the Americans produced their own savior for Vietnam—Ngo Dinh Diem, who was thrust in to serve as premier in Bao Dai's government.

During a period of foreign refuge, Diem had made a most favorable impression on many American political figures, including John F. Kennedy. The Vietnamese was a certified patriot who had refused to collaborate with either the French or the Japanese. He had been raised in an upper-class family and thus was equipped with the educational advantages and the attitudes of a mandarin. In addition to his assets of background and temperament, Diem was a Roman Catholic of renowned piety in a country where co-religionists, including many who had fled from the Communist north, made up a tenth of the population. Catholic Vietnamese were inclined to look to Diem for leadership and protection; he reciprocated by trusting few others.

The premiership was too modest an office for a messiah. By late October 1955 Diem had eased Bao Dai out to languish on the Riviera and in Paris, and had transformed South Vietnam into a republic with himself in the presidency. His rise to full authority had required him to overcome formidable enemies, most particularly the criminal gang that controlled Saigon as its own warlord satrapy. The Cao Dai and Hoa Hao sects, politico-military powers in their own right, also had to be brought into line. Not the least of Diem's tasks in the process of winning authority was the mobilization of loyal support among the officers of the South Vietnamese army, many of whom had risen to command as protégés of the French or favorites of Bao Dai. Diem earned the reputation of a political virtuoso in subduing his many adversaries, and at the time of his assumption of the presidency he seemed to some to be the one man who could lead his country to stability and security. American officials were especially unrestrained in their admiration and optimism. Eight years of deterioration in South Vietnam were to pass before Washington grew cool toward Diem, and when that negative reappraisal was made, the consequences were violent.

The new president's failings were legion, though they were largely hidden in the initial phase of his administration, when the country was weary of war and appeared to be moving in an encouraging direction. But the optimistic interlude was of short duration. According to the terms of the international accords that ended the First Indochina War, a plebiscite on the reunification of all Vietnam was to be held by July 1956. With the backing of his American enthusiasts, however, Diem refused to grant the people the promised opportunity to express themselves. He had his reasons. A nationwide vote would undoubtedly have favored Ho Chi Minh's government at Hanoi. Not only was Ho the best-known and probably the most admired patriot, north or south, the population above the seventeenth parallel was somewhat greater than that of the south and could be expected to cast a disciplined, monolithic vote. Thus, even though Diem himself had already established an ability to command virtual unanimity in rigged elections, ending the national division by plebiscite would surely have put all Vietnam under the sway of the Communists.

The instinct for political survival that caused Diem to prevent the holding of the plebiscite may have been sound, but the consequences that followed his decision were immediate and terrible. Early in 1957 the Communists opened a campaign of assassinations to bring about the destruction of village administration across South Vietnam. In widespread rural areas, Saigon's authority was soon broken; the Communists and their supporters had largely succeeded in confining Diem's forces to urban centers, isolated strongpoints, and the main roads. The situation was virtually identical to that of the early years of the first Indochina conflict, except that Diem's troops had replaced the French as the targets of revolutionary warfare.

In his presidential palace, Diem long tried to minimize the threat. His ego and the confidence of his American patrons would be injured if the magnitude of the crisis were acknowledged. Moreover, in the classic ignorance of the despot whose subordinates fear reporting bad news, the president was late to sense danger. Increasingly, as the military situation deteriorated, he turned for guidance to his brother, Ngo Dinh Nhu, and to his beautiful, venomous sister-in-law. By the end, Diem was a hollow figure. Dressed in the white suit of the old colonial officialdom, he grew verbally incontinent in his marathon discourses on the politics and philosophy of "personalism," an authoritarian ideology that proclaimed that dignity and national salvation could best be promoted through public obedience to the leader. It was an unappealing and largely unintelligible message to an afflicted populace. Diem's concept of human dignity had no meaning for landless peasants sunk in poverty, no reality for the citizens of a corrupt police state at war.

Even if Diem had been perceptive and progressive in coping with his country's difficulties, his dependence upon American backing in itself would have discredited him in a land of nationalist passions. Ho Chi Minh had the distinct and decisive advantage of a reputation for independent patriotism; Diem, like his successors, was tainted by his reliance on the United States. In exploitation of that circumstance, Communist statements and writings invariably linked Diem's name to that of America with a hyphen to emphasize the servility of the Saigon regime in contrast to the self-reliance claimed for Hanoi. Yet there was no way for South Vietnam to rid itself of the foreign encumbrance without sacrificing the vital support that was needed more with each passing day.

Though Diem's credibility as a national leader was eroded by the American presence, his downfall was the product of local and more traditional forces: oppressed Buddhists and ambitious military men. The Catholic minority of South Vietnam had enjoyed preferential treatment, especially in government service, under a Catholic president who was both intensely religious and the brother of Ngo Dinh Thuc, the archbishop of Hué. Diem's displays of favoritism toward religious fellows was long an annoyance to the Buddhist majority population; but when outright persecution replaced discrimination early in 1963, smouldering frustration gave way to open defiance. When the official prohibition of a public celebration at Hué of the 2506th anniversary of the birth of the historic Buddha was ignored, the local authorities struck in frightened rage, killing eight. Instead of punishing the perpetrators of the tragedy, the Diem government attempted to justify the action and opened a general campaign against the Buddhist community, particularly its clergy. At pagodas, as Buddhist temples are known in Vietnam, monks and lay sympathizers massed in protest. Efforts to dislodge them merely exacerbated the tension.

The anxiety grew until, to dramatize the plight of the Buddhists, a monk in Saigon, his robe drenched with gasoline, set himself aflame and died, hands in an attitude of prayer. A press photograph of the immolation shocked the world and did more than anything that had been reported previously to weaken Diem in Washington's estimation. The situation was not bettered when the president's sister-in-law publicly referred to the dreadful suicide as a "barbecue."

The seething discontent of the Buddhists and the brutality of the police in meeting it ultimately persuaded the Americans that Diem was a liability who had to be replaced for the sake of the war against the Communists. Kennedy ordered the suspension of a portion of the financial aid that kept the South Vietnamese regime's head above water. The rebuke was precisely what was required to encourage Saigon's senior military officers to plan a coup, one that would succeed where prior attempts had been foiled because of American support for Diem. To ensure that the generals understood the promise of the altered situation,

American intelligence operatives passed the word that the plot could unfold free of foreign obstruction.

Inspired by the shift in Washington's affections, the military moved early in the afternoon of November 1, 1963. Tanks ringed the presidential palace, while inside, protected by a thin guard of loyal soldiers, Diem and his brother Nhu engaged in futile negotiations by telephone with the leaders of the rising. A call to the American ambassador produced only an expression of pious hope that the two Ngo brothers would be granted safe conduct if they left the country for exile overseas.

Despite all, the brothers remained confident of eventual victory or perhaps they were merely in a state of shocked irrationality. Some time late in the day of the coup, the two Ngos escaped from the palace by a hidden passage and set up new headquarters at a church some miles away. There, the next morning, the president and his brother were captured and loaded into a truck from which they were not to emerge alive; both were shot as the vehicle rumbled across the city.

Though embarrassed by the summary executions, the Americans were delighted that the government of South Vietnam would henceforth be led by generals dedicated to defeating the Communists. The cloud of despondency that had hung over the White House and the Pentagon was wonderfully dispelled. Men who had built careers by professing to "see light at the end of the tunnel" or other beckoning mirages were restored in their naïveté and in their reputations. Rework plans for rural pacification; make just one more push; unleash a bit more firepower; and "the hearts and minds of the people" would be won.

Nothing of the sort happened, of course. The war went from bad to worse to hideous and hopeless. By 1967, over half a million American troops were to be in the field, supported by sizable South Korean units and token contingents of Australians, Filipinos, and Thais. Together with the South Vietnamese army, the total strength of the forces of the "free world" came to 1,300,000, one soldier for every fifteen civilians in a tortured land that had known war for a generation. Vietnam, north and south, suffered heavier aerial bombardment than had been inflicted on the Axis powers throughout the entire Second World War. Still there was no promise of peace. The escalation of the Washington-Saigon side was met by the deployment of fresh Communist-led forces, recruited locally or, increasingly, marched southward from North Vietnam.

The futility of the effort was long concealed from most Americans at home by the artful claims of Washington. Not to be hidden, however, was the horror of the conflict, the use of chemicals to strip trees of their foliage and fields of their crops, the incineration of villages and villagers by jellied gasoline dropped from the air, the atrocities committed against the helpless. The massacre at My Lai was unique in scale, perhaps, but not in kind.

The revulsion of the American public finally had telling effect. The disgrace and the internal divisions of the United States became intolerable, though the United States endured years of national anguish before its combat forces were finally withdrawn from Vietnam. And the withdrawal came only after the war had been territorially expanded into neutral Cambodia, and only when extensive preparations had been completed to ensure the continuation of hostilities by Washington's South Vietnamese surrogates.

A turning point of sorts came in 1968, when Lyndon Johnson resigned from electoral competition in acknowledgment of the failure of his presidential policies in Vietnam. His successor in the White House, Richard Nixon, destined to become a national humiliation in his own right, at first tried to avoid the inevitable with one final offensive, the invasion of Cambodia in 1970.

The justification for the assault on a neutral kingdom lay in the fact that eastern Cambodia had been used as a staging area for Communist forces fighting in adjacent South Vietnam. In the view of Prince Sihanouk, the de facto independence won from a harassed France in 1953 and made de jure by Cambodian constitutional amendment two years later could only be safeguarded through a policy of non-alignment in international politics. Thus, the small kingdom had sought at almost any cost to keep clear of the flames that raged in Vietnam and sputtered in Laos, where the independence gained in 1953 had been endlessly endangered by a contest among ineffectual neutralists, a right wing backed by the United States, and the Pathet Lao, largely under North Vietnamese Communist sponsorship.

For years, unable to deny use of his territory to the Communists, Sihanouk had chosen to ignore their presence. That posture, plus the Cambodian leader's frequent and normally bumptious verbal assaults on

American self-righteousness, had made the neutralism of the prince seem like pro-Communism to the domino theorists of Washington. It is one of history's ironies that Sihanouk was toppled, and Cambodia all but destroyed as a country, just when the prince had begun to manifest tolerance toward the American position in Southeast Asia and irritation with the Communists within his frontiers. Be that as it may, in mid-March 1970, General Lon Nol, who had become Sihanouk's premier the previous August, took advantage of the prince's absence abroad to seize power in Phnom Penh. From then on Cambodia slid, and was pushed, toward disaster as Lon Nol, under American manipulation, sought to clear eastern Cambodia of Communists. Within six weeks, United States and South Vietnamese forces had invaded the country to take over the task.

Though the Americans stayed only till the end of June, the consequences were frightful. The South Vietnamese soldiers who had arrived under American protection went on a rampage of looting in the homeland of their ancient enemies, the Khmers. The economy of the country was all but destroyed by the military action, and the ensuing flight of rural refugees to the dubious security of Phnom Penh and other towns. As ought to have been anticipated by Washington, fresh Communist units were promptly dispatched to Cambodia from Vietnam and recruited locally to offset the escalation of the other side. In a matter of weeks the tranquil kingdom had become a battleground, scarred from one end to the other. The Lon Nol government ruled little more than Phnom Penh and its immediate environs. Elsewhere, even at the glorious ruins of Angkor Wat, now damaged by shellfire, the Communists were victorious. The Americans had snatched defeat out of the jaws of stalemate.

The Cambodian fiasco, the disgust of the American public, and—once again—United States relations with China now determined the course of American actions toward Vietnam. With respect to the Chinese element in the equation, it should be observed that Nixon's trip to Peking early in 1972 transformed international politics in East Asia, including Indochina. With Sino-American détente, the myth of Southeast Asian dominoes falling under Chinese blows became less credible than ever. Furthermore, the establishment of a channel of diplomatic communications between Washington and Peking opened a new route for peace feelers to be transmitted to or from Hanoi. Simultaneously, improved Russo-American relations served a like purpose.

Plans to repatriate American combat personnel that had been in limited operation even before 1972 were rapidly pushed ahead to completion in the course of that year. But the process of American withdrawal, the "Vietnamization" of the war, by no means ended the conflict. Greatly expanded tonnages of supplies were shipped to the Saigon army, while United States aircraft flew combat missions from bases in Thailand. In December, North Vietnam was subjected to massive bombing to demonstrate continuing American resolve. By then, however, both sides wanted rest.

In January 1973, peace talks that had dragged on for months finally produced an agreement for the cessation of hostilities. Though the cease-fire accord was reaffirmed the following June, it never was effective. The killing continued among Vietnamese; Cambodia remained a theater of war; only Laos, always a backwater, came to enjoy relief from violence under a newly constituted coalition regime that brought the Pathet Lao down from the hills and into Luang Prabang and Vientiane to dominate the entire country. Meanwhile, American power remained in the region, based in Thailand and the Philippines and afloat in the western Pacific. It seemed possible that the twilight between war and peace might extend over several years, but that was not to be.

The first months of 1975 brought the Second Indochina War to a close; by the end of April, the Communists of North Vietnam and their allies—the National Liberation Front in South Vietnam and the Khmer Rouge in Cambodia—were victorious. Saigon's armies, after disintegrating in the face of an offensive in the highlands, fled to the thickly settled coast. One after another, starting with Hué, the coastal cities were abandoned. Saigon, the last to be surrendered, was taken by the Communists, as the staff of the American Embassy was evacuated by helicopter. Over 130,000 South Vietnamese, including defeated military commanders and discredited officials, became refugees abroad. The Communist-directed provisional government of South Vietnam that then came to power has since worked to inaugurate socialism and to achieve Vietnamese reunification under the authority of Hanoi.

The war in Cambodia ended even before the one in Vietnam. During the last weeks of the conflict, Phnom Penh was isolated by the closing of all land and water routes to the city. After the capital's airport was overrun by Communist troops, Phnom Penh itself was captured, virtually without a shot fired. By then, Lon Nol had moved to Honolulu. His brother and some other senior officials of the former government were captured and executed.

At the time of their triumph, the Khmer Rouge initiated a resettlement policy without historical precedent. Phnom Penh and lesser cities were all but emptied of people. Without time to prepare for the journey, the urban populations were ordered to march to country districts to labor as peasants. There is no ready explanation for the suddenness and the harshness of the action—even hospital patients were compelled to join the exodus. The Communists may have feared American bombing of the cities; perhaps the shortage of food in Cambodia dictated the Draconian recruitment of an agricultural labor force; or the Khmer Rouge may have simply decided to inflict massive punishment on those Cambodians—and overseas Chinese—most likely to cling to bourgeois values.

Prince Sihanouk paid one brief visit to his native land after the Communists came to power, but he subsequently indicated that he intends to live abroad indefinitely. Meanwhile, the new rulers of Cambodia appear determined to avoid subservience to any outside power—Russian, Chinese, or Vietnamese.

Defeat for the Indochinese clients of the United States has accelerated efforts by the Philippines and, more particularly, Thailand to disengage from cold-war partisanship. American bases are in the process of being dismantled in Thailand; the Philippine government actively seeks accommodation with the People's Republic of China; SEATO is to be liquidated by 1977.

THE CHINESE SHADOW

The government of the People's Republic of China has never treated Southeast Asia as a region of primary concern. The coming of Communism to China brought no change of substance to a traditional pattern of relative detachment from the affairs of southern neighbors. The style of Chinese international conduct has been remoulded to accord with current necessity or dogma, as manifested in the preference for revolutionary language; but preoccupation with problems of administration and economic development at home, and with defense against military threats—first from the Americans in Korea and later from the Soviets—has not allowed the Chinese leadership to invest in major undertakings to the south.

There is, of course, no certainty that restraint born of realism will always govern Chinese behavior in Southeast Asia. Nor is it to be assumed that China is forever destined to be held in check by commitment to the realization of domestic goals or by fear of the Soviet Union. The goals may be attained or abandoned, and rapprochement with Moscow is presumably possible, but, for the discernible future, it is sound to assume that the People's Republic will follow an established course. Trading opportunities will be developed; diplomatic advantages will be sought; and provided the costs are modest and the risks few, support will be extended to revolutionary allies.

Despite the fact that Peking has endeavored to promote its interests with caution and with minimal resources, China has played more than a peripheral role in the recent history of Southeast Asia. For one thing, generated by economic jealousy and ethnic differences, the anti-Sinicism so deeply rooted among the indigenous peoples of the region for generations has been politicized. Since 1949, the union of old prejudice with fear of Communist advance has produced general Sinophobia—that is to say, dread of the "yellow peril" has lately been reinforced by anxiety over Maoist revolutionary plans. China has therefore come to occupy a far greater place in the imaginations and the affairs of her neighbors than can be justified by the facts of history. For example, without the spectral menace of China, there could have been no domino theory of collective Southeast Asian vulnerability to forces born of civil war in Vietnam. Even by doing nothing, China could thus confound her enemies; and of course, Peking has not been solely a passive observer of world events.

In the first years of the People's Republic, the tasks of consolidating internal power and of waging war in Korea were so demanding that there was no time to develop a strategy for Southeast Asia. Protection was promised overseas Chinese; the region's nationalist leaders, from Sukarno to U Nu, were denounced as lackeys of the West; Communist-led insurrections were applauded; material aid was shipped to Ho Chi

Minh's forces. Such actions represented either the continuation of patterns from the past or demonstrations of ideological orthodoxy. When the initial phase of the Maoist revolution had been completed at home and when the danger of an American attack from Korea had passed, however, pragmatism began to supplement habit and doctrine in the shaping of Chinese foreign policy. The change was directed by the greatest pragmatist of them all, Chou En-lai, and it was signaled by the staging of the Bandung conference of 1955.

The convening of the assembly of Asian-African leaders in the western Java city was a stroke of political genius. Chou had quite effortlessly maneuvered Sukarno into hosting a meeting that, in the Indonesian President's imagination, would promote the island republic to leadership in the post-colonial world. For Peking, the conference was a perfect setting for demonstrating the new Chinese posture of peaceful coexistence with friendly or nonaligned states, not by coincidence, just when the United States held cold-war neutralists to be international pariahs. Moreover, Nehru was challenged in the role he had assumed as the spokesman and the conscience of the non-Western world. To rub salt in the wound, Jakarta later decreed that the Indian Ocean had been renamed the "Indonesian Ocean." Finally, at Bandung, by emerging from beneath the Russian wing, China became a bona fide Asian power, no longer the junior partner in a bilateral bloc. Indeed, it is far from fanciful to regard the Chinese debut of 1955 as having marked the start of the Sino-Soviet split.

The Bandung spirit, as the benign mood was known, radiated with particular warmth toward Burma, Cambodia, and Indonesia. The People's Republic forged diplomatic friendships with all three. Chinese economic aid was invested in the building of tangible evidence of the new amity. The exchange of state visitors was seemingly uninterrupted. Cultural missions and other agents of good will were endlessly on tour. Resident Chinese in the three favored countries were told by Peking to be law-abiding and loyal to their adopted homelands.

Within a decade of its beginning, the amiable offensive appeared to have won near total victory. Burma and China in 1960 had settled a border dispute that dated from the nineteenth century. Furthermore, Rangoon had pledged not to enter into any defense agreement with a third power in the absence of Chinese approval. Sihanouk seemed to act like a modern tributary prince in his dealings with Peking. Indonesia moved to merge its international policy with that of China, as was most forcefully expressed by Sukarno's resignation from membership in the United Nations. Yet, in a period of less than two years, bitterness and suspicion replaced friendship.

Disintegration came first in Indonesia, where China was charged with complicity in the Gestapu rising of 1965. The backlash of anti-Communism that ensued not only broke the PKI; the explosion of public fury and official reprisal brought death to thousands of local Chinese whose only crime was their ethnicity and shattered the bonds between Jakarta and Peking. Anti-Communist demonstrators invaded the embassy and consulates of the People's Republic, effectively putting those establishments out of official business. Formal diplomatic relations, ended in 1967, have yet to be restored. Even American abandonment of hostility toward China has left the generals who rule Indonesia unmoved and unforgiving.

Both Burma and Cambodia experienced shock waves from the Great Proletarian Cultural Revolution that convulsed the People's Republic in 1966 and 1967. In the latter year overseas Chinese students in Rangoon, in emulation of the youthful Red Guards of China, barricaded themselves in their school to resist official Burmese orders that a halt be put to the display of Maoist emblems and to public demonstrations of revolutionary ardor. The police were not gentle, nor were the riotous students passive when fighting began. Casualties were suffered on both sides, but that was not the end of the affair. Throughout the city and in some provincial towns enraged citizens attacked individual Chinese residents, striking with patriotic wrath against an alien minority that seemed contemptuous of Burmese sovereignty. The government of the Union expelled Chinese diplomatic and aid personnel, denouncing them as subversives. For months thereafter, official charges of Chinese treachery were repeatedly voiced; in response, Peking urged the Burmese peoples to overthrow the regime of Ne Win.

The comparatively peaceful confrontation in Cambodia resulted, inevitably, from injury done to Sihanouk's pride. To permit Chinese diplomats, lesser officials, and residents to conduct their own small-scale cultural revolution would be to give the aliens extraterritorial political rights and erode the authority and dignity of the prince. Consequently, Peking's journalists were expelled; the Sino-Cambodian Friendship Association was shut down; the embassy of the People's Republic was obliged to restrict its activities to the routine and sterile tasks of diplomacy. An actual rupture of relations between Phnom Penh and Peking was avoided only at the eleventh hour; in October 1967, Chou En-lai reportedly appealed to Sihanouk as a friend and promised that there would be no further Chinese acts of *lèse-majesté* in Cambodia. The aberrant interlude of the Cultural Revolution has passed; the work of rebuilding bridges to Southeast Asia lay ahead.

In remarkably short order, the Chinese re-established harmony with Burma and Cambodia, though the restructured relationships were cool and correct in comparison with the bonds of earlier years. Neither Ne Win nor Sihanouk could afford to isolate himself from China. Burma had trouble enough coping with dissident minorities and rebellious bands without alienating the giant to the north. Pinched between Vietnam and Thailand, Cambodia quite properly held diplomatic flexibility to be the *sine qua non* of national survival.

Elsewhere in the region, China used her trading resources and the art of "peoples' diplomacy" to win acceptability. Chinese exports of modestly priced consumer goods satisfied a growing number of customers in most countries; imports began to be significant, especially in the case of Malaysian rubber. The volume of shipments north and south expanded steadily, although Southeast Asia's trade with China still amounted to less than one-sixteenth of the business done with Japan. So far as "unofficial" contacts were concerned, there were the usual trips by journalists, theatrical groups, and, *de rigeur*, ping-pong teams. The move toward ending the isolation of the People's Republic was given decisive impetus by the Sino-American thaw of 1971-72. China now has formal diplomatic relations or at least regularized government-to-government communications with all the states of Southeast Asia, except Indonesia.

The question of Peking's involvement with insurrectionists is necessarily the most elusive aspect of China's policy toward Southeast Asia. At one time or another, encouragement has been given to disaffected militants in all the countries of the region. Chinese support has ranged from arming and training rebels to the passive, yet influential, provision of a revolutionary symbol and guide. As examples, minority insurgency in the hills of northern Thailand has been materially sustained; the esprit of the jungle terrorists of Malaysia has been kept high by the beacon of inspiration that shines from the distant northern horizon. Expressions of support for wars of national liberation are routinely presented in Chinese publications and radio broadcasts. Even when relations between the People's Republic and neighboring states are officially friendly, revolutionary propaganda may continue, though possibly reduced in volume and stridency, for the diplomacy of the Chinese government and the propaganda work of the Chinese Communist party are alleged to be independent of one another. All things considered, however, there is no persuasive evidence to show that China is the prime mover in any of the unrest that plagues Southeast Asia. If Peking were to halt all its activities in support of rebellion, the insurgents would continue their campaigns, motivated by local forces and local bitterness.

The unique nature of the Sino-Vietnamese relationship merits separate consideration. The legacy of strong cultural ties originally formed in antiquity, geographical propinquity, and the Marxist-Leninist foundations of the Hanoi government dictate close Chinese interest in the course of events in the Democratic Republic of Vietnam. In the final years of the First Indochina War, arms from China contributed, perhaps decisively, to the defeat of the French; and the pattern of material support was continued in the American phase of the fighting.

That the processes of making North Vietnam socialist resemble those of China is not surprising in view of the fact that the two countries were and remain overwhelmingly agrarian. The peasants of both nations have experienced the upheaval and the hope of land reform and, subsequently, felt pressures for collective endeavor. They are similarly obliged to meet state demands for manpower and capital accumulation, since the villagers and their harvests are the main resources to be exploited in the building of socialism. In the cities of both countries, as must be anticipated, high production levels are expected of the labor force, and intellectuals are required to conform to ideological orthodoxy. China and North Vietnam alike have gone through periodic mass campaigns to promote the mobilization of their populations.

However great the similarities between China and North Vietnam may be, Hanoi has by no means followed a path set by Peking. For one thing, the Vietnamese leaders, like all national Communists, are jealous of their independence; for another, the determination to resist Chinese domination is rooted in the distant past and shows no sign of evaporating solely because of recent changes in the ideological climate. Even in their most imperiled hour, the North Vietnamese did not ask for

Chinese troops to bolster their defenses against American attack. Soldiers from China reportedly stood guard along the rail line that runs through Tonkin to connect the Chinese provinces of Kwangsi and Yünnan, but no "volunteers" from the People's Liberation Army were sent into combat, as they were in the Korean war.

Peking occasionally displays a like unwillingness to sacrifice independence of action for the sake of Sino-Vietnamese cooperation. In 1967, when outside supplies were most urgently needed by an embattled ally, rail shipments moving across China from the Soviet Union to Vietnam were interrupted. At the time, the Chinese appeared to be more concerned with scoring points in the Sino-Soviet quarrel than with supporting Hanoi's war effort. In the same spirit, China apparently did not consult with North Vietnam as moves toward détente with the United States were made; and once the secret was out, Chou En-lai had to fly to Hanoi to explain the development, just as Henry Kissinger was obliged to rush to Tokyo to try to mollify the Japanese. In 1974 the Chinese employed armed force to advance their claims of sovereignty over two groups of uninhabited islets in the South China Sea between Vietnam and the Philippines—both of which had claims of their own. South Vietnam unsuccessfully resisted and loudly protested the Chinese action, while Hanoi maintained a pregnant silence, refusing to support China. In the present age of off-shore oil exploration, the conflicting territorial claims of the parties to the dispute involve far more than considerations of national prestige, and could well bring the Chinese and Vietnamese Communists into open confrontation.

The most suggestive example of differences between Hanoi and Peking is the highway the Chinese have built across northern Laos running from the Yünnanese frontier almost to the Mekong. In view of the fact that a road connection between China and the great river via Dienbienphu has existed since colonial times, it is reasonable to conclude that this construction effort was designed to strengthen Chinese influence in Laos, and possibly in northern Thailand, independent of North Vietnamese control—perhaps even in opposition to Hanoi. Time should provide a fuller explanation.

Finally, to bring into sharper relief the picture of China's marginal involvement in Southeast Asia, it is useful to consider some of the activities of the People's Republic elsewhere in the world. Pakistan, hardly a model of popular democracy, has been singled out for highly favored treatment, both diplomatically and economically. The reasons for this pattern of particular favoritism are clearly attributable to the chronic Sino-Indian dispute. Even the brutality of the Pakistani army in seeking to put down a genuine war of national liberation in East Bengal did not deflect Peking from its custom of not allowing revolutionary emotions to interfere with the promotion of state interests.

Farther from home, China is deeply and somewhat inexplicably involved in Africa and the Middle East. There can be no historic explanation for the active animosity of China toward Israel. No rational economic analysis can account for the magnitude of Chinese aid projects in sub-Saharan countries, notably in Tanzania, where railway construction dwarfs all of Peking's developmental undertakings in Southeast Asia. There must have been some special importance attached to the role of the Chinese embassy in Cairo that permitted it to remain under an ambassador during the Cultural Revolution, while all other top diplomats were ordered back to Peking. The primacy given activities in historically and geographically distant lands can be accounted for only by the fact that Sino-Soviet competition for "Third World" leadership is most intense in Africa and the Middle East, not in the region to China's south.

THE FUTURE

Needless to say, the United States and China are not the only great powers with Southeast Asian interests. The Soviet Union has invested heavily in the region both economically and politically. The Vietnamese Communists have been, and doubtless will remain, far more dependent on the Russians than on the Chinese for military equipment and economic aid. China simply has not been able to compete with the industrially advanced Soviet Union in gaining material ascendancy in Hanoi, and there is no likelihood that the comparative disadvantage of the Chinese will soon be overcome. That hard fact alone would oblige Hanoi to avoid entanglement in the Sino-Soviet dispute.

Beyond Vietnam, as well, Soviet aid has overshadowed Chinese efforts. Burma, Indonesia, and Cambodia, the three countries long favored by China, were extended especially generous help by the Russians, who unlike the Chinese, never gave major offense to local nationalists. Obviously, in that connection, there is no general Slavophobia in the region comparable to the indigenous fear and hostility that handicaps the Chinese. Few in the area have ever seen a Russian, but all Southeast Asians are aware of the Chinese in their midst and most are infected with anti-Chinese prejudices.

The industrial affluence of the Soviet Union that supports open-handed aid projects also endows the Russian market with the power to buy relatively large quantities of Southeast Asian products. Huge cargoes of rubber, as well as forest and agricultural products, are carried away by the fleet of Soviet merchant vessels now active in the region's shipping lanes.

On the political side, among revolutionaries, Soviet ideological guidance is relatively ineffectual in competition with the power of national Communism or even the restricted appeal of Maoism. At the diplomatic level, the Russians are both industrious and conspicuous. Their embassies are large and heavily staffed. The establishments can also be show-places of Soviet wealth and power. A new one in Singapore's most fashionable neighborhood, for example, complete with tiled swimming pool and the latest in American-made air-conditioning equipment, is the finest embassy in the republic.

The purpose of a major Soviet fleet in the Indian Ocean is primarily supportive of Russian influence in East Africa, the Middle East, and South Asia, but it must be recognized that the presence of the red navy in the waters west of Southeast Asia has strategic significance for that region as well. By stationing ships in the Indian Ocean, the Russians have achieved the power to outflank the Chinese in the East Asian tropics. In acknowledgment of that potentiality, China has tacitly encouraged the United States to develop a naval counterweight based on the island of Diego Garcia—much to the displeasure of the Soviet Union and of India, where the memory of American threats to intervene on the subcontinent, possibly to abort the birth of Bangladesh, is still fresh and disturbing.

Whatever value there may be in speculative musings on the purposes and directions of the policies of the United States, the People's Republic of China, and the Soviet Union in Southeast Asia, none of those three countries is soon likely to gain or seek hegemony over the region. The Americans have now been compelled to reallocate their resources by reducing military investment in the Far East for the sake of greater flexibility in other parts of the world. The Middle East, explosive in the best of times, since the start of the international economic crisis stimulated by Arab-Persian oil pricing policies, has become the focal point of the anxieties of the Americans and their chief allies. The Chinese are fully occupied with domestic matters and with the strategy and tactics of the Sino-Soviet unpleasantness. The Russians are primarily committed to promoting their interests in Europe and in the eastern Mediterranean and to containing and thwarting China wherever possible. Thus none of the three states under discussion can now assign top priority to Southeast Asia in their policy formulations. The same cannot be said of a fourth great power, Japan.

The Japanese economy, the third most productive in the world, is notoriously susceptible to diseases of foreign origin. Over a hundred million people live on an archipelago smaller than California and not much larger than Malaysia, that nature has blessed with little more than impressive scenery. To survive, the Japanese must have reliable access to raw materials and markets abroad. For that reason, Southeast Asia is more important to Japan than to any other power.

Under normal conditions, the Japenese nation could be fed by the surplus harvests of Burma, Thailand, and Vietnam. All the lumber Japan could ever use for construction is in the jungles of the Philippines or Malaysia. Japan's needs for rubber, tin, bauxite, and various lesser non-ferrous ores are now satisfied by Southeast Asia. The same is not true for coal and iron, but there are limited deposits of those basic materials in the region. Eighty percent of Indonesia's petroleum exports go to Japan; with newly found reserves coming into production, as in Sarawak, Southeast Asian oil will certainly gain in significance. Even while Japan remains primarily dependent upon Middle Eastern oil, the tankers that carry it from the Persian Gulf must have free passage through the Malacca Strait. That circumstance causes Tokyo to react apprehensively to the proposals of Malaysia and Indonesia for drawing the boundary between Sumatra and the peninsula down the middle of the waterway, thus bilaterally ending its international status.

Although tropical customers do not yet have enough purchasing power to keep Japanese industry at full employment, with each passing day Japanese goods gain a larger share of the Southeast Asian market. This is most readily seen in the sales of radios, television sets, and motor vehicles. Japanese shipping and banking similarly play expanding roles.

Investment capital from Japan, much of it to finance local construction and industrial growth, all of it to profit the investors, is welcomed virtually everywhere. Indonesia alone has received over a billion dollars in Japanese funds, though no economic benefits have yet trickled down to the village level. Bands of Japanese tourists seem to be everywhere; the overexpanded hotel industry of Singapore would surely collapse without them.

In short, Japan is the region's paramount trading partner. None of the countries, possibly excepting those of Indochina, can afford to ignore that reality. The Japanese for their part could get along without the cooperation of any single Southeast Asian state, though exclusion from them collectively could bring economic disaster. Seldom has the world seen such economic interdependence, both established and potential. The goals of the Greater East Asia Co-prosperity Sphere have been surpassed, and the end is not in sight.

Yet the Japanese relationship with the region is in fact anomalous. It is simply contrary to the rules of history for Japan to be inextricably linked to Southeast Asia economically without having to assume concomitant political and military burdens. This is particularly true today, when the uncertainties and fears arising from global inflation and recession can be expected to stimulate economic nationalism everywhere. That retrograde development would certainly encourage greater Japanese political activity in her economic colonies to the south. With American disengagement, it is likely that Japan might well ultimately feel obliged to devise military means to reinforce jealous political guardianship. Political efforts through diplomacy and state visits, such as the tour of Prime Minister Tanaka early in 1974, have been in progress for some years. Rearmament at home and the sale of militarily useful equipment abroad, notably to Indonesia, appear to be the initial phases of Japanese military intervention.

The expectation, then, is that Southeast Asia will come under increasing Japanese influence, though the multilateral division of power among the great states of the world ought to ensure that a measure of international balance in the region will be maintained for years to come. That being the case, Southeast Asians can be expected to guide their individual and collective destinies just as they have always shaped their past. As throughout history, this Asian meeting place of cultures, forces, and ambitions will preserve its own vitality and its own identity.

READINGS

Adams, Nina S., and Alfred W. McCoy, eds., *Laos: War and Revolution,* New York: Harper and Row, 1970.

Armstrong, John P., *Sihanouk Speaks,* New York: Walker, 1964.

Barnett, A. Doak, *Communist China and Asia,* New York: Council on Foreign Relations, 1960.

Buss, Claude A., *The Arc of Crisis,* Garden City, N.Y.: Doubleday, 1961.

Buttinger, Joseph A., *A Dragon Defiant,* New York: Praeger, 1972.

Chawla, Sundershan, Melvin Gurtov, and Alain-Gerard Marsot, eds., *Southeast Asia under the New Balance of Power,* New York: Praeger, 1974.

Cohen, Jerome A., ed., *The Dynamics of China's Foreign Relations,* Cambridge: East Asia Research Center, Harvard, 1970.

Cole, Allan B., ed., *Conflict in Indochina and International Repercussions: A Documentary History, 1945-1955,* Ithaca: Cornell University Press, 1956.

Dake, Antonie C. A., *In the Spirit of the Red Banteng: Indonesian Communists between Moscow and Peking, 1959-1965,* The Hague: Mouton, 1973.

Darling, Frank C., *Thailand and the United States,* Washington: Public Affairs Press, 1965.

Dommen, Arthur I., *Conflict in Laos: The Politics of Neutralization,* rev. ed., New York: Praeger, 1971.

Ellsberg, Daniel, *Papers on the War,* New York: Simon and Schuster, 1972.

Fairbairn, Geoffrey, *Revolutionary Warfare and Communist Strategy: The Threat to South-East Asia,* London: Faber and Faber, 1968.

Fall, Bernard B., *Anatomy of a Crisis: The Laotian Crisis of 1960-1961,* Garden City, N.Y.: Doubleday, 1969.

———, *The Two Vietnams: A Political and Military Analysis,* 3rd ed., New York: Praeger, 1966.

———, *The Viet-minh Regime: Government and Administration in the Democratic Republic of Vietnam,* Ithaca: Institute of Pacific Relations, 1956.

———, *Viet-Nam Witness, 1953-66,* New York: Praeger, 1966.

Fifield, Russell H., *Americans in Southeast Asia,* New York: Crowell, 1973.

———, *The Diplomacy of Southeast Asia, 1945-1958;* Hamden, Conn.: Archon Books, 1968.

———, *Southeast Asia in United States Policy,* New York: Praeger, 1963.

Fitzgerald, Frances, *Fire in the Lake: The Vietnamese and the Americans in Vietnam,* Boston: Little, Brown, 1972.

Fitzgerald, Stephen, *China and the Overseas Chinese,* London: Cambridge University Press, 1972.

Goodman, A. E., *Politics in War,* Cambridge: Harvard University Press, 1973.

Gordon, Bernard K., *The Dimensions of Conflict in Southeast Asia,* Englewood Cliffs, N.J.: Prentice-Hall, 1966.

———, *Toward Disengagement in Southeast Asia: A Strategy for American Foreign Policy,* Englewood Cliffs, N.J.: Prentice-Hall, 1969.

Gould, James W., *The United States and Malaysia,* Cambridge: Harvard University Press, 1969.

Grant, Jonathan S., comp., *Cambodia: The Widening War in Indochina*, New York: Washington Square Press, 1971.

Gurtov, Melvin, *China and Southeast Asia: The Politics of Survival*, Lexington, Mass.: D. C. Heath, 1971.

Halberstam, David, *The Best and the Brightest*, New York: Random House, 1972.

———, *The Making of a Quagmire*, New York: Random House, 1965.

Halpern, A. M., ed., *Policies toward China: Views from Six Continents*, New York: McGraw-Hill, 1966.

Henderson, William, ed., *Southeast Asia: Problems of United States Policy*, Cambridge: Massachusetts Institute of Technology Press, 1963.

Hickey, Gerald C., *Village in Vietnam*, New Haven: Yale University Press, 1964.

Hinton, Harold C., *China's Turbulent Quest*, New York: Macmillan, 1970.

———, *Communist China in World Politics*, Boston: Houghton Mifflin, 1966.

Honey, P. J., *Communism in North Vietnam: Its Role in the Sino-Soviet Dispute*, Cambridge: Massachusetts Institute of Technology Press, 1964.

Hyde, Douglas, *The Roots of Guerrilla Warfare*, London: Bodley Head, 1968.

Iriye, Akira, *The Cold War in Asia: A Historical Introduction*, Englewood Cliffs, N.J.: Prentice-Hall, 1974.

Johnstone, William C., *Burma's Foreign Policy*, Cambridge: Harvard University Press, 1963.

Kahin, George McT., *The Asian-African Conference, Bandung, Indonesia, April, 1955*, Ithaca: Cornell University Press, 1956.

———, and John W. Lewis, *The United States in Vietnam*, rev. ed., New York: Dial, 1969.

Kirk, Donald, *Wider War: The Struggle for Cambodia, Thailand and Laos*, New York: Praeger, 1971.

Lacouture, Jean, *Vietnam: Between Two Truces*, New York: Random House, 1966.

Leifer, Michael, *Cambodia: The Search For Security*, New York: Praeger, 1967.

McCoy, Alfred W., *The Politics of Heroin in Southeast Asia*, New York: Harper and Row, 1972.

McLane, Charles B., *Soviet Strategies in Southeast Asia*, Princeton: Princeton University Press, 1966.

Modelski, G. A., ed., *SEATO: Six Studies*, Melbourne: Cheshire, 1963.

Neuhauser, Charles, *Third World Politics*, Cambridge: Harvard University Press, 1969.

Nuechterlein, Donald E., *Thailand and the Struggle for Southeast Asia*, Ithaca, Cornell University Press, 1965.

Ojha, Ishwer C., *Chinese Foreign Policy in an Age of Transition*, Boston: Beacon, 1969.

Pike, Douglas, *Viet Cong: The Organization and Techniques of the National Liberation Front of South Vietnam*, Cambridge: Massachusetts Institute of Technology Press, 1966.

Schoenbrun, David, *Vietnam: How We Got In, How To Get Out*, New York: Atheneum, 1968.

Shaplen, Robert, *The Road from War: Vietnam, 1965-1971*, New York: Harper and Row, 1971.

Sihanouk, Prince Norodom, *My War with the CIA*, New York: Pantheon, 1973.

Smith, Ralph Bernard, *Vietnam and the West*, Ithaca: Cornell University Press, 1971.

Smith, Roger M., *Cambodia's Foreign Policy*, Ithaca: Cornell University Press, 1965.

Stevenson, Charles A., *The End of Nowhere: American Policy Toward Laos since 1954*, Boston: Beacon, 1972.

Taylor, Jay, *China and Southeast Asia*, New York: Praeger, 1974.

Van Ness, Peter, *Revolution and Chinese Foreign Policy*, Berkeley: University of California Press, 1971.

Warner, Dennis, *The Last Confucian*, New York: Macmillan, 1963.

Williams, Maslyn, *The Land in Between: The Cambodian Dilemma*, New York: Morrow, 1970.

Wilson, David A., *The United States and the Future of Thailand*, New York: Praeger, 1970.

Zacher, Mark W. and Robert Stephen Milne, eds., *Conflict and Stability in Southeast Asia*, Garden City, N.Y.: Anchor, 1974.

Zagoria, Donald S., *Vietnam Triangle: Moscow, Peking and Hanoi*, New York: Pegasus, 1967.

GENERAL READINGS

Allen, Sir Richard H. S., *A Short Introduction to the History and Politics of Southeast Asia*, New York: Oxford University Press, 1970.

Bastin, John, and Harry J. Benda, *A History of Modern Southeast Asia*, Englewood Cliffs, N.J.: Prentice-Hall, 1968.

Benda, Harry J., and John A. Larkin, eds., *The World of Southeast Asia*, New York: Harper and Row, 1967.

Cady, John F., *Southeast Asia: Its Historical Development*, New York: McGraw-Hill, 1964.

Hall, D. G. E., *A History of South-east Asia*, 3rd ed., New York: St. Martin's Press, 1968.

Harrison, Brian, *South-East Asia: A Short History*, 3rd ed., New York: St. Martin's Press, 1966.

Purcell, Victor, *The Chinese in Southeast Asia*, 2nd ed., London: Oxford University Press, 1965.

Steinberg, David J., ed., *In Search of Southeast Asia*, New York: Praeger, 1971.

Tarling, Nicholas, *A Concise History of Southeast Asia*, New York: Praeger, 1966.

Index

READINGS

Adams, Nina S., and Alfred W. McCoy, eds., *Laos: War and Revolution,* New York: Harper and Row, 1970.

Armstrong, John P., *Sihanouk Speaks,* New York: Walker, 1964.

Barnett, A. Doak, *Communist China and Asia,* New York: Council on Foreign Relations, 1960.

Buss, Claude A., *The Arc of Crisis,* Garden City, N.Y.: Doubleday, 1961.

Buttinger, Joseph A., *A Dragon Defiant,* New York: Praeger, 1972.

Chawla, Sundershan, Melvin Gurtov, and Alain-Gerard Marsot, eds., *Southeast Asia under the New Balance of Power,* New York: Praeger, 1974.

Cohen, Jerome A., ed., *The Dynamics of China's Foreign Relations,* Cambridge: East Asia Research Center, Harvard, 1970.

Cole, Allan B., ed., *Conflict in Indochina and International Repercussions: A Documentary History, 1945-1955,* Ithaca: Cornell University Press, 1956.

Dake, Antonie C. A., *In the Spirit of the Red Banteng: Indonesian Communists between Moscow and Peking, 1959-1965,* The Hague: Mouton, 1973.

Darling, Frank C., *Thailand and the United States,* Washington: Public Affairs Press, 1965.

Dommen, Arthur I., *Conflict in Laos: The Politics of Neutralization,* rev. ed., New York: Praeger, 1971.

Ellsberg, Daniel, *Papers on the War,* New York: Simon and Schuster, 1972.

Fairbairn, Geoffrey, *Revolutionary Warfare and Communist Strategy: The Threat to South-East Asia,* London: Faber and Faber, 1968.

Fall, Bernard B., *Anatomy of a Crisis: The Laotian Crisis of 1960-1961,* Garden City, N.Y.: Doubleday, 1969.

———, *The Two Vietnams: A Political and Military Analysis,* 3rd ed., New York: Praeger, 1966.

———, *The Viet-minh Regime: Government and Administration in the Democratic Republic of Vietnam,* Ithaca: Institute of Pacific Relations, 1956.

———, *Viet-Nam Witness, 1953-66,* New York: Praeger, 1966.

Fifield, Russell H., *Americans in Southeast Asia,* New York: Crowell, 1973.

———, *The Diplomacy of Southeast Asia, 1945-1958;* Hamden, Conn.: Archon Books, 1968.

———, *Southeast Asia in United States Policy,* New York: Praeger, 1963.

Fitzgerald, Frances, *Fire in the Lake: The Vietnamese and the Americans in Vietnam,* Boston: Little, Brown, 1972.

Fitzgerald, Stephen, *China and the Overseas Chinese,* London: Cambridge University Press, 1972.

Goodman, A. E., *Politics in War,* Cambridge: Harvard University Press, 1973.

Gordon, Bernard K., *The Dimensions of Conflict in Southeast Asia,* Englewood Cliffs, N.J.: Prentice-Hall, 1966.

———, *Toward Disengagement in Southeast Asia: A Strategy for American Foreign Policy,* Englewood Cliffs, N.J.: Prentice-Hall, 1969.

Gould, James W., *The United States and Malaysia,* Cambridge: Harvard University Press, 1969.

Grant, Jonathan S., comp., *Cambodia: The Widening War in Indochina*, New York: Washington Square Press, 1971.
Gurtov, Melvin, *China and Southeast Asia: The Politics of Survival*, Lexington, Mass.: D. C. Heath, 1971.
Halberstam, David, *The Best and the Brightest*, New York: Random House, 1972.
——, *The Making of a Quagmire*, New York: Random House, 1965.
Halpern, A. M., ed., *Policies toward China: Views from Six Continents*, New York: McGraw-Hill, 1966.
Henderson, William, ed., *Southeast Asia: Problems of United States Policy*, Cambridge: Massachusetts Institute of Technology Press, 1963.
Hickey, Gerald C., *Village in Vietnam*, New Haven: Yale University Press, 1964.
Hinton, Harold C., *China's Turbulent Quest*, New York: Macmillan, 1970.
——, *Communist China in World Politics*, Boston: Houghton Mifflin, 1966.
Honey, P. J., *Communism in North Vietnam: Its Role in the Sino-Soviet Dispute*, Cambridge: Massachusetts Institute of Technology Press, 1964.
Hyde, Douglas, *The Roots of Guerrilla Warfare*, London: Bodley Head, 1968.
Iriye, Akira, *The Cold War in Asia: A Historical Introduction*, Englewood Cliffs, N.J.: Prentice-Hall, 1974.
Johnstone, William C., *Burma's Foreign Policy*, Cambridge: Harvard University Press, 1963.
Kahin, George McT., *The Asian-African Conference, Bandung, Indonesia, April, 1955*, Ithaca: Cornell University Press, 1956.
——, and John W. Lewis, *The United States in Vietnam*, rev. ed., New York: Dial, 1969.
Kirk, Donald, *Wider War: The Struggle for Cambodia, Thailand and Laos*, New York: Praeger, 1971.
Lacouture, Jean, *Vietnam: Between Two Truces*, New York: Random House, 1966.
Leifer, Michael, *Cambodia: The Search For Security*, New York: Praeger, 1967.
McCoy, Alfred W., *The Politics of Heroin in Southeast Asia*, New York: Harper and Row, 1972.
McLane, Charles B., *Soviet Strategies in Southeast Asia*, Princeton: Princeton University Press, 1966.
Modelski, G. A., ed., *SEATO: Six Studies*, Melbourne: Cheshire, 1963.
Neuhauser, Charles, *Third World Politics*, Cambridge: Harvard University Press, 1969.
Nuechterlein, Donald E., *Thailand and the Struggle for Southeast Asia*, Ithaca, Cornell University Press, 1965.
Ojha, Ishwer C., *Chinese Foreign Policy in an Age of Transition*, Boston: Beacon, 1969.
Pike, Douglas, *Viet Cong: The Organization and Techniques of the National Liberation Front of South Vietnam*, Cambridge: Massachusetts Institute of Technology Press, 1966.

Schoenbrun, David, *Vietnam: How We Got In, How To Get Out*, New York: Atheneum, 1968.
Shaplen, Robert, *The Road from War: Vietnam, 1965-1971*, New York: Harper and Row, 1971.
Sihanouk, Prince Norodom, *My War with the CIA*, New York: Pantheon, 1973.
Smith, Ralph Bernard, *Vietnam and the West*, Ithaca: Cornell University Press, 1971.
Smith, Roger M., *Cambodia's Foreign Policy*, Ithaca: Cornell University Press, 1965.
Stevenson, Charles A., *The End of Nowhere: American Policy Toward Laos since 1954*, Boston: Beacon, 1972.
Taylor, Jay, *China and Southeast Asia*, New York: Praeger, 1974.
Van Ness, Peter, *Revolution and Chinese Foreign Policy*, Berkeley: University of California Press, 1971.
Warner, Dennis, *The Last Confucian*, New York: Macmillan, 1963.
Williams, Maslyn, *The Land in Between: The Cambodian Dilemma*, New York: Morrow, 1970.
Wilson, David A., *The United States and the Future of Thailand*, New York: Praeger, 1970.
Zacher, Mark W. and Robert Stephen Milne, eds., *Conflict and Stability in Southeast Asia*, Garden City, N.Y.: Anchor, 1974.
Zagoria, Donald S., *Vietnam Triangle: Moscow, Peking and Hanoi*, New York: Pegasus, 1967.

GENERAL READINGS

Allen, Sir Richard H. S., *A Short Introduction to the History and Politics of Southeast Asia*, New York: Oxford University Press, 1970.
Bastin, John, and Harry J. Benda, *A History of Modern Southeast Asia*, Englewood Cliffs, N.J.: Prentice-Hall, 1968.
Benda, Harry J., and John A. Larkin, eds., *The World of Southeast Asia*, New York: Harper and Row, 1967.
Cady, John F., *Southeast Asia: Its Historical Development*, New York: McGraw-Hill, 1964.
Hall, D. G. E., *A History of South-east Asia*, 3rd ed., New York: St. Martin's Press, 1968.
Harrison, Brian, *South-East Asia: A Short History*, 3rd ed., New York: St. Martin's Press, 1966.
Purcell, Victor, *The Chinese in Southeast Asia*, 2nd ed., London: Oxford University Press, 1965.
Steinberg, David J., ed., *In Search of Southeast Asia*, New York: Praeger, 1971.
Tarling, Nicholas, *A Concise History of Southeast Asia*, New York: Praeger, 1966.

Index